Child of a Turbulent Century

CHILD OF A
TURBULENT
CENTURY

VICTOR ERLICH

NORTHWESTERN UNIVERSITY PRESS
Evanston, Illinois

Northwestern University Press
www.nupress.northwestern.edu

Copyright © 2006 by Northwestern University Press. Published 2006.
All rights reserved.

Printed in the United States of America

10 9 8 7 6 5 4 3 2 1

ISBN 0-8101-2350-9 (cloth)
ISBN 0-8101-2351-7 (paper)

Library of Congress Cataloging-in-Publication Data

Erlich, Victor, 1914–
    Child of a turbulent century / Victor Erlich.
        p. cm. — (Jewish lives)
    Includes bibliographical references.
    ISBN 0-8101-2350-9 (cloth : alk. paper) — ISBN 0-8101-2351-7
(pbk. : alk. paper)
        1. Erlich, Victor, 1914– 2. Critics—Biography. 3. World War, 1939–
1945—Biography. I. Title. II. Series.
PG2947.E75A3 2006
891.709—dc22

                                                              2006009870

For Mark and Henry

Contents

Child of a Turbulent Century

Author's Note

As I look back on the trajectory stretching from First World War Petrograd to New Haven at the beginning of the new millennium, I am reminded of the title of a nineteenth-century memoir, *Confessions d'un enfant du siècle* (*Confessions of a Child of the Century*), by Alfred de Musset. My selective recollections will contain few "confessions." But the phrase "a child of the century" is singularly apposite. I was born in 1914, at the threshold of what the great Russian poet Anna Akhmatova called the "real twentieth century" in her retrospective "A Poem Without a Hero." Moreover, my place of birth—or rather its uncommonly short-lived name, Petrograd—was indelibly marked by that century's violent dislocations and upheavals: in 1914, in a burst of patriotic fervor, the German-sounding "Petersburg" was Russified into "Petrograd," which was displaced in turn by "Leningrad" only ten years later, in deference to the dead architect of new Russia, Vladimir Lenin.

More important, much of the story that follows reflects the lethal nature of the "real twentieth century." The fate of my family was shaped by the fearful symmetry of the age of totalitarianism. My grandfather, the distinguished Jewish historian Simon Dubnov, was felled in December 1941 by a Nazi bullet. My father, Henryk Erlich, a Jewish socialist leader, took his life in one of Stalin's prisons in May 1942.

Another major twentieth-century theme that will loom large in these pages is that of displacement—both geographic and cultural—as the inevitable cost of a precarious rescue and a prelude to personal and professional fulfillment in the New World.

3

In a World of My Own

Life with Grandfather

M y first memories, which hark back to the fifth year of my
life, are inevitably dim and often derivative, that is, largely
shaped by what I was told later by adults. Since I was barely three
when Russia careened from the nearly bloodless democratic February revolution to the Bolshevik seizure of power in October
1917, I was too young in those turbulent days to hear "the noise
of time" (as Osip Mandelstam's remarkable memoir was titled).
Like all of the progressive Russian Jewish intelligentsia, my
parents welcomed the collapse of the czarist regime with enthusiasm. Nor were they merely cheering spectators. My mother,
Sophie Dubnov, was a contributor to the independent socialist
journal *Letopis* (*Chronicle*), edited by Maksim Gorky, and an active member of the Jewish Labor Bund, an influential political
party that campaigned for socialist revolution and endeavored to
unite the aims of Jewish workers with their Russian counterparts'. The Bund was founded in Vienna in 1897. My father,
Henryk Erlich, was born and raised in Poland but settled on the
eve of the First World War with his wife in St. Petersburg. He
was a rising star in the Bund and an influential spokesman for
democratic socialism in what was in 1917 a left-wing alternative
government, the Petrograd "Soviet" (Council) of Workers' and
Soldiers' Deputies. A principled opponent of Bolshevism, he
joined the Menshevik faction in walking out on the historic meeting of the Petrograd Soviet, described by John Reed in *Ten Days
That Shook the World,* in protest against the October coup.

My brother, Alexander, two years older than I, proved more responsive than I could be to revolutionary rhetoric. It seems that several times in the course of the fateful summer of 1917, our nanny, who was supposed to take Alex for walks, would schedule trysts with her Bolshevik sailor friend in front of the balcony of the famous palace from which Lenin would harangue the crowds, proclaiming his vehement opposition to the Russian "imperialist" designs on Constantinople and the Bosporus straits. I understand that after one of these excursions, Alex urgently claimed my parents' attention to declare in no uncertain terms his total disinterest in the "straits." It took my parents a while to decode his deeply held beliefs.

Father's, and the Bund's, critical attitude toward the new regime made his, and his associates', position increasingly precarious. Another matter of concern to my parents in 1918 was the acute food shortage in civil war–battered Petrograd and its impact on the two "growing boys"—Alex and me. This, I was told, was the main reason why, after some soul-searching, my parents decided to accept a rather urgent invitation from my paternal grandfather, Moses Erlich, who owned a flour mill in Father's native Lublin, in central Poland. The immediate objective of the visit was to build up the emaciated "kids." The westward move was apparently seen as temporary, but by the end of the year, it became clear that Poland would be our home for an indefinite period. The political situation in Soviet Russia was rapidly deteriorating. While a few Bundist activists seceded from the Jewish socialist mainstream to join the Yiddish-speaking section of the Russian Communist Party, the bulk of the movement stood firm and was about to share the fate of other opponents of what was in effect a one-party dictatorship. As my maternal grandfather, Simon Dubnov, who at the time was still unhappily trapped in Petrograd, was signaling to my parents, most of Father's associates were either under arrest or forced into emigration.

No less important, in November 1918, after a century and a half of tripartite occupation, Poland regained its independence. With the Jewish labor movement being reconstituted on the territory of the new nation, Father's proven skills and commitments were sorely needed. I was told that in the fall of 1918, Vladimir Medem, one of the most charismatic figures in the movement—he was to become subsequently my special hero—journeyed from Warsaw to Lublin to urge Father to assume a leading role in the Polish Bund. "We are in greater need of living leaders," he is said to have argued, "than of martyrs or prisoners languishing in Russian jails."

For Father, the decision to remain in his fatherland was, to coin a phrase, overdetermined. Mother, who was steeped in Russian culture and whose best years were spent in prewar Petersburg, reluctantly recognized the inescapability of this choice but found permanent separation from Russia wrenching. Though she fully mastered Polish and became an active participant in Poland's cultural life as a literary and drama critic, essayist, and educator, she never ceased pining for her homeland. Toward the end of her long life, she was to put it succinctly in a deeply personal poem:

An émigré? No, simply a daughter
Torn away from her mother.[1]

With Father shuttling between his native town and the capital, the project of feeding the underfed was proceeding apace. The standard Jewish mother's injunction "Eat, child, eat" (*Es, Kind, es*) was being vigorously implemented by three Jewish mothers on the premises—our somber grandmother Sarah; Father's oldest sister, the kindly and placid Gustava; and our youngest aunt, Manya, a warm and vivacious brunette who promptly became Alex's and my favorite. After a couple of months of this regimen, we were no longer the "skin and bones" lamented by Father's family after our arrival in Lublin.

One of the early episodes of our becalmed Lublin existence involved my impressionable brother. I have already mentioned his formative exposure to Lenin's forceful speechifying. At the time, Alex was given to talking in his sleep. Once, in the middle of a dark Lublin night, he got up on his bed, cried in Russian while still asleep, "Long live the proletarian revolution!" and went down. I can only speculate, in retrospect, about the impact he made on our stolidly "bourgeois" relatives.

Though it is naturally the ladies who were in charge of building Alex and me up, the key figure in this patriarchal household was my paternal grandfather. The image of Moses Erlich which I have been harboring for many decades rests in part on early exposure and in part on what I was told later or was able to piece together during our annual visits to Lublin through the 1920s and the early 1930s. (Every April we would repair to Lublin to attend large-scale family seders.) My first impressions are dominated by the sense of a vaguely agitated presence. The habit of Moses Erlich, which I recall distinctly, was getting up every morning at the crack of dawn and, without rousing anyone in so many words, racing through the house several times so as to make it extremely difficult for anyone to remain asleep. I figured out somewhat later that this morning restlessness was closely related to my grandfather's going to bed very early, which in turn had something to do with his diabetes, which by the time I got to know him was a major concern and an important aspect of his identity.

It seems that diabetes, or rather its detection, proved to be a turning point in Grandfather's spiritual life. He had been for years a fervent Hasid; as a typical true believer, he would make regular pilgrimages to the court of the "wonder-rabbi" (*rebe*). On such occasions, along with the somewhat unsanitary custom of eating "leftovers" (*shirayim*) from the *rebe*'s dish, one would imbibe significant amounts of kosher vodka known as *peysakhovka*. At some point during a regular checkup, the family doctor detected in Moses Erlich a strong proclivity for diabetes. Kosher vodka had to be eliminated from his diet forthwith. I am not prepared to claim that the prospect of a good swig was a major motive for Grandfather's ritualistic attendance of Hasidic get-togethers. It appears, though, that shortly after the diagnosis, his religious zeal visibly abated. He dropped his habit both literally and figuratively (a Hasid could be recognized by his distinctive black garb) and became a secular thinker by exchanging a rather zealous brand of Orthodox Judaism for "spiritual Zionism." This secular doctrine, formulated by an influential Russian Jewish thinker, Ahad HaAm (Asher Ginsburg), in contradistinction to the political Zionism of Theodor Herzl, disposed with the concept of the Jewish state to postulate a cultural "radiation"—to use de Gaulle's phrase, *rayonnement français*—of the exemplary Palestine settlement (*yishuv*) upon Diaspora Jews.

The way Moses Erlich presided over the many Passover meals our family had occasion to attend in Lublin was a characteristically counterproductive compromise between a residual attachment to the Jewish tradition and a recognition of the impinging secular realities. He would read the entire Haggadah text prior to the meal without skipping a single word, but with ten grandchildren—more keenly interested in matzo balls than in the ritual—breathing down his neck, he would deliver the text at breakneck speed so as to make it virtually unintelligible.

Sometime in 1919, the Lublin prelude to my Polish period drew to a close. The "eat, child, eat" project had by that time run its course. Father had lined up a modest but adequate apartment at the edge of Warsaw's teeming Jewish quarter. What with the party commitments piling up, he must have been eager to bring us all to the capital. Mother, though fully appreciative of the family's solicitude and hospitality, was becoming restless in the overstuffed Jewish provincial setting. I do not remember either our move to Warsaw or my first impression of the city. What stands out in my mind as one of my first authentic memories is a trying moment in the summer of 1920, which Mother, Alex, and I spent in the dramatically scenic mountain resort of Zakopane. I was ill and feverish. My condition was diagnosed as dysentery, an acute gastric disease. Mother was very anxious—the medical resources of Zakopane were vastly inferior to those of Warsaw. Since Father was away, my barely eight-year-old brother had to assume the role of the man of the house. He was dispatched to the other end of the village to fetch a doctor. I recall vividly the gentle face of a young pediatrician looming over me with visible concern. His intervention must have helped. The crisis was over, and we returned to Warsaw ahead of schedule.

Shortly after my bout with dysentery, I contracted scarlet fever. This time the family anxiety level was appreciably lower. Medical treatment was easily available, and the case was relatively mild. In fact, I think back to the leisurely recovery with some pleasure. I was reading *Les Misérables* in either Polish or Russian (my French at the time wasn't good enough). I fell in love with this panoramic melodrama. Jean Valjean, Cosette, and Javert became major presences in my childish universe. Above all, at this early stage of my involvement with fiction, I had the best cry of my entire life.

I dwell on my medical condition in 1920 since this sequence of events did much to shape my way of life for the following seven years. I must have been enfeebled by the siege, but I'm afraid the image of me as a physically vulnerable child lodged itself too firmly in Mother's mind. A person of luminous intelligence and considerable good sense, in dealing with her younger child she tended to be overanxious and overprotective. Thus, she overgeneralized what was a temporary condition and concluded that I was too frail to go to school. I have a distinct impression that Father was not entirely sold on this notion, but as an overtime public figure and a part-time lawyer, he was so swamped as to leave some domestic decisions to Mother.

My own feelings must have been mixed: I was being deprived of the company of my peers, enjoyed by Alex, who had been out in the world since the age of eight. But being tutored at home had its advantages: I never liked getting up in the morning (in fact, I still don't); also, I had lots of time to myself. My education was blatantly lopsided. My oldest and favorite cousin, who became a close friend of the family—he was in fact the only relative of Father's to become a strong Bundist sympathizer—taught me math and Latin. I was making considerable strides in French and imbibing history and literature, partly by osmosis. (Mother was a woman of letters—a fine essayist and a minor but good poet. Eventually, I grew to appreciate the spare, disciplined lyricism of her verse.) Natural science was a yawning gap. It remained so during my two years at high school because our chemistry teacher was an unmitigated disaster.

For Alex and me, reading became a consuming passion. We both managed to skip most of children's literature, though Alex in his "Russian" period managed to savor, and partly commit to memory, the delightfully whimsical poem "The Crocodile" by the splendid children's writer and all-around man of letters Korney Chukovsky. We had a brief exposure both in Russian and in Polish to deservedly obscure adventure writers such as the prolific hack Karl May, who spent much of his life in German jails fantasizing about cowboys and Indians. But early on we went for classics or near classics—Alexandre Dumas père, Victor Hugo, Walter Scott, Robert Louis Stevenson, and, above all, Charles Dickens!

Our birthdays were commemorated jointly. Father's friends and associates, members of the Bundist elite, would attend, bringing more or less appropriate gifts. On one such occasion— I may have been eight, Alex ten—one of our favorites, whose name will recur in these pages, the dashing, charismatic Victor Alter, sauntered in, exuding his usual joie de vivre. "Boys," he announced cheerfully, "I'm bringing the best thing there is." Even though his hands were unmistakably empty, in total denial of reality, we cried in unison, *"David Copperfield!"* "No," said Alter. "Hope." (I'm afraid this hope never materialized.)

A few minutes later, another Bund leader, a popular if occasionally maudlin orator, Beynish Mikhalevich, a man of remarkable sweetness, entered carrying a good-size package. It clearly did not look like *David Copperfield.* We opened it somewhat apprehensively; it contained a soccer ball. My brother could not suppress his disappointment. "What a fool you are," he said to the gray-haired revolutionary. "You couldn't bring a book?" Father, who was generally slow to anger, was properly outraged by Alex's wanton rudeness.

Predictably, in our involvement with literature, Russian classics had the pride of place. When I turned seven, Mother gave me a precious volume—the *Selected Works* by her favorite Russian fiction writer, Nikolai Gogol. I was spellbound. Naturally, I was responding more readily to Gogol's early romantic goblin tales, too airily dismissed by Vladimir Nabokov in his brilliant but willfully lopsided *Nikolai Gogol,* than to such later masterpieces as "The Overcoat," where the fantastic obtrudes upon the quotidian. In any case, I was so taken with the volume that I found reading and rereading it too passive a response. At some point, I began to copy the book page by page. By the time I reached page 100, my older cousin dropped by; he was about five years my senior, a bright and witty teenager, who was considerably more reality-oriented than I. Having witnessed for a while my medieval monk-type labors in silence, he inquired, "What are you doing?"

"I'm copying this book," I answered.

"Why are you doing this?" he wondered.

"I really like it," I confessed.

"But you've got it," he insisted, pointing to the hefty volume.

Unable to produce a single plausible reason for my activity, I muttered, "Suppose the house burns down."

"So would the copy," retorted my cousin sensibly.

The fact of the matter is that my exertions lacked any pragmatic justification. They answered a need to do something about, or with, a book that meant a great deal to me, to get inside the text. It occurs to me it is this sort of need that at a considerably later stage of my development guided me toward literary criticism.

While at the age of seven or eight this kind of engagement with the text was not available to me, there was nothing to prevent me, what with a considerable amount of time on my hands, from grotesquely inadequate attempts to emulate the works I admired, that is, from plunging into "creative writing." In fact, the years 1921 to 1930 proved, in retrospect, to be the most productive period of my life.

After a mercifully brief bout with verse (in Polish), I switched to prose fiction and stayed with it until my junior year. My strong literary identification with Mother became apparent in more ways than one. My stories were couched in Russian. (I was effectively bilingual). Moreover, the notebooks which contained my scribblings bore a portentous title, *Collected Works of Victor Erlich-Dubnov* (I was using the reverse of Mother's literary signature).

I began with a homespun story about the vicissitudes of a feisty Russian boy, "The Adventures of Mishka Sepkin." Soon Russian themes and settings were supplanted by Western ones— echoes of Dumas, Scott, and Stevenson. One of the novellas centered around a Robin Hood–like figure. The ending was not a happy one. The high-minded outlaw is captured by the authorities, convicted, and sentenced to death by hanging. As I was mourning with some intensity the hero John Chesterfield's impending death, a friendly but somewhat imperious neighbor, the forceful lawyer Esther Iwińska, dropped by to say hello. My parents were away, and I was alone grieving.

"Why are you crying?" Mrs. I. inquired brusquely.

"I'm not crying," I muttered unpersuasively, doing my best to suppress residual sobs.

"Yes, you are," insisted the neighbor, "and you shouldn't be. You are a big boy. What's the matter?"

"John Chesterfield is going to die," I averred.

"Who is John Chesterfield?"

"He is the hero of my story."

"In that case," Mrs. I. proclaimed confidently, "there is no problem. He doesn't have to die. It's up to you."

I was genuinely taken aback by this nonliterary approach to the narrative. I was not articulate enough to point out that the author actually is not omnipotent, that once unleashed, events narrated acquire an autonomy and logic all their own, that a point of no return can be reached. All I could offer was, "No, it's too late, by now he has got to die." Mrs. Iwińska remained unconvinced. She left in some bafflement, urging me to shape up. When somewhat later I related this conversation to Mother, she was clearly on my side. Though she had not read the story, she was inclined to believe that "by now" no other outcome would have been credible.

By the time I turned twelve, I was done with noble English bandits. I was embarked on a more ambitious venture, a historical novel in two parts, set in Paris, at the height of the French Revolution.

Though my involvement with the subject in 1926 may well appear a bit precocious, interest in the French Revolution was endemic within the milieu in which I was raised, the early twentieth-century East European radical intelligentsia. Suffice it to mention the prominence of such terms as "Jacobin" or "Thermidor" in Leon Trotsky's eloquent if fiercely partisan *History of the Russian Revolution.*

My sense of that era was dominated by the massive presence of Victor Hugo, whose poetry and fiction I was imbibing in inordinate amounts under the tutelage of my maternal grandfather. I am not speaking here of the Hugo of *Les Misérables* but of the author of a lesser-known but no less remarkable novel, *Quatre-vingt-treize,* built around a confrontation between two types of revolutionaries: the intrepid and profoundly humane Gauvain and a somber but pure Jacobin Simourdain. (Though both protagonists are admirable, the author's, and certainly this reader's, sympathies were strongly engaged by the gentle warrior.) True, I had managed to do a bit of historical research: I read the florid *Histoire des Girondins* by A. de Lamartine and somehow came across an obscure Belgian semidocumentary novel, *L'histoire d'un paysan* by Erkmann-Chatrian, but the tenor of my efforts and my view of the Terror were unquestionably shaped by Victor Hugo.

If Dickens's *A Tale of Two Cities,* which, needless to say, I devoured, is Dickens at his most romantic, *Quatre-vingt-treize* is Hugo at his most theatrical. The scene in which Danton, Robespierre, and Marat confront each other across the table of the famous Paris café Chez Maxime made a profound impression on me when I first read the book and, for better or worse, shaped for years my image of the formidable triumvirate. Revisited

many years later, at a less impressionable age, the staccato dialogue with its deadly repartees and epigrammatic growls struck
me as totally, if brilliantly, implausible. But the melodramatic
staginess of the novel's manner should not blind us to the tragic
resonance of its central theme—that of the conflict between the
initial humanitarian impulse of the revolution and the impla-
cable exigencies of revolutionary action.

Though, obviously, I was unable to put it this way, while
scribbling my large-scale novel, I was preoccupied by what I recognized later as the problems of revolutionary ethics. I installed
at the center of the proceedings a most implausible protagonist,
an enlightened and high-minded peasant residing on the Left
Bank in "the stormy year" spanning 1793 to 1794. I have scant
recollection of the plot. I must have relied heavily on the major
historical events and otherwise indulged in some pontification.
Pierre Rouge, the authorial mouthpiece, though not exactly a
Girondin, took a very dim view of the Jacobins. In a word, he was
a Menshevik avant la lettre. I don't remember how he made his
living, but he clearly got around; at some point he was giving
Danton a piece of his mind. In responding to criticism of his
disheveled personal life, the tempestuous tribune of the people
declared, "Why fuss over honor, as long as the revolution is well
served." Pierre Rouge is moved to sententiousness: "Honor is one
thing we cannot afford to sacrifice on the altar of the revolution."
I'm afraid I made my thoughtful peasant sound like a bit of a prig.
I suppose I was trying to convey rather early in the game what I
managed to formulate many years later in my last book, *Modernism and Revolution.* In an essay on Evgeny Zamyatin, I maintained
that for the author of the antiutopian novel *We,* revolutionary
engagement was a moral obligation rather than a moral alibi.

As I look back on my overly ambitious literary undertaking,
I am struck by my early awareness of the theme which stayed
with me through much of my adult life—the means-versus-ends
dilemma. When some twenty-five years later I came across the
somber epiphany of the Bukharin-like protagonist Rubashov in
Arthur Koestler's *Darkness at Noon,* "The means have swallowed

the ends," I had a shock of recognition. This happened to be one of my parting shots when in 1985 I was winding up the last undergraduate course I taught at Yale, Literature and Revolution.

Whether or not I could be credited in retrospect with ideational precocity or prescience, I suspect that the literary vehicle I devised for my preoccupations was less than promising. I'm saying "I suspect" since for more than half a century I have not been in a position to assess the quality of my literary efforts. My oeuvre went up in smoke in September 1939 when an incendiary bomb destroyed our Warsaw house shortly after our departure. Thus, I have to rely on my early judgment. When at the "mature" age of fourteen I reviewed the second draft of *In Stormy Years,* I arrived at the firm conclusion that I was not cut out to be a fiction writer. Some years later, I told my wife, Iza, about this verdict. She thought it might have been too precipitous, but I feel in my bones that I was right. In fact, this moment of truth may have been an early high point of my career as a literary critic.

But I am getting ahead of my story. The self-critical diagnosis occurred in the wake of a school year which is especially worth recalling, a year which took us away from our respective Warsaw routines and made it possible for Alex and me to get to know more closely a man who since my early childhood was an important presence in our lives—our maternal grandfather, the distinguished Jewish historian Simon Dubnov.

Only during the first three years of my life, a period of which any memories are less than vivid, did we all live in the same city (Petrograd), indeed in the same house. Yet with so much goodwill on both sides—in spite of some political differences, my father had a higher regard for Simon Dubnov than for his own father—there was ample motivation in two subsequent decades to overcome the distance that separated Warsaw from Berlin and Riga and to contrive occasions for family reunions, whether on shared vacations at the German seaside or visits to my maternal grandparent's home. Throughout my adolescence, Grandfather affected my intellectual development in many ways and across a wide spectrum. To indicate the scope of his influence, let me mention two widely disparate instances. It was Grandfather who was largely responsible for my falling under the spell of Victor Hugo and for my resulting fascination with the drama and the moral dilemmas of the French Revolution. It was Simon Dubnov who managed to take enough time from his exacting schedule to teach me the Hebrew-Yiddish alphabet.

Perhaps I should add that in making use of these cultural acquisitions, I must have been guided by a desire, conscious or otherwise, to merge Grandfather's teachings with models provided by my parents. Thus, when I was embarking on my historical novel, I was clearly seeking to combine Simon Dubnov's vocation with my poet mother's commitment to imaginative literature. By the same token, I would for years, before my exposure to the classics of Yiddish, I. L. Peretz and Shalom Aleikhem, exercise my Jewish literacy primarily by reading the organ of the Jewish Labor Bund, *Naye Folkstsaytung,* edited by Father.

In my fond recollections of life with Grandfather, the years 1925 and 1926 have the pride of place. With Father embarked on a coast-to-coast speaking tour in the United States on behalf of Poland's Jewish labor movement, Mother eagerly accepted an invitation to do some research in the Bund archives, located then in Berlin, in order to spend a full school year with her parents, who had settled in Berlin in 1922, and to reimmerse herself in the congenial milieu of Russian Jewish intelligentsia which since leaving Petrograd she never ceased to miss. (In the 1920s, Berlin became a refuge for the Menshevik elite, who brought out the journal the *Socialist Courier,* containing some of the most sophisticated analyses of Soviet politics and culture, and inevitably spent much time arguing about what went wrong in 1917 and 1918.) For Alex and me, this extended visit offered a golden opportunity to get to know Simon and Ida Dubnov and to become initiated into their way of life.

The Dubnov apartment, located in a quiet residential section of a teeming metropolis, seemed at times a rare instance of controlled bustle. Somehow Grandfather's rigorous writing schedule was made to absorb a stream of visitors, close associates, and

Jewish community leaders, self-assured pundits and timid apprentice historians. (One of the latter, I recall, was nearly turned away by Grandmother, who mistook him for an obnoxious Berlin peddler. Muttering her habitual "wir broykn nikht," a somewhat Yiddish version of the German for "We don't need this," she was about to shut the door in the hapless young scholar's face when Dubnov emerged in time to recognize the visitor.)

Above all, it was a household dominated by steady work. I have never since met anyone more methodical, more productive, more fully committed to writing than was Dubnov. (That's how he managed to write the ten-volume *World History of the Jewish People,* along with some other scholarly and polemical tracts.) On visitor-free days, the exacting routine would be interrupted by two daily "constitutionals." Actually, "interrupted" is hardly the right word; the walks were an integral part of the writing schedule, clearly indispensable to the demanding pace Dubnov was determined to maintain. A man of modest if not austere habits where food, clothing, and housing were concerned, he would allow himself one luxury: a pleasant residential location, within walking distance from a park or woods.

I would often accompany him on these walks and got to learn their immutable pattern by heart. While we strolled down the quiet, tree-lined streets of the Grunewald, he would engage me in conversation or, more typically, hold forth on a topic of mutual interest. Yet as soon as we would enter the path, he would stop talking, even if it meant interrupting himself in the middle of a sentence, raise his finger, and say with feeling: "Vitya, breathe." For some fifteen or twenty minutes, we would breathe together in silence as leaves rustled under our feet. If the story had not run its course or the point had not been made, the narrative or discursive flow would be resumed on our way back.

It was clear to me that Grandfather's insistence on "breathing" was not simply a matter of body hygiene, of expanding one's lungs by imbibing maximal amounts of healthful air. The silence which followed the injunction suggested a quasi-religious reverence. Arguably, it is at such moments of wordless communion with nature that Dubnov came as close to a religious stance as he ever did.

It is a well-known fact that Dubnov was in the main a secular thinker. His attitude toward Judaism had evolved since his rebellious youth, when he was an *epikoyres,* a militant challenger of the rabbinical establishment. The premier historian of Jewry was bound to acquire a rich appreciation of Judaism's contribution to Jewish survival. But he never became an observant Jew, though he would attend the synagogue on the High Holidays, partly in deference to tradition, partly out of fondness for Kol Nidre (the song sung on the Day of Atonement). Predictably, his favorite Jewish holiday was Passover. He found its symbolism particularly congenial and enjoyed celebrating it in the company of friends.

As it happens, one of the most vivid memories of our Berlin year involved a seder to which the Dubnovs were invited, with Mother, Alex, and me tagging along. The host, Dr. Isaac Steinberg, was a colorful and distinctive figure among the Russian Jewish émigrés in Berlin. During the revolution of 1917, he was one of the leaders of the ultraradical group the "Left-Wing S.R.s" who seceded from the Socialist-Revolutionary Party and joined Lenin's first government only to walk out on it in 1918 in protest against the burdensome peace treaty with Germany in Brest-Litovsk. What made Dr. Steinberg a unique if not bizarre phenomenon is that he managed throughout to be a rigorously observant Jew. (It was rumored that, during his brief tenure as a commissar of justice, he refused to work on the Sabbath, much to Lenin's dismay.)

A spellbinding orator in at least three languages (Russian, Yiddish, and German), Dr. Steinberg seemed to me more a rhetorician than a thinker. In any case, his outlook was so different from Dubnov's that I have often wondered what had brought the two men together. I assume that the initial link was provided by Isaac's younger brother Aaron, an intellectual historian of depth and subtlety. Aaron Steinberg became a much-valued friend and collaborator of Dubnov's as a splendid German translator of his magnum opus and coauthor of the masterful three-volume abridged version of this monumental work. Yet I also suspect that Grandfather was fascinated by the coexistence of revolutionary maximalism with Orthodox Judaism in Isaac Steinberg's ideological makeup.

Quite predictably, the seder at the Steinbergs' turned out to be a relentlessly ritualistic affair, in fact, the most protracted and Orthodox seder I have ever attended. The festivities were preceded by an awkward moment. As we were about to sit down at the table, the host produced skullcaps for all males present. My brother, who at thirteen was a committed socialist and a principled atheist, balked at the skullcap. The ensuing tension was relieved by Dubnov's quiet diplomacy. He took Alex aside and said something like, "Believe me, I could just as well dispense with a skullcap myself, but since we are in Isaac's house, we should respect his feelings." My brother grudgingly relented. There was something beguiling about the spectacle of an architect of Jewish secular nationalism pleading with his teenage socialist grandson to show consideration for the religious beliefs of the first Soviet commissar of justice.

One of the fringe benefits of our year with the Dubnovs was the chance it gave my brother and me to see Grandfather "in the round," to glean facets of his personality to which only few intimates were privy. Among them was a lively and at times unexpectedly zany sense of humor. Once, as we were having our evening tea, Grandmother, usually somewhat reticent, was in a reminiscent mood. She began to relate an incident reaching back to the youth of my maternal uncle Yasha, who at the time of the storytelling was professor of mathematics at the University of Moscow. "When Yasha was in Kishinev," she began, only to be briskly interrupted by her husband. "He was never in Kishinev," he announced. "You must have confused Yasha with Pushkin." The far-fetched notion produced a great deal of merriment around the table. Grandmother, whose story was whimsically undercut, was naturally reluctant to join in the laughter. She responded with a characteristic verbal shrug, "Oy Semyon," roughly a cross between "there you go again" and "boys will be boys." Ida Dubnov was too sober a person to side openly with "Semyon's" jeux d'esprit, but she was too good-natured really to resent them.

There was nothing staid about Grandfather; even at his most didactic, he was never pedantic or ponderous. Age failed to dim his vitality, to diminish his zest, even if inevitably it affected some of his responses. He could be sturdily and unabashedly old-fashioned. His attitude toward modern technology, including such eminently useful inventions as the telephone, was decidedly wary. I remember a scene when Mother got up from the dinner table and proceeded in the general direction of the telephone. "Where are you going, Sonia?" Dubnov asked, somewhat apprehensively. "I have to call Mr. X," answered Mother, whereupon Grandfather remonstrated, "Is it necessary? He'll call you." Being a reasonable man, he reluctantly conceded that since it was she who needed some information from Mr. X, it was logical for her to call. But back in 1926, he clearly tended to view the telephone as the last resort. A positive obverse of this stance was his awe-inspiring promptness in answering letters. (Clearly, correspondence was for him a much more natural activity than telephone conversation.) When congratulated on this admirable habit, he expressed genuine surprise. "What else? Postponing for days, let alone weeks, an answer to a letter is as rude as not responding immediately when one is greeted in the street."

Another area in which Dubnov showed himself unmistakably a nineteenth-century man was his literary taste. His abiding love of poetry forged early on a powerful link between him and his favorite daughter, Sonia, who learned to appreciate verse on her father's knee only to become an accomplished poet in the second decade of this century. Though Grandfather's intellectual outlook was shaped by positivism, he was keenly responsive to the romantic and the lyrical. He was steeped in classical Russian poetry, finely attuned to the luminous genius of Alexander Pushkin, the romantic turmoil of Mikhail Lermontov, the civic muse of Nikolai Nekrasov, the haunting music of Alexander Fet, the meditative eloquence of Fyodor Tyutchev. He knew by heart many poems of Heinrich Heine and Victor Hugo. But his literary sensibility stopped at the century's edge. He found the quasi mysticism of the Russian symbolists too murky, their eroticism too enervating and "decadent." Needless to say, Grandfather had even less use for the verbal experimentation of the Russian futurists, the more so since their most resonant spokesman, Vladimir Mayakovsky, became an ardent Bolshevik. It seems that at some point, Mother and Dubnov agreed to disagree on "modernism," but there were moments when he could not quite contain himself.

I recall one such moment in the Dubnov Berlin apartment. Grandfather picked up a volume of Mayakovsky's verse, which would have belonged to Mother, and opened it to the poem "Versailles," where the rhythmic flow, in a true futurist manner, was broken into short lines consisting of a single word or a word cluster. The opening sequence of the poem, in literal translation, would read like this:

> On this
> Highway
> Hastening to the palace
> Innumerable Louises
> Shook
> In the silk
> Of gilded carriages
> Their heavy flesh.

Dubnov viewed the text with undisguised revulsion and proceeded to recite, deliberately exaggerating the abrupt, staccato quality of the verse and pausing after each miniline. Having gone on in this fashion to his total dissatisfaction, he turned to Mother: "Do you call this poetry? This is hiccups!"

The subsequent decade offered precious little room for humor or facetiousness. The sky over Europe, most notably over Germany, grew darker every day.

There was a shorter, cheerless visit with the Dubnovs in the

summer of 1932. The city in which they had sought, and for
a while had found, a peaceful haven was now inundated by
the "brown battalions" of Nazi thugs. With a heavy heart, the
Dubnovs began to brace themselves for a new move. Shortly after
they had settled into their new residence in Riga, Dubnov sustained a painful loss. His faithful companion of more than fifty-
five years, the quietly brave and undemonstratively caring woman
who had stood by him through years of penury, often straining
her resourcefulness to enable her husband to pursue his calling,
died after a protracted illness. Dubnov's growing concern over
Europe's future and the deadly menace to European Jewry was
compounded, and for a while overshadowed, by an acute sense of
bereavement, of loneliness.

In 1935, Mother and I journeyed to Vilna to join Grandfather
at the Second Congress of Yivo (now known as the Yivo Institute
for Jewish Research in New York). Dubnov was one of the institute's founders in 1925 and its honorary chairman. In her fine
biography of Dubnov, Mother has spoken aptly of the "atmosphere of a major cultural festival." Yet it was an unmistakably
Eastern European Jewish festival—intense, tumultuous, occasionally abrasive, teeming with ideas and projects, with ideological and methodological controversies. I vaguely recall a spirited debate about the relationship between scholarship and
politics, in the course of which a forceful spokesman of the
Bundist faction, Shlyoma Mendelson, took issue with the stance
of the Yivo leadership represented by Dr. Max Weinreich. I remember being impressed both by Mendelson's challenge and
Weinreich's counterattack, though as a budding Bundist I must
have been leaning toward the former. Yet as far as I was concerned, this was no more than an interesting sideshow. The main
reason Mother and I came to Vilna was to hang around Grandfather, to see him in action. What I saw was consistently impressive. Dubnov clearly was one of the commanding presences
at the congress. His impassioned speech at the opening session,
delivered in crisp Yiddish, visibly stirred the large and attentive

audience. His paper "On the Current State of Jewish Historiography" was one of the high points of the proceedings. During the same week, he delivered a moving eulogy of an old friend, the beloved Jewish community leader Tsemakh Shabad, speaking at his grave in Vilna's Jewish cemetery.

The outpouring of attention and admiration for the doyen of Jewish historians must have been deeply gratifying. It offered palpable evidence of the vitality of many fields of Jewish scholarship which Dubnov helped pioneer. But the hectic pace of the congress was draining. It seemed a good idea to adjourn for a few days to a quiet summer place near Vilna. In the small Jewish rooming house (pension) in which we landed, we were joined by Marc and Bella Chagall, who had come to the congress in conjunction with an exhibit of Chagall's Bible drawings. We saw a great deal of them during our brief stay in the pension. The Chagalls chose to take their meals with us and often accompanied us on our walks in the woods.

Our breakfast routine was especially memorable. Each morning a pert waitress would confront us with a thoroughly ethnic choice, one between chopped liver and herring; I recall that whenever Chagall's turn came, he would turn to his wife, his large blue eyes pleading inability to tackle so mundane a matter, and say, "Bella, what do I feel like this morning?" It was noteworthy that Bella had no difficulty answering this query.

I must have been tickled to share the table with an internationally known painter. But I was fully aware that while he seemed to enjoy Mother's company and expressed at some point painterly interest in one of my profiles, which he fancifully labeled "Ethiopian" (I've been looking for such a profile ever since), the real magnet in our trio was Grandfather. It stands to reason that a Jewish artist as mindful of his roots as Marc Chagall would thrill to the opportunity to commune with the most distinguished Jewish historian of his time. But this, I assume, was only part, even if a major part, of the story. What may well have captivated Chagall was a rare blend of intense seriousness with what I do not hesitate to describe as youthfulness—the blend which was Simon Dubnov at seventy-five.

It is this latter quality that dominates my recollection of what turned out to be our last meeting. The time was late spring of 1940, the place was once again Vilna. But in the meantime, both the ancient city and our personal fortunes had undergone drastic changes. We were no longer visitors to the "Jerusalem of Lithuania" but refugees faced with the Nazi invasion and the fourth partition of Poland. As I shall report in a later chapter, our family had expanded by including my sister-in-law and my wife, Iza, but it was brutally truncated when Father was arrested by the NKVD in Brest-Litovsk, Vilna, which after September 1939 had been occupied by the Red Army and then temporarily ceded to independent Lithuania pending the creeping Sovietization of the entire country that was to begin in the summer of 1940.[2]

It was during this interlude, laden with uncertainty and anxiety, that Grandfather came down from Riga to see his friends and colleagues and to visit with us. He fully shared our intense worry about Father and viewed Hitler's designs with increasing dismay. Yet characteristically he refused to yield to gloom, let alone despair. He was full of plans for further activities and as vigorous, involved, and energetic as ever. What stands out most vividly in my memory is the brisk way he ran up the four flights of stairs leading to our Vilna apartment on the day of his departure. I remember thinking that this octogenarian was in spirit one of the youngest men I knew.

The rest is history, which in 1941 meant nightmare. In December of that year, as Riga's Jewish population was being annihilated, the great historian was felled by a murderous bullet—a fate he could have easily avoided had he accepted a long-standing invitation to the United States rather than, as he put it, remaining with his people and bearing witness to this ordeal.

As I think back to our last glimpses of Grandfather, I am reminded of the closing lines of a late Pasternak poem, "Fame," a poem which, I am sure, he would have found congenial:

You must not for a single instant
Betray your nature and pretend.
But be alive, that only matters,
Alive and living to the end.[3]

My staggered account of life with Grandfather has led me far afield. Let me retrace my steps and return to the dreamy teenager who, having returned to Warsaw in 1926, was gradually moving toward normalcy.

Just in case, I took an entrance exam to one of Warsaw's major high schools. I'm saying "just in case" because what was at issue was not actually entering the school in question but testing myself vis-à-vis the system by assessing the level of my proficiency. The results were generally satisfactory, though I had unexpectedly considerable trouble with one of my favorite subjects, mathematics. The fact of the matter is that my examiner was a man who was yet to be recognized as one of the most creative mathematical logicians of his generation, Alfred Tarski. It was testimony to the prevalence of anti-Semitism on the Polish campuses that this eminent scholar was reduced to teaching math at a Warsaw high school. He must have converted somewhat later, changing his original name of Tajtelbaum to Tarski, a move which enabled him to land a junior position at the University of Warsaw. (He was not granted a full professorship until emigrating to Berkeley.) Naturally, he resented his status in 1926 and 1927 and seemed to be taking it out on me by asking sophisticated, essentially philosophical questions which a high school sophomore could not have been expected to tackle. I found the famous logician stringent and more than a bit crabby. (I would like to believe that there was nothing personal about his crabbiness.) In any case, it was a trying experience, and I barely squeaked through.

I was not slated to enroll for another year. It seems that the notion of my being frail was still shaping the agenda. It was decided, with the strong support of at least one prominent pediatrician, that I should spend my two years of high school in a healthful environment, notably in the pine woods of Otwock, a town located some twenty miles from Warsaw, which in addition to balmy air boasted a relatively enlightened coeducational gymnasium.

This decision required some rearranging of the family way of life. Alex had just graduated from high school and was all set to leave the nest to study social sciences at the University of Berlin, while staying with the Dubnovs. Mother and I would settle in Otwock for two years. Father would join us during the weekends. Whenever he had to do some larger-scale writing for the Bundist *Naye Folkstsaytung,* the calm of the modest resort would be more conducive to reflection that the hectic pace of our Warsaw apartment.

The period of my adjustment to the high school regimen was relatively brief. For a while I projected the image of a weirdo; I would hang on to my briefcase during recess, but I promptly abandoned this habit. I was doing well enough in my classes and decided early on that the presence of girls was a definite asset. In fact, sometime during my junior year, I developed a mild crush on a vivacious brunette with laughing brown eyes. She probably never knew about this: I was absurdly shy. (I guess one cannot spend much of one's adolescence at home with total impunity.)

One of the most acute symptoms of my inordinate shyness was an inability to "sound off" in the classroom. Those who have known me for the last fifty years or so will be astonished to hear that whenever I had to perform, I spoke so softly as to be barely audible. (My wife repeatedly complained that in some social situations, especially during a heated political discussion, I had trouble keeping my volume down.) The fact of the matter is that when asked a question in the Polish literature class, I would usually know the answer, but I would offer it in the form of a fairly coherent mumble. Our astute literature teacher, who was also an effective and popular principal, would typically assume that I was making some sense, since she approved of my written work. But on one occasion, when I was presenting a paper at our literary club, she was moved to intervene rather forcefully. It was testimony to the liberal ethos of my school that every other meeting of our literary club would be devoted to antiwar fiction. I was asked to speak about a novel which created quite a stir in the 1920s: *The Controversy over Sergeant Grisha* by Arnold Zweig. After the first few minutes of my presentation, Mrs. Izdebska, who was chairing the meeting, virtually tore the paper out of my hands. "Sit down, Erlich," she said brusquely. "You are murdering a good paper. Let me read it." And read it she did. My feelings, understandably, were mixed. I was glad that my paper was good enough to be read by Mrs. Izdebska. But I was embarrassed to have to depend on her mediation.

A few months later, at the beginning of my senior year, our class was engaged in a production of a comedy by a popular Polish playwright, B. Hertz, *A Young Forest.* Though not a masterpiece, it was a lively and performable play, set in a Warsaw high school in 1905, the year of a general school strike directed against the Russian authorities. One of the protagonists, a half-comical, half-melodramatic figure, was a pathetically ineffectual French teacher beset by an obstreperous, disrespectful class. Late into the rehearsals, the director was faced by a crisis—the boy who was to play the French teacher was taken ill. An immediate replacement was needed. The situation got so critical that someone was moved to mutter, "How about Erlich? He gets As in French." The reaction was all too predictable. "Erlich? But he mumbles. Nobody will be able to hear him." Finally, since no other option was available, out of sheer desperation, I was offered the part.

To everyone's surprise, I carried it off. I could be heard in the last row. I was a success. The local barber's wife was moved to tears.

Actually, what happened could be easily explained. I found my voice by being someone else, by impersonating a character very much unlike myself. What matters is that my playing a part in a minor play proved a turning point for me vocally. From then on I had no trouble projecting, even if for a while the circumstances under which I found my voice exerted some influence. Some months after the performance of *A Young Forest,* I was once again called upon to present a paper at a meeting of the literary club. This time I was perfectly audible. When the session was over, one of my best friends in the class, a very bright boy with pronounced leftist leanings, congratulated me on my delivery and then added, "No one had any trouble hearing you this time, but I have a question. There was nothing particularly sad about what you were saying. But why did you sound so sad?" I had to reflect for a minute until I realized that the wistful if not lachrymose tenor of my presentation was a direct throwback to what was vocally my finest hour. It took me a while to shake off the hapless French teacher's tonality. The amplified volume stayed with me, for better or worse, through the rest of my life.

One of the dubious benefits of my brief high school career, preceded by years of what was essentially a hothouse existence, was belated exposure to stupidity. In terms of intelligence, our class was something of a cross section of humanity. I remember distinctly two bright Jewish girls. Miss G., an ambitious and assiduous all-around A student, had a decidedly uninteresting mind. Miss C., moody and apparently neurotic, had a genuine literary sensibility and an incurable allergy to math. At the other end of the spectrum were the Baybuk brothers. The older one, who was merely stupid, was referred to by our French teacher as *le meilleur Baybuk* (the better Baybuk). Upon graduation, he failed to gain admission to the University of Warsaw medical school—a fact which may have not been entirely due to the Jewish quota—and landed in Grenoble. I once received from him a postcard in which he praised the French for not telling one what they thought of him. It occurred to me that for someone like the older Baybuk, this was a very precious quality.

Yet in comparison to his younger brother, *le meilleur Baybuk* was a wizard. I still recall with acute embarrassment a Polish literature class where the pathetic young man was enjoined to engage in textual analysis. The text in question was a sonnet by the great Polish romantic Adam Mickiewicz, "Sea Calm," which contained the following lines: "Sunlit water is playing with its quiet breasts/like a young bride dreaming of happiness."[4] Asked to explicate this metaphor, Baybuk junior blabbered, "A young bride sits in the water and plays with her quiet breasts." Mrs. Izdebska's response was curt: "Sit down, Baybuk. You are a fool."

My brief bout with high school was drawing to its close. On the whole, my academic record was creditable, though I came dangerously close to flunking physical education through a combination of uncommonly poor performance and dismal attendance. Another subject in which I did not excel, but neither did anyone else, was Jewish religion.

Since interwar Poland did not believe in separation of church and state, one could not graduate from high school without a passing grade in religion. As my family was staunchly secular, it would have been more accurate to write in filling out the questionnaire "nonbeliever" or "nondenominational" (*bezwyznaniowy*). But one would put down "Jewish" under "religion" so as not to appear to try "to pass." In the face of growing anti-Semitism, it was essential to own up to one's Jewishness. Thus, during my senior year, about 25 percent of the graduating class became the captive audience of an ineffectual elderly man who was trying to convey to us in faltering Polish the fundamentals of Judaism. I've said "trying" since no one listened. Our teacher, who would have felt more at home in a Jewish religious grade school, the so-called heder, than in a Polish gymnasium, could not make himself heard above the din of brazenly loud conversation and occasional insults. Every meeting of his class was pandemonium. Now and then our hapless instructor in Judaism was pelted by pieces of paper. Though I had scant interest in what our teacher was attempting to impart, I found this harassment objectionable and refrained from the more unseemly activities. Toward the end of the term, the beleaguered instructor paid me a hedged but unexpectedly subtle compliment: "Erlich does not believe in anything but respects everything."

Between Socialist Politics
and Neo-Romantic Literature

In the summer of 1932 it was time to bid farewell to the Otwock pines and return to the capital. My student days were about to begin.

I elected to enroll not at the traditional University of Warsaw but at a private and relatively liberal institution located on the outskirts of the city, the Free Polish University (Wolna Wszechnica Polska), which numbered among its faculty some left-leaning historians and economists.

It took me no more than a few weeks to choose my field of study. (In contradistinction to American colleges, at Polish—and, more broadly, continental—universities, it was customary to declare one's major at the beginning of the first year and to pursue it steadily, with little attention to "breadth requirements.") For a short while I was torn between two principal strains in my family—literature and politics. Thus, I toyed briefly with the idea of majoring in political philosophy only to turn to literature, more specifically, Polish literature, with a strong Russian minor. (Russian literature was taught at the Free Polish University by a somewhat melancholy and intelligently eclectic Russian émigré.)

Since the advanced degree toward which I began to work was one in Slavic philology, I needed a few credits in linguistics, including a course in Old Church Slavonic, the first Slavic written language, taught by the highly competent but dry-as-dust scholar Professor S. Slonski. As I recall, my bout with this gateway to Slavic philology was less than a success. During my oral final examination, I proved reasonably sound on the Old Church Slavonic grammatical patterns, such as its distinctive verbal aspects, but I was somewhat foggy at identifying the canonical texts. When I was asked to place a passage which I was trying to analyze, I muttered, "I think this is *Codex Marianus.*" My examiner was not impressed: "Here one doesn't think, here one is supposed to know." (Incidentally, I have never found out whether my guess was right or wrong.) Clearly, historical linguistics as taught by Professor Slonski was not my cup of tea. It took me nearly fifteen years to realize, when converging on Columbia University with Roman Jakobson, that linguistics could be as exciting as literature.

If my choice of a major was of a piece with my early involvement with prose fiction, my extracurricular activities were increasingly shaped by the fact of my having been raised in the family of a Bund leader.

Unlike my brother, Alex, and many other Bundist progeny, I had not become affiliated with the movement until after my graduation from high school. My brother, who at the age of six shattered the complacency of a bourgeois household by shouting revolutionary slogans in the middle of the night, was clearly predisposed for an early engagement. Some four years later he woke up Father in midmorning to announce: "I'm not sure whether I'm a socialist, but I'm sure I'm a revolutionary." (Father absorbed this news with equanimity, though he might not have been convinced it was that urgent.) At the age of fifteen, Alex was "sure" on both counts. By the time I graduated from high school, he was an active and prominent member of the Bundist youth movement Tsukunft ("Future"). With his acute sense of social justice and his instinctive bias in favor of anyone who could be plausibly construed as an underdog, Alex was one of the most organic socialists I have ever known.

Need I say that for a number of years I lived in a world of my own? It is noteworthy that Father never pressured me to get involved. He seems to have been intrigued by my literary efforts, and, while he must have assumed that sooner or later I would declare myself politically, he wanted me to do so at my own pace. Predictably, my childhood and adolescence were strongly colored by distinctively Bundist themes and concerns. After I had mastered the Hebrew-Yiddish alphabet at the age of thirteen and acquired a rudimentary reading knowledge of Yiddish, I would regularly plow through the pages of the party's daily paper, *Naye Folkstsaytung*. While still a teenager, I would attend special Bund events along with my family. I remember vividly one such occasion—an imposing rally held in 1927 to commemorate the thirtieth anniversary of the Bund. The festively decorated hall, one of the largest in Warsaw's Jewish quarter, was filled to overflowing. Father's speech was the centerpiece of the celebration. He spoke in clear and resonant Yiddish, with what I would later recognize as his customary blend of passion and lucidity. I suspect that I had a bit of trouble following his argument both because of lacunae in my Yiddish and because some of what he was saying was inevitably over my head. But I must have been aware that he was cutting a fine figure at the podium, looking trim and distinguished in his black suit, and that the audience was listening to him raptly. My primary, and essentially nonpolitical, response was one of childish pride: "It is *my* father up there!"

Yet something of the event's ambience must have rubbed off on me. In describing it in the diary that I kept assiduously in those days, I noted rather lamely, "The atmosphere was very Bundist." Had I been able to elaborate on this unexceptionable if unilluminating observation, I might have spoken of the combination of a fierce loyalty to the Bundist tradition—a "boundless fidelity to the Bund," in the words of the party's anthem "Di Shvue" ("The Oath")—with a warm family feeling (*mishpokhedikayt*), a sense of mutual affection and trust between the speakers and the audience, the leaders and the rank and file.

Some five years later, as I was enrolling at the Free Polish University, I was ready, indeed eager, to join the Bundist student group Ringen ("Links"), known in Polish as Ogniwo. Over the course of the decade, I assumed an increasingly prominent role in that organization.

Let me say that to be a Bundist student activist was not, at least in some respects, a typical Bundist experience. It meant that one was affiliated with a relatively weak segment of a vital mass movement which toward the end of the interwar period became a significant force in Poland's Jewish community. A Yiddish-oriented and primarily working-class party, the Bund held scant appeal to the linguistically assimilated Jewish middle-class professionals. Consequently, our recruiting efforts had limited success. Yet there were two factors which mitigated against despondency and kept our morale on an even keel. First, and most important, there was a sense of being indeed a link in a firm chain, a sense of relatedness to a dynamic movement, anchored in a shared ideological commitment and kept alive by participation in rallies, May Day demonstrations, and elections. We also engaged in grassroots campaigns, such as those on behalf of the Bundist press, when we would fan out through the teeming streets of Warsaw's Jewish quarter hawking the latest issue of *Naye Folkstsaytung.*

Another boost to our morale was our close and harmonious relationship with the Polish socialist student organization ZNMS (Union of Independent Young Socialists). Our political affinity with it was often reinforced by personal friendships. Since the ZNMS was consistently to the left of its mother party, the PPS (Polish Socialist Party), our alliance, though limited in scope, was less impeded than was the relationship between the Bund and the PPS.

There were many issues on which Ogniwo and our Polish counterpart saw eye to eye. No issue was more pressing to the socialist and liberal students in Warsaw in the 1930s than the rising tide of fascism and bigotry. During that decade, most notably in the late 1930s, the major Polish universities became hotbeds of right-wing hooliganism and blatant anti-Semitic discrimination. I refer to the infamous "bench ghetto"—that is, the physical segregation of Jewish students. During that last prewar decade, individual Jewish students would protest this outrage by standing rather than occupying the classroom seats assigned to them. But the situation called for organized political action as well. A total mobilization of the student Left seemed necessary, an alliance or coalition that would include, in addition to the two socialist groupings, the predominantly, though not exclusively, Jewish procommunist organization Zycie ("Life").

One of our first joint ventures was an unauthorized protest rally staged in the hostile territory of the University of Warsaw. Predictably, it proved very brief. As a spokesman of the Polish socialists held forth, the hastily assembled audience was invaded almost simultaneously by anti-Semitic hoodlums and the campus police. The former burst upon the scene looking for Jewish faces. Having sighted mine, two or three of them pounced on me, trying to drag me away from the crowd. While they were pulling me to the right, two husky campus policemen grabbed me in an attempt to drag me in the opposite direction. (Their objectives, and indeed their overt stance, were, to put it mildly, ambiguous.) I was miraculously rescued from this predicament when my brother, who was one of the chief organizers of the rally, surprised everybody, including himself, by exclaiming, "I know this guy! He is OK!" Stunned by this totally unexpected, though heartfelt, testimonial, both sets of my attackers let go of me. Naturally, the rally could not be resumed.

Though impelled by a brutal and ubiquitous threat, the united front of left-wing Warsaw students proved precarious. I must confess that I found having to deal with my "progressive" or "anti-fascist" fellow students—since the Polish Communist Party had been outlawed, the followers and sympathizers had to adopt these euphemistic labels—increasingly intolerable. Their mindless apologies for Stalin's purges, including the infamous "Moscow trials," turned nearly every discussion of Soviet policy into a shouting match. Yet, ironically, our coalition foundered not on Communist dogmatism but on their opportunism, which at times assumed truly grotesque proportions. (Anyone who was politically active on the Left during the Popular Front era can testify that the Communists managed to be as extreme in their "pragmatism" as they often were in their sectarianism.) Thus, at some point the political strategists of Zycie arrived at the notion of broadening the base of our struggle against anti-Semitism on the Polish campuses to include, along with "bourgeois liberals," those Endeks—that is, followers of the right-wing, anti-Semitic National Democratic Party—who did not actually beat up on Jews. The apparent aim of this maneuver was to isolate the fascist hooligans politically.

Needless to say, such a strategy was more than we could stomach. It fell to me to dissociate Ogniwo from this patently absurd position and to conclude, not without some personal satisfaction, that this orgy of broad-mindedness made our further cooperation impossible. The parting of ways occurred in a small apartment somewhere in Warsaw South, at a meeting that brought together the representative bodies of Ogniwo and Zycie. Confronted by the aforementioned proposal, I denounced it in no uncertain terms and walked out of the room. If I now recall my declaration with somewhat mixed feelings, it is because of its tone rather than its substance. I certainly do not regret having been so intractable; the break with the "progressives" was, if anything, overdue. But considering the nature, or rather the scale, of the occasion, I could have been a trifle less solemn. Budding political activists often lack a sense of perspective, and I was no exception. The gravity of my rhetoric made my perfectly legitimate exit sound a bit too much like, say, the walkout of the representatives of the Democratic-Socialist factions on the historic meeting of the Petrograd Soviet of Workers' and Soldiers' Deputies in October 1917.

On at least one memorable occasion, our politics of protest took the form of a national rather than a united front, though even there the fierce political differentiation of Polish Jewry made itself felt. In the fall of 1937, all of Warsaw's Jewish student organizations chose to stage a three-day mass hunger strike in order to dramatize our campaign against the bench ghetto policy. Not uncharacteristically, this act of Jewish solidarity provided an occasion for a competitive parade of major political creeds within Poland's Jewish community. As we set up camp uncomfortably, but zestfully, in the rickety building known as the Jewish Students' Home, the leaders of nearly all the Jewish parties came to pledge their support, to vow solidarity, and in the process to make a bid for the hearts and minds of the demonstrators. The most skillful, if somewhat demagogic, speech was delivered by the canny Zionist orator M. Kleinbaum, who later became a highly controversial left-wing figure in Israel under the name of Moshe Sneh. Citing the well-known notion that the status of the Jew in a given society is a reliable yardstick of its relative moral health, he cried out passionately, "We are tired of serving as a barometer of other people's righteousness!" Though my comrades and I appreciated Kleinbaum's rhetorical effectiveness, the speech that brought us to our feet cheering was given in Yiddish by S. Mendelson, who urged those present to view our challenge to anti-Semitism as an integral part of a wider struggle for a democratic and socialist Poland.

It has often been argued that the fate which befell Polish Jewry during and after the Second World War marked these hopes as naive and utopian. I have some difficulty with this view. I admit that our long-range optimism rested in part on an overly Marxist interpretation of anti-Semitism. Today, while recognizing a connection between the overall political climate of the country and the relative virulence of ethnic discrimination, I would be inclined to insist that no social class, however "progressive," is inherently immune to anti-Semitism, and no socioeconomic system, however otherwise desirable, is a guarantee of a constructive solution to the "Jewish question." But I'm not prepared to criticize either myself or my former comrades-in-arms for having associated our struggle for the dignity of the Jewish masses with a generous vision of Poland as a land of freedom, decency, and justice or, for that matter, for having linked our personal and political aspirations with the country we lived in. It occurs to me that it is this sense of rootedness in the soil of the Eastern European Diaspora, often expressed by the concept of *doikayt* (liter-

ally, Yiddish for "hereness"), that accounts in large measure for
the remarkable vigor and unswerving consistency of the Bund's
moral and physical resistance to the anti-Semitic blight, a resistance which in the last years before the war earned our party
support and trust well beyond the confines of its natural constituency. During the last prewar elections of the Warsaw City
Council, held in the fall of 1938, the Bund garnered an absolute
majority of the capital's Jewish vote. Judging by a rough version
of an exit poll, a large number of Hasidim voted for the first time
in their lives for the anticlerical Bund, which fought for their
rights, rather than for the Orthodox Agudath Isroel, whose operatives persisted in their increasingly incongruous role of "court
Jews."

Speaking in more personal terms, one of the fringe benefits of
my political activism lay in bringing me closer to Father. Whenever the family would get together in the evening around the
kitchen table, sometimes no earlier than midnight, both Alex
and I would have an opportunity to try out on Father some of the
positions we had just taken in an intraorganizational dispute.
One such instance comes to mind: Ogniwo was asked to respond
to a statement issued by a Ukrainian student group decrying the
repressive official policy toward Poland's Ukrainian population.
Our personable secretary, Yasha Zlatin, mindful of the anti-
Semitic strain in Ukrainian nationalism, thought our support of
this declaration was unwarranted. I maintained that since the
grievances voiced in it were legitimate, we should join in protest-
ing the Polish government's mean-spirited nationalities policy
without endorsing the overall philosophical position of our
Ukrainian classmates. It was a matter of great satisfaction to me
that when I reported the stand that I had taken, Father said quietly, "You were right."

Those of us who entered the Bundist movement in interwar
Poland were fortunate to be initiated into socialist politics under
the aegis of two remarkable men, Henryk Erlich and Victor Alter.
Some years later their names were to become indissolubly linked
in a tragedy that befell them in Stalin's Russia. Back in the

1930s, at the peak of their influence, they were an uncommonly appealing and effective team; they complemented each other both functionally and temperamentally. Father was editor in chief of the *Naye Folkstsaytung,* chairman of the Bundist caucus in the Warsaw City Council, the party's main spokesman, and its principal representative in the Socialist International. Alter was the leader of the Jewish trade unions, the Bund's popular alderman and its freewheeling theorist. As personalities, they were at once akin and different. They were both strikingly handsome, with Father looking like a statesman and Victor Alter like a film star, the Cary Grant of Jewish labor. (He was quite irresistible to women and demonstrably responsive to them.) They were akin in their unswerving commitment to principle, their humanity, and their luminous intelligence. But where Father was judicious, thoughtful, controlled, Alter was volatile, combative, impetuous. There was also, especially throughout the thirties, a distinct difference of temperament. We, the family, knew that Father had an exquisite sense of humor because we were privy to his rare moments free from public cares, during his all-too-brief vacations in the mountains or at the seashore. But as W. H. Auden's "low, dishonest decade" wore on, I sensed in him a growing sadness, not a personal, but, if I may say so, a historical sadness.[1] A man who felt history in his bones, he was visibly weighed down by the sense of a mounting threat which the rise of Hitler presented to everything he held dear. Victor fully shared Father's overall assessment of the international situation. But there was something irrepressible about his congenital high spirits. It seemed impossible to get this "happy warrior" down.

Alex and I greatly enjoyed Victor Alter's impromptu visits. For a number of years he lived across the street from us. He would breeze in now and then for a few minutes to share with Mother something interesting or amusing he had just read. I remember his delight in the opening sentence of Yuri Olesha's *Envy,* a remarkable early Soviet novel which many years later I was to discuss in my last academic book, *Modernism and Revolution.* "In the mornings he sings in the john."[2] (The "he" is the ebullient Soviet entrepreneur Andrey Babichev.) "Isn't this a great way to launch a novel?" Victor exclaimed. In five minutes, he was on his way.

Does the somewhat overused phrase "role models" describe accurately the way I felt, when growing up, about Henryk Erlich and Victor Alter? Yes and no. Though I admired both and was demonstrably influenced by them, I did not aspire to emulating them. One does not emulate charisma.

All in all, I was preceded by difficult acts to follow—my maternal grandfather was a world-famous historian, my father a distinguished public figure, my mother a wide-ranging woman of letters. I could have experienced this eminent ancestry as a burden, but I do not think I did. My parents' expectations of me were not overly specific or, to coin a phrase, structured. They probably assumed that I would grow up into an intelligent and decent human being with the right set of values. Also, in view of my early fling with narrative fiction, they must have expected me to land at some intersection of politics and literature, which is indeed what happened. As indicated earlier, I bade farewell to creative writing at the age of fourteen. In my early twenties I was increasingly drawn to literary criticism.

My initial approach to the study of literature was bound to be somewhat affected by my political engagement. Marxism or historical materialism as a philosophy of culture came with the Bundist territory. In fact, only one of my early sorties into print, featured in the Polish-language Bundist biweekly *Nowe Zycie* (*A New Life*), was unabashedly Marxist. The title of the essay, occasioned by the death of an aged man of letters, Alexander Swietochowski, was "Prisoner of [His] Class." The "class" in question was the Polish bourgeoisie. My thesis was that the blind spots of this mildly conservative standard-bearer of Polish nationalism mirrored the stance of the segment of the mid-nineteenth-century Polish society which had nurtured Swietochowski. Yet, when all is said and done, my commitment to the Marxist approach to literature was less than wholehearted. As a budding literary critic, I was expending more intellectual energy cautioning against the overly simplistic applications of the method than actually applying it. I was clearly uneasy about the Marxist potential for reductionism, the tendency to treat culture in general and literature in particular as an epiphenomenon, as a direct reflection or a by-product of socioeconomic forces. I was wary of the readiness of my "leftist" classmates to overpoliticize literature, to care more about politically correct interpretations of the literary texts than about the texts themselves.

An episode which occurred in 1936 or 1937 at a meeting of the Free Polish University Literary Club seemed to me paradigmatic. Professor Orzęcki, whose course in philosophy of law I was attending at the time, volunteered to present a paper on the parallel between Stavrogin, the chief protagonist of Dostoevsky's *The Devils,* and Steerforth, the glamorous troublemaker in Dickens's *David Copperfield.* A portly, flamboyant, and somewhat irascible man, Prof. O. was known for his rhetorical skills and his short fuse. (I had once drawn his ire for paying undue attention during one of his verbal fireworks to the whispering of an attractive neighbor. I'm afraid I was never very good at shutting up comely young women.) At the meeting of the club, I found Prof. O.'s argument deft and quite persuasive. However, Mr. Stasiak, a strapping young man and one of our most vocal leftist graduate students, felt duty-bound to take issue with the speaker's interpretation and inject the Marxist point of view. His strictures had a transparent flaw: the more strenuously he harangued his audience, the more apparent it was that his grip on the plot of *The Devils* was, to put it mildly, tenuous, a fact which did not escape the alert lecturer's attention. When his turn to respond came, Professor Orzęcki did his best to put his arms around his opponent and declared, "My dear colleague Stasiak, I have high regard and affection for you, but you've not read *The Devils.*" I cannot reconstruct the evidence adduced; all I recall is that it was conclusive. Mr. Stasiak was not half as embarrassed as he should have been. Clearly, what mattered to him was to have been methodologically sound. In retrospect, the case of "colleague Stasiak" appears to me as a crude illustration of a dictum by a relatively thoughtful early Soviet critic which I had occasion to quote fifteen years later in my first book: "There is no point in discussing the sociological implications of literary facts, as long as the facts themselves are not established."[3]

My growing dissatisfaction with Marxist determinism made me vulnerable to "revisionist" heresies. True, I felt somewhat reassured by F. Engels's emendation that allowed the "ideological superstructures" a degree of autonomy and some dynamics of their own. But in the late thirties, along with a few like-minded young Bundists, I found myself receptive to a book by the Belgian socialist Henri de Man, *Psychologie du Socialisme,* which argued the importance of the "subjective factor" in the social process. (The deplorable fact that several years later Henri de Man, who incidentally was Paul de Man's uncle, turned out to be a leading collaborationist in occupied Belgium is not directly relevant here, since there was no discernible connection between de Man's prewar "revisionism" and his wartime record.) Characteristically, it was Victor Alter who called de Man's book to the attention of the party intelligentsia. I say "characteristically" since Alter was more drawn to theoretical innovation and more apt to seek a conceptual basis for our policies than were most Bund leaders. It was he who injected into our debates about the nature of the Soviet regime the concept of the leader principle (*Führerprinzip*). In a move that was totally unpalatable to left-wing Bundists, Alter sought to anchor some of the excesses of the Stalin regime in the authoritarian, centralist structure of the Russian Communist Party laid down by Lenin.

Alter's readiness to use a Nazi term in dealing with Soviet communism meant a principled repudiation of Bolshevism rather than a mere revulsion from Stalinism—a stance which as an author of a juvenile Menshevik novel about the French Revolution I found totally congenial. Already in my student days I was prepared to be as anti-Bolshevik as the Bundist traffic would bear.

By 1937, my studies at the Free Polish University were drawing to a close. After a total immersion in Polish romantic poetry and a bout with the Polish realistic novel, I focused on the turn-of-the-century literary ferment variously labeled "Neo-

Romanticism" or "Young Poland." When the time came to pick a subject for my M.A. thesis, I chose one of the most seminal and controversial literary intellectuals of the period: the brilliant, quirky, fiercely polemical Stanislaw Brzozowski (1878–1911), whose brief and tumultuous career ranged over narrative fiction, philosophy of culture, and literary criticism. I dealt with the latter dimension of his oeuvre.

Brzozowski's involvement with early Polish modernism is not easily summed up. As Czeslaw Milosz writes in *The History of Polish Literature*, "he shared the adventures of 'Young Poland,' first as a fervent supporter of the *Moderna*, then as its detractor in a book that created quite a stir called *The Legend of a Young Poland* (*Legenda Mlodej Polski*, 1909)."[4] He spoke for many of his contemporaries, especially the strongly Western European–oriented intelligentsia, in his relentless debunking of that consummate storyteller and national morale builder Henryk Sienkiewicz, whose immense popularity he saw as the epitome of parochial self-congratulation. While strongly drawn to the activist, engagé strain in Polish Neo-Romanticism, Brzozowski tended to excoriate those aspects of the fin de siècle culture which smacked of aestheticism and "decadence." All in all, his attitude toward the powerful romantic tradition in Polish letters was profoundly ambivalent. He once described the romantic rebellion against the "given," in a memorable phrase with a distinct Marxian flavor, as a "revolt of a flower against its roots." Marx was indeed one of the major influences on Brzozowski's thought, but his impact was significantly modified by exposure to other thinkers—Vico, Proudhon, Sorel—and, finally, by the Christian personalism of Cardinal Newman.

My interest in Brzozowski's critical legacy was testimony to a growing preoccupation with what T. S. Eliot called "the nature and uses of literary criticism," as well as a predisposition toward a sociocultural approach to literature. Moreover, my attraction to an eclectic maverick who, as Czeslaw Milosz reminds us, "launched a call: Revisionists of all churches unite!"[5] was indicative of my growing restiveness over Marxist orthodoxy.

My M.A. essay must have been good enough to earn me an M.A. degree, but I have an inkling that it was a somewhat immature piece of writing. In 1939, I had occasion to return to Brzozowski, most notably to his attitude to Marxism, in a polemical article which took issue with the strictures of two radical intellectuals, M. Boruchowicz and Jerzy Borejsza. The former was to become known as an Israeli man of letters; the latter was slated to be one of postwar Poland's leading ideologists. My "Brzozowski and Marxism" landed in a fairly high-level left-wing literary journal *Sygnaly* (*Signals*), based in Lwów and edited by the thoughtful and independent Karol Kuryluk. The fate of my essay was bizarre: it appeared on the brink of the Second World War, in the September 1939 issue of *Sygnaly.* Needless to say, it never reached me. Many years later, I was able to read the piece at the New York Public Library and found it one of my more creditable early literary efforts.

If the reader gets the impression that back in my graduate student days I was a bookish and somewhat abstract young man, he or she will not be altogether wrong. In matters sexual, I was unquestionably a later bloomer, held back as I was by inhibitions and residual shyness. Yet by 1937, I was ready for an emotional involvement. It was my good fortune to meet at that juncture a vivid, keen, and feisty young woman. Her name was Iza Sznejerson (Shneerson). Iza's ancestry could be traced back to the charismatic founder of Hassidism, Zalmen Shneur. The famed Lubavitcher Rabbi Menachem Shneerson was a very distant relative. Iza's father, a personable and thoughtful lawyer, was a second-generation secular Shneerson; he was drawn to the Bund, mainly, I believe, because of his high regard for Father. Since Iza's family and mine knew one another, I had been aware of her existence as "old Shneerson's daughter" early on.

Actually, our first encounter was less than momentous. As a bright-eyed girl of thirteen, Iza embarked on a rather ambitious school project—a paper on the origins of religion. Her father suggested to her that she turn to Alex and me for some guidance. Alex, who at the early age of twenty was a budding Marxist scholar, assumed his role readily, if a bit too gravely. Standing in front of the fireplace, speaking cogently but slowly, with an audible gulp after each sentence, he held forth about the standard Marxist study of the subject by the German Social-Democratic pundit H. Cunow. I just stood there, not in deference to my older brother, but because I had nothing essential to add. The addressee of the somewhat impeded lecture appeared to listen closely, but, as she was to tell me several years later, as soon as the door closed behind her, she broke into laughter and giggled uncontrollably all the way down to the street. Iza's merriment was totally unrelated to the substance of Alex's disquisition and was only partly provoked by its delivery. It seems that she found the sight of two gangly and skinny young men irresistibly funny. (Separately we probably looked fairly normal, but together we must have been a rather ungainly spectacle.) Having returned home, she asked her father, "How come Mr. and Mrs. Erlich are fine-looking people but their sons look as if they had just come off a tree?" Iza's old man was, or pretended to be, scandalized. "That is no way," he presumably exclaimed, "to talk about two intelligent young men who are considerably older than you!"

I don't recall too vividly my response to our irreverent visitor. I must have found her bright and rather cute. But in 1932, she was too young to bother with. When the parties are respectively eighteen and thirteen, the five-year difference is apt to be crucial. In 1937, encountered as a university freshman at an Ogniwo meeting, "old Shneerson's daughter," radiating intelligence and vitality, definitely merited attention.

Iza's decision to join a Bundist organization was almost unexpected. Being totally "assimilated" linguistically, she would have probably turned to the Polish counterpart of Ogniwo, ZNMS, had it not been for a contrarian streak in her makeup. Her stepmother, a cultivated if somewhat obsessive student of art history, suffered from an acute case of Jewish self-hatred. (Eventually Cecily came to view me as an honorable young man, but initially she found my unmistakably Semitic nose aesthetically offensive.)

In any case, I could only applaud Iza's choice. As it happens, my interest in her received a totally unnecessary organizational endorsement. Iza lived in a suburb of Warsaw, but whenever she had a downtown evening engagement, she would stay overnight with her maternal grandparents, who lived a few blocks down from my house. Before the meeting adjourned, our well-informed and vigilant secretary took me aside and wondered if I couldn't possibly walk the "new comrade" home. "She looks rather critical-minded," he added. The idea was that she could use some ideological reinforcement. I accepted the assignment with some alacrity, though I might have taken it a bit too seriously. Sometime later I asked Iza if I had not bored her the first time around (I was not incapable of ponderousness). Her response was uncharacteristically evasive. I guess she did not mind my preaching since she rather liked my looks.

In the course of the academic year 1937 to 1938, Iza and I saw a great deal of one another, though things were not moving as rapidly as they might have because of my persisting shyness. As it is, another political contingency proved an enabling act—on the eve of our 1938 First of May demonstration, I was charged with a double mission. I was to teach Iza how to sing the Bundist anthem "Di Shvue" ("The Oath") and the Yiddish version of the "Internationale." The mission was doomed to failure. For one thing, Iza knew no Yiddish; for another, while she had a pleasant speaking voice, she tended to sing off-key. It is fair to say that we got sidetracked. To maintain that instead of teaching Iza the Bundist songs, I married her would be to telescope a process that was to take another year and a half. What actually happened on that memorable evening was that we kissed for the first time. With or without the "Internationale," we were launched.

When I look back to May 1, 1938, I see it as one of the sunniest moments of an increasingly ominous decade. The day was brilliant, the mobilization of the Bundist troops exemplary. As we marched in the ranks of Ogniwo through the streets of Warsaw's Jewish quarter, hailed by thousands of friendly bystanders, we did not always sing in unison but, to use a corny cliché, our hearts beat as one. As our demonstration was winding down, Iza and I were delivering the Ogniwo banner to the headquarters of the Warsaw Bund. (I cannot figure out at this point how we managed to carry the flag jointly and hold hands at the same time.) We were about to deposit the banner when we ran into Father, who had just delivered the closing speech. He beamed at us approvingly.

In retrospect, I find it hard to believe that we could be so happy on the brink of Armageddon. I guess it helps to be young, to share a cause, and to be in love.

The fact that Iza and I were getting hooked up was not lost either on our families or on mutual friends. The feisty Bundist lady lawyer, Mrs. Iwińska, who fifteen years earlier had failed to understand that John Chesterfield had to die, bumped into Iza's father, a good friend and a favored colleague, and informed him that "Iza had won a lottery ticket." Though "old Shneerson" was well-disposed toward me, he responded with some heat, "It is Victor who won a lottery ticket."

Without false modesty, Iza's father was right. Though she was five years my junior, she was in some ways more mature, more worldly, than I. It took her pluck and enterprise to bring me out. And bring me out she did. Through the academic year 1938 to 1939 we did an incredible amount of running around Warsaw together. We enjoyed each other's company in the most disparate and scattered locales, from a "sophisticated" coffee shop to a grove at the city's outskirts. It was on a suburban wooded path that we had occasion to test the longevity of our relationship. When we asked a cuckoo how long we would stay together, the answer was "five." Iza said, "Five months?" "How about five years?" I ventured hopefully. Though we were increasingly committed to one another, Iza, who after all was only nineteen, had a residual resistance to the idea of going steady. Of course, we were both wrong. Our union was to last more than five decades, for nearly sixty years!

Inevitably, there was a price to be paid for so much "messing around." By the fall of 1938, I was done with my M.A. thesis, and my duties as assistant literary editor of the Polish-language biweekly *Nowe Zycie* were less than onerous. Within my baili-wick the main casualty, I'm afraid, was the middle-aged Russian Jewish lady, Mrs. Zuckerman, whom I was tutoring in Polish; I was unconscionably late in showing up for our lessons. Iza paid a higher price. As a second-year law student at the University of Warsaw, she was expected to bear down on such subjects as Pol-ish constitutional law. The final examination was arduous, and Jewish students were held to exorbitantly high standards. In order to pass, Iza had to recite the locations of all the gates lead-ing to the field where kings were elected in seventeenth-century Poland. Needless to say, Iza failed to memorize this information and flunked the exam. As I recall, she was not exactly crushed; though back in 1939 she did not anticipate landing in the United States three years later, somehow she had a hunch that Polish con-stitutional law would not loom too large in her future.

We spent two weeks of the last prewar summer in a scenic va-cation spot which was especially popular with the intelligentsia, Kazimierz on the Vistula. The late medieval town was atmos-pheric, and the picturesque ravines along the banks of the Vis-tula had a special appeal to young lovers. Yet, though duly ap-preciative of the scenery, we spent a lot of time indoors. We clung to each other as if anticipating the perils that loomed ahead.

Though the international situation looked ominous, my parents, Alex, and I managed before the end of the summer a brief visit with my recently bereaved grandfather in Riga. (As indicated previously, he had lost his indispensable Ida several years earlier.) Our presence gave this resourceful man a badly needed lift. We sang together some of his favorite Yiddish and Russian songs, including the stirring Soviet "Yesli Zavtra Voina" ("If Tomorrow the War"). By common consent, we would skip the lines extolling the Soviet leaders—"Our own Stalin is with us/And Voroshilov's iron hand/Leads us to victory." Our stay was cut short. We had to rush back to Warsaw. In response to Hitler's brutal shouts about Germany's claims on the so-called

Polish corridor (Gdansk and its environs), the government declared a mobilization.

For a while, the bleakly authoritarian Polish regime of the so-called colonels who ruled Poland after the death of the charismatic if increasingly willful Marshal Józef Pilsudski had toyed with the idea of a modus vivendi with Nazi Germany. Now, in the face of Hitler's blatant territorial designs, the Polish government assumed an intransigent posture. The official pronouncements breathed defiance along with rather unconvincing bravado. Slogans such as "We don't covet what's theirs, but we shall not surrender what's ours," or "We shall not yield not only the coat but a single button on it," in view of Poland's unmistakable military unpreparedness, had a wishfully hollow ring.

Though we welcomed the regime's belated anti-German stance, its posturing seemed strangely off-key. We found more congenial a note struck by our favorite left-wing poet, Wladyslaw Broniewski, who managed to combine uncritical enthusiasm for Soviet industrialization with romantic patriotism—during the First World War he fought in the ranks of Pilsudski's Legions—and political engagement with genuine lyricism. In April 1939, in the short poem "Let Us Fix Our Bayonets!" he wrote: "There are many wrongs in this country/Which a foreigner's hand will not erase/But no one will grudge his blood/We'll draw it from our breasts and our songs." In his determination to repeal the attack on our land without forgetting about its iniquities, Broniewski spoke for the bulk of Poland's Left.

Looking back on this call to arms, I cannot help but note the characteristically Polish bent of the poem's imagery. The notion of close combat was clearly anachronistic at a moment when Hitler's *Panzerdivisionen* were preparing to roll across Poland's plains.

On the Road

On September 1, 1939, Hitler's armies crossed the German-Polish borders and began to move toward Warsaw. Their advance was swift. Polish cavalry was no match for the German tanks. From the first day on, the *Luftwaffe* was raining death on the capital. Father was named the chief air warden in our apartment house, and I became his assistant. I am embarrassed to recall that, since in those days I was a much sounder sleeper than I am today, I had to be roused during one of the air raids.

By September 5, the threat to Warsaw was imminent. The initial strategic plan was to declare Warsaw an open city and to erect a second defense line on the banks of the Bug River, some 150 to 200 miles east of the capital. (About a week later the authorities decided to defend the city rather than surrender it.) The mayor of Warsaw, Stefan Starzyński, called all the able-bodied young men who had not yet been drafted—Alex and I fell into this category—to go east in order to be available for the retreating army. At the same time, he urged a number of public figures who were especially threatened by the Nazi invaders, most notably the Jewish socialist leaders such as Father and Victor Alter, to leave the city forthwith. The night of September 6 to 7 witnessed a large-scale exodus that included my parents; Alex and his intense, dark-haired activist wife, Rachel; and a number of prominent Warsaw Bundists. At the last moment it became clear that Iza would not be able to join us; she could not bring herself to leave behind her father, who had a heart condition—a decision which, needless to say, was very hard on both of us. I was leaving the capital in an emotional daze.

In the final paragraph of her fine memoir, *Bread and Matzoth,* which brings her life story to the outbreak of the Second World War, Mother captured the anxiety-laden moment:

> We walked down to the blacked-out streets toward a spot where a van was supposed to wait for us. It turned out that it had been pre-empted by another group. In the car in which Henryk's Central Committee associates were waiting for us two seats were reserved for my husband and me. We pushed into it resisting Alex and Rachel (because of a congenital foot deformation she was unable to do much walking). . . . The three of us, H., Vitya, and I entered a crowd of pedestrians, slowly swaying under a somber sky, bound for the outskirts of the city. Carts rumbled on the cobblestones of the pavement, brim full of people and bags, Warsaw . . . was on the move.[1]

During what turned out to be an arduous nine-day trek, we must have walked from shtetl to shtetl, or, rather, from one small-town Bundist organization to another, or, still more precisely, from one Yiddish secular school to another. One of the key figures in our group was the previously mentioned S. Mendelson, who, in addition to being the most compelling Bund orator, was a leading Jewish educator.

Since we were walking down the Polish army's routes of retreat, we were strafed by the *Luftwaffe* much of the time. The most stressful attack was the air raid we experienced in the town of Międzyrzec, about thirty miles east of Warsaw. We were camping in a deserted Yiddish school building located in the immediate vicinity of the railroad station, apparently the Germans' main target. The bombs landed dangerously close to the site. The rickety building was shaking, the glass of its windows shattered. The prospect of being buried under the rubble must have been more frightening than that of being hit en plein air. Embarrassingly enough, I fainted. (The anguish of having to leave Iza behind may have contributed to my momentary collapse.) By the time the air raid subsided and we were ready to leave our precarious haven, I had recovered sufficiently to trot along.

The next day, the *Luftwaffe* once again invaded the cloudless September skies. Somehow the situation was more tolerable—the claustrophobic menace was lifted. Yet when the German planes appeared overhead, everyone hit the ground—everyone, that is, but Victor Alter. When urged to go down, he replied serenely, "According to the probability theory, the statistical chance of my being hit is very small." This incident exemplified vintage Alter—indestructible optimism, almost unnatural immunity to physical fear, bolstered by a scientific formula.

Two days later, our paths diverged. The bulk of our group pressed eastward, in the general direction of Pinsk, one of the largest cities in northeastern Poland. Alter, with several associates, chose the southern route—they went first to Lublin and then to Kovel, a town in Volhynia.

In retrospect, I find it difficult to comprehend how a heterogeneous group comprising a number of middle-aged women, one of whom was pregnant, managed to cover so much ground (about 150 miles) in nine days, largely on foot. Our progress was marginally facilitated by a totally unexpected encounter. A couple of days after we left Warsaw, we ran into a character who could have stepped out of the pages of Sholem Aleikhem. He was a big, strapping Jewish coachman (*balagole*) who was driving down our road at a pace that was just barely ahead of the weary pedestrians. The minor advantage of having him in our midst was the opportunity to place in his coach, on a rotational basis, three or four of the most needy or exhausted among us. The coachman exercised strict control over the number of his passengers so as not to overburden his horse. At times he would actually slow us down by giving the horse another "rest." "A horse is not a human being," he would say in a sententious Yiddish. "A horse is a delicate thing [a *delikate zakh*]. A horse needs to rest."

Once, when it was Father's and my turn to mount the coach, on a childish impulse I cuddled up to Father. He put his arm around me. The wife of a Bundist activist who was walking beside us said approvingly rather than censoriously, "You are a soft family, aren't you?" "I guess we are," answered Father without a trace of embarrassment. (Little did I know that I would see him for the last time in less than three weeks!)

Some two days before we reached Pinsk, the bombing stopped. This could have been a tip-off, but it was not. In any case, the moment of truth was not far off. On September 16, we reached our objective and proceeded directly to the home of the local Bund leader for whom Father had high regard. As soon as we plopped on Comrade S.'s porch, our host turned on the radio. The first voice we heard was that of the Soviet minister of foreign affairs, Vyacheslav Molotov: "I have just given the order to our heroic Red Army to cross into Poland in order to liberate our blood brethren, the Western Belorussians and the Western Ukrainians, from the yoke of feudal Poland (*panskaya Polska*). . . . Feudal Poland has ceased to exist."

Clearly, we had underestimated the Molotov-Ribbentrop nonaggression pact, concluded in August 1939. We had thought that it merely assured Hitler of Soviet neutrality in case of his attack on Poland. We were not privy to the secret clause of the agreement that stipulated their intended partition of Poland.

The next day, the first Red Army units marched into Pinsk. The "liberators" were welcomed by a fair-size demonstration. I was less than thrilled to recognize in one of the first rows of the motley parade one Lutski, a former member of Ogniwo, who hailed from Pinsk. Lutski was not one of my favorite people. During my brief tenure as chairman of Ogniwo, he would frequently bait the board from what was ostensibly a left-wing position though often on fairly picayune grounds. (Our secretary, Yasha, and I were staunchly mainstream.) Sometime in 1938, Yasha talked me into co-opting Lutski to the board. The Machiavellian move achieved its immediate objective. Access to power made Lutski considerably less argumentative. Now that I saw him marching close to the head of a pro-Soviet demonstration, I wondered if he had been a bona fide left-wing Bundist or a Communist infiltrator.

We spent several days recovering from the trip and weighing various options. We were facing incontrovertible facts along with rumors, some of which proved false. One of these rumors was the notion that Father's native town, Lublin, wound up east of the demarcation line between the two occupation zones. Father promptly came to the conclusion that, whatever the future under the Soviets held for him and the Bund—he did not seem too sanguine on that score—it would make more sense for him, both personally and politically, to operate in a familiar setting rather than remain in Pinsk. Consequently, he decided to proceed forthwith to Lublin. By September 30, the trains began to roll again. Father's plan was to leave on the first westbound train. He claimed that the four of us traveling together would attract more attention than he would by himself. Actually, he was the only member of the family who was apt to attract attention—he was well known all over Poland. Perhaps he would have been less readily recognizable had he chosen to shave off his goatee. But, though he was quite apprehensive about Stalin, he clearly was not prepared to go underground under the Soviets. The last we saw of Father was on October 1, 1939. The train that he boarded never reached Lublin. The demarcation line between the two zones was drawn east of Lublin, through the town of Brest-Litovsk. It was there that Father had to get off the train. At the railroad station, he was recognized by a Jewish Communist from Warsaw who pointed him out to an NKVD officer. A local Bundist who witnessed the arrest took the train to Pinsk to tell us what had happened.

Within a few days after the news reached us, we decided to take a train to Vilna. Since it was the largest city in what until September 17, 1939, was northeastern Poland, we thought that Father was likely to have been transferred to the Vilna jail. Mother's inquiry was met by a brusque refusal to discuss the matter. "I can't tell you whether he is or is not here," declared a grim-faced bureaucrat. (As we found out at a considerably later date, Father was never in Vilna; he was transferred directly to the notorious Lubyanka prison in Moscow.)

Seeking information about Father's fate proved futile. It was also risk-laden. In Russia of 1939, close relatives of political prisoners were routinely either arrested or interned. As it was, we were granted a brief reprieve. In October, the Soviets ceded the Vilna province to Lithuania, which had coveted the area ever since the end of the First World War. This seemingly generous gesture failed to deceive the more clear-sighted locals, who muttered, "We've gained Vilna, but we are about to lose Lithuania." In July 1940, the old-timers were proven right.

By November, nearly all our fellow travelers on the Warsaw-Pinsk trek had found their way to Vilna. I remember an impromptu policy session in an apartment of a local comrade. The lines of authority were blurred: the motley gathering included some members of the Central Committee and a number of second-string Warsaw Bund activists such as my brother, Alex, who was fairly prominent in our youth movement. I was there, I suppose, more as Henryk Erlich's son than as a former chairman of Ogniwo. We were trying to take stock of the situation, most notably to redefine our position vis-à-vis the Soviet regime in light of the partition of Poland and the arrest of our leaders. (During the brief Soviet occupation, two leading Vilna Bundists were seized by NKVD.)

Even before the war, I managed to be as anticommunist as a Bundist could be. This time, facing Stalin's brutal assault on our country and our party, I let myself go in what was, in retrospect, one of the two most effective political speeches I ever delivered. (I spoke in Polish; my Yiddish was not fluent enough.) For too long, I argued, even as we deplored crimes committed by the Stalinist regime, we tended to muffle our outrage in deference to the hopes aroused by the Russian Revolution and our common, Marxist roots. It is high time, I insisted, to confront the truth: there is no longer any common ground between Stalinist dictatorship and libertarian socialism. (We preferred "libertarian" to "democratic" in those days so as not to sound too much like the mainstream Social Democratic Party.) Soviet communism is not a perverted form of "socialism" but its betrayal, a lethal threat to everything we stand for.

If a thoughtful member of the Central Committee, Emanuel Szerer, with whom I had worked closely in putting out our bi-weekly *Nowe Zycie* (*A New Life*), found my position a bit extreme, I received wholehearted support from one of the Bund's most popular journalists and speakers. Borukh Szefner, who had leavened his political analyses with wit, was something of a Bundist Russell Baker. He was visibly pleased, indeed energized, by my outburst. "What you said," he cried, "was right on the money, and it was long overdue!"

Though it was good to let off some steam, we were aware of the precariousness of our confab. We were speechifying in a vacuum, dislodged into the periphery of the encroaching Soviet empire, bereaved of our best leaders, physically cut off from our constituency. Apprehensive as we were about its fate, we could not foresee the horrors that were in store for Polish Jewry.

Before long, my political ally became a close associate in a vital personal enterprise. The fact of the matter is that ever since we landed in Vilna, my growing worry over Father's fate was accompanied by a concern with Iza's being trapped in Nazi-occupied Warsaw. Szefner's daughter, Mary, shared Iza's predicament and was eager to join her father. By early December, Szefner and I were plotting to bring the two young women to Vilna. We had found out through underground channels that the movement had at its disposal trustworthy guides who might facilitate if not insure a passage from Warsaw to Vilna—at best an arduous and risk-laden proposition as it entailed illegally crossing the German-Soviet and the Soviet-Lithuanian borders. It appeared that Iza and Mary chose to take the risk and to do so together.

For Iza this was not an easy decision. She had to leave behind her father, whom she loved dearly and for whom she was the most important person in the world. It was Leon Sznejerson who at a crucial moment prevailed upon Iza to go east. "In the long run," he said, "you belong with Victor."

Traveling over the treacherous terrain in December was often fraught with danger. In one literally chilling moment, when the two friends were crossing an ice-covered river, their plight came

perilously close to that of Eliza in *Uncle Tom's Cabin*. But the
main threat faced by the travelers came from the soldiers guard-
ing the borders. The first encounter at the German-Soviet demarcation line proved unexpectedly benign. The German guard
turned out to be an Austrian Social Democrat who was in full
sympathy with Iza's and Mary's project. Not only did he let
them go, he also suggested the optimal route. Yet the Red Army
man into whom the young women ran several miles down the
road was less tractable. What saved the day was Iza's newly discovered ability to speak Russian and her truly remarkable presence of mind. When confronted rather rudely by the Red Army
guard, Iza surprised her travel companion and herself by producing a perfectly intelligible Russian sentence. (As a child, she
had heard some Russian at the home of her maternal grandparents—her favorite uncle sang Russian lullabies and told Russian
fairy tales to Iza and her younger cousin. Under pressure, this
seemingly buried "linguistic competence" suddenly surfaced.)
No less impressive was the use made of this prowess. When
asked, "Where do you think you're going?" she offered a dazzling
piece of misinformation: "We are going from Bialystok to Warsaw." "No, you don't!" exclaimed the guard. "You're going back
to Bialystok!" whereupon he escorted Iza and Mary to what was
actually their immediate destination.

The second illegal border crossing presented less of a problem. The Lithuanian guard who "caught" the trespassers was
entirely amenable to bribery. He was keenly interested in the
watch of Iza's father. However, there was a momentary hitch.
The Lithuanian apparently was quite taken with Iza and was reluctant to let go of her. As far as he was concerned, Mary was free
to proceed. Now it was Mary's turn to rise to the occasion. She
became absolutely hysterical. The guard reluctantly let both
women go. Soon they found themselves in a snow-covered
Lithuanian village, under the protection of a benevolent local
priest. I do not recall how word of this reached the Vilna Bundists. All I'm sure of is that toward the end of December, the
denizens of the hamlet were treated to an unusual sight: a good-

size black car stopped in front of Iza and Mary's haven. The personable young man who emerged from the car was a Vilna Bundist activist, Abram Feinsilber. It was thus that the weary travelers arrived in Vilna on the night of December 31, 1939.

A few weeks after Iza had joined our family kibbutz on the outskirts of Vilna, our hard-won togetherness seemed to be threatened once again. It was rumored that the Lithuanian authorities were not too happy with the influx of Jewish refugees from central Poland and were considering a scheme whereby some of the newcomers to Vilna would be relocated to a few smaller towns. While the distances involved were not staggering, the prospect of Iza's and my landing in two different Lithuanian backwaters—an outcome which was not implausible if the relocation were to be guided by the alphabetical principle—was dismal. Though, to begin with, formalizing our relationship had not been on our minds, the possibility of being separated made marriage a matter of some urgency. Thus, by the end of January, I was actively engaged in a search for a rabbi. (In Lithuania, as in prewar Poland, there was no such thing as a civil marriage; moreover, neither a Reform nor a Conservative option was available.) I had to turn without much enthusiasm to the thoroughly Orthodox Rabbi Rubenstein. He turned out to be a very busy man—partly, I believe, because of the aforementioned contingency (which, incidentally, failed to materialize). It took me some time to hunt him down. When I finally did, Rabbi Rubenstein was clearly impressed by my ancestry. Upon hearing that I was Simon Dubnov's grandson, he gave me a firm date and waived his fee.

That, however, was only part of the story. Since Iza was still a minor—she was twenty—she could not marry without her father's permission. I had every reason to believe that Leon Sznejerson would be happy to bless our union, but since he was under the German occupation, to coin a phrase, he could not be reached for comment. In what was, without any doubt, the only fraudulent act of his life, Alex dashed off a letter to the effect that he had no objections to his daughter Iza marrying one Victor Erlich and

signed for my father-in-law. Nor was this permission the only requirement to be met. Rabbi Rubenstein insisted on a statement
by two respected Jewish communal leaders testifying that the
bride was a virgin. I turned to the aforementioned S. Mendelson
and the prominent Yiddish educator S. Kazhdan. They did not
need much persuading to coauthor an inaccurate document.

The ceremony itself, held on February 27, 1940, had all the
earmarks of an emergency occasion. Both Iza and I were casually,
indeed shabbily, dressed. I was wearing a ski cap, Iza a peasant-
type kerchief which made her look so goyish that the rabbi took
me aside to be assured once more that her maiden name was
Shneerson. Since I could not afford a ring, Mother, who was one
of the three witnesses, lent me the ring with which she had wed
Father in 1911; throughout the brief ritual she kept muttering:
"Don't lose it, don't lose it." At some point I came dangerously
close to undercutting the proceedings by taking off my ski cap
to thank the rabbi for officiating free of charge. At the last second I thought better of it. (It was essential to keep headgear on
at all times.) All in all, it was a precarious launch for a union that
was destined to last for nearly fifty-seven years.

The rest of the winter was relentlessly bleak and generally uneventful. We huddled together in our frigid suburban hideout,
listening to the increasingly grim news on a barely audible radio, waiting and reading. The absentee house owner's library offered a less-than-balanced diet but contained some surprises.
Among them was the *Complete Works of Henrik Ibsen*—in Russian.
Arguably this was more Ibsen than was good for anyone, but, on
the whole, I was grateful.

Sometime in the dead of the harsh Vilna winter, a number of
us, natives and refugees alike, gathered together in an unheated
hall of the Vilna Yiddish high school to hear S. Mendelson speak
about the distinguished Yiddish writer I. L. Peretz. For more
than a decade, Mendelson was a significant and vivid presence in
my life—no wonder his name keeps cropping up in these pages.
One of the architects of the Yiddish school network Tsisho,
Mendelson was passionately committed to and profoundly

steeped in modern Jewish culture and literature. He was one of the most charismatic speakers I have ever encountered. If Henryk Erlich and Victor Alter mastered Yiddish and became effective Yiddish speakers and writers because they were socialists who chose to cast their lot with the Jewish laboring masses, Mendelson was an ardent Yiddishist who became a Bundist because he saw the Bund as the only major Jewish political movement committed to the cause of Yiddish.

Mendelson's lecture on Peretz was one of his classic performances; it was both illuminating and moving. He spoke with insight and penetration about Peretz's oeuvre. He was especially effective in dealing with Peretz's drama *Di goldene Keit* (*The Golden Chain*), most notably with its larger-than-life protagonist Reb Shloyme, who, in a supreme challenge to routine and contingency, refuses to perform, when the time comes, the ritual duty of announcing the conclusion of the Sabbath, and proclaims: "*Shabes zol zayn oyf der welt!*" (Let Sabbath go on!)

If Reb Shloyme's existential defiance of the established order became strangely stirring in Mendelson's renditions, another Peretz quotation he seized upon spoke more directly to our predicament. Shortly before closing, Mendelson's rich voice projected into the hushed hall Peretz's clarion call: "*Oysgelayzt fun payn un shrek muz vern di velt!*" (The world must be liberated from pain and fear!) The words still reverberate in my mind when I think back to that extraordinary evening in Vilna. And as I do, I cannot help but feel that there was something singularly appropriate, indeed symbolic, about the spectacle of the Bund's most eloquent spokesman drawing solace and strength, at one of the darkest moments in Jewish history, from a master of modern Jewish imagination.

The advent of summer confirmed the pessimistic prognosis described earlier. By July 1940, the Soviet Union installed military bases all over Lithuania as a prelude to its formal incorporation into the USSR. Creeping Sovietization meant inexorably a gradual penetration of the Lithuanian polity by the NKVD. Sometime in mid-July, as Iza and I returned from a walk to our

flat—by that time we had relocated to "downtown" Vilna—we
were told by our landlady that two men were inquiring about the
Erlich family. The description of our visitors left little doubt as
to the nature of their mission. Clearly, it was time to move.

A family conclave, drawing on advice from the locals, concluded that we ought to impersonate a group of vacationers and
spend the rest of the summer in Verki, a pleasant village in the
environs of Vilna. With indispensable assistance from the local
comrades, most notably a resourceful and warm young Vilna
Bundist, L.G., who was to become one of our most valued
friends, we rented a cottage owned by a remarkably congenial
peasant couple. The youngest member of the Balukiewicz family,
a spunky girl of five, proved a constant source of mirth. She once
ventured on her own into the highway and greeted the Red
Army unit marching down the road, exclaiming gaily in a mix-
ture of Russian and Polish, "Good morning, Jews!" We had every
reason to believe that her parents were totally free of anti-
Semitism; somehow the insidious right-wing notion of a symbiotic relationship between Jews and Communists must have
rubbed off on Lilka without the concomitant hostile affect.

The enforced vacation had its charms. Our walks along the
banks of Walja were enhanced by friendship. In addition to L.G.
there were the Aleksandrowicz brothers—two prominent Bund
activists from Kraków. The older, Ignacy, was closer in age to my
parents than to Iza and me. A lawyer and a member of the
Kraków City Council, he was the more learned of the two and a
mite more ponderous. The younger, Max, had a common touch
and a delightful sense of humor. A popular figure in Kraków's
Bundist youth movement during the prewar decade, he had a
definite affinity for our left-wing faction, but a brief exposure to
Soviet realities cured him of whatever illusions he may have had
about the Stalin regime.

By September, our companions and most of the real vacationers were gone. The days were clear but increasingly breezy and
chilly. Yet we were in no hurry to leave our pastoral refuge. Our
hosts must have sensed that we had serious problems with the

new dispensation. At some point, B. took Mother aside. "If you'd rather spend the winter here," he said shyly, "we'll manage. I'm going to kill our pig and there'll be enough food for everybody." Though genuinely moved by the offer, we would not consider being a burden to our uncommonly decent hosts. Since returning to Vilna was out of the question, we had to cast about for another solution. I don't remember which of our counselors suggested that we steer clear of the major cities. All I can say is that shortly after our departure from Verki, we found ourselves in a bleak shtetl in the Kaunas province. Our landlady, a lower-middle-class, motherly Jewish woman, seemed to respond to the Soviet occupation with chronic depression. "You think it's my house?" she said in mournful Yiddish, pointing to our rickety abode. "This is Stalin's house!"

Our room-and-board arrangement was Iza's first exposure to kosher cuisine, and mine to what might be called its greasy provincial variety. More important, we realized early on that for a family such as ours, staying in Garliava was a dubious and counterproductive way of going underground. Not unpredictably, we had considerable trouble blending into the shtetl landscape. Hence a hasty farewell to the dispossessed matron and to Stalin's shabby piece of real estate. Once again it was necessary to hit the road.

This time we opted for Kaunas. Having arrived in the capital, we were advised to diffuse the risk by breaking down into three units. Mother was placed in a relatively safe apartment, Alex and Rachel found another location, Iza and I still another. We landed on the outskirts of Kaunas, renting a room from a friendly, Russian-speaking young widow with a girl of six.

Strange as it may seem, I look back with some affection on the two months we spent in that cozy cottage. To be sure, we were never free from a nagging worry about Father. Our own situation was precarious enough; we were hoping against hope that, what with Lithuania in the throes of gradual Sovietization, the liaison between the Vilna NKVD and its Kaunas counterpart would for a while remain tenuous. Being young unquestionably helped. The constant sense of risk, though a bit unnerving, was adding spice to our life. More important, for the first time since Iza's arrival in Vilna, we were on our own.

During this modest and belated honeymoon, we somehow managed to have a good time in a snug circle of friends which included Iza's travel companion, Mary S., the elder Aleksandrowicz, and, last but certainly not least, a newly acquired soul mate, the freewheeling radical Warsaw intellectual Antoni Pański. A tall, somewhat stooped, bespectacled man over forty, "Pan Antoni" combined luminous intelligence with a gentle sense of humor. He promptly became one of the most reliable participants in our small get-togethers, including some spontaneous "sings." (He once paid me a hedged compliment by calling me a "zestful singer.") But what mattered most to Iza and me were long, leisurely conversations which often centered around the built-in limitations of Marxism and, more broadly, the pitfalls of any overarching system, any encompassing weltanschauung. I do not recall what Antoni's academic credentials were; he had studied both philosophy and sociology and was Bertrand Russell's first Polish translator. Talking to him was our first exposure to a mode of thinking significantly different from the intellectual tradition on which we were raised and which we were increasingly inclined to call into question. Antoni's "otherness" may well have been part of our attraction to him. In any case, we found his principled yet undoctrinaire stance, his lucid skepticism which never degenerated into cynicism, singularly appealing.

In retrospect, I wonder why Antoni chose to spend as much time with us as he did. He was at least fifteen years older than I—at twenty-five I was still in some respects a callow youth. It occurs to me that he may have relished the company of my vivacious, incisive, witty Iza. Also, he may have enjoyed the role of a mentor. At some point, Antoni may have been close to the Communist Party, though he was too much of a free spirit to have ever toed the line. By the time we met, he was clear-eyed about the Soviet regime and openly contemptuous of the intellectual crassness of Stalinist culture and the brazen mendacity of

Soviet propaganda. In the fall of 1940, a glaring example of this mendacity was staring in our faces. At an early stage of Sovietization, the new authorities began to transport to the center all kinds of produce requisitioned in relatively prosperous Lithuania. As the Kaunas-Moscow trains groaned under the weight of these goods, the omnipresent posters proclaimed an urgent need for raising Lithuania's standard of living to that of the Soviet sister republics.

If I may get ahead of my story, Antoni's candor ultimately cost him his life. Shortly after our departure from Kaunas, in January 1941, he was arrested by the NKVD. Apparently, he had been denounced by a fellow displaced Warsaw intellectual who was a true believer. Pański's reckless talk, claimed the zealot, was damaging to the cause. (It seems that in this instance, ideological vigilance was in part a screen for sexual rivalry.) The arrest proved lethal. Antoni was still in jail when the Germans entered Kaunas. Arrested by the Soviets, he was executed by the Nazis. His fate was as grim as it was symbolic. When in June 1943 Iza gave birth to our older son, we named him Henry and gave him the middle name Anthony.

In November 1940, Iza and I left with some regret our suburban hideout and moved to a somewhat tawdry hotel bearing an inappropriate name, Noblesse, where we registered under Iza's maiden name. The central location was essential. We had learned through the Bundist grapevine that we had a fighting chance to get out of what was about to become another Soviet republic. A New York–based organization, the Jewish Labor Committee, founded by influential figures in the American trade union movement such as David Dubinsky, was working hard trying to rescue Bundist activists stranded in semi-Soviet Lithuania. Drawing on its connections with Franklin Delano Roosevelt's White House, these spokesmen for Jewish organized labor managed to generate a number of emergency ("visitor's") U.S. visas and to underwrite the travelers' passage via Russia and Japan. (In the winter of 1940 to 1941, this circuitous route was the only available option.) However, in order to embark on this far-flung journey, the prospective immigrants had to meet two additional formal requirements. They had to obtain Japanese transit visas and Soviet Lithuanian exit permits.

We did not appreciate at the time how lucky we were to be able to secure the former without much ado. One of the advantages of being part of the movement, or, frankly, being a member of the family of the leader, is having access to skillful operatives who would attend to technical matters on behalf of the group. Thus, at some point we were presented with five Japanese transit visas. Since we did not have to deal with the Japanese consul in Kaunas directly, we never met, to my recollection, the remarkable man who acquired posthumously the reputation of a Japanese Schindler for enabling the rescue of a significant number of Polish Jewish refugees. (If Bundists benefited from institutional relief, a much larger number of Warsaw Jews stranded in Lithuania were assisted by their U.S.-based relatives.) As we found out many years later, without any authorization on the part of the Tokyo government, Mr. and Mrs. Sugihara produced within a couple of weeks hundreds of Japanese transit visas.

Obtaining exit permits from Soviet Lithuanian authorities was quite another matter. Granting individuals, who through no fault of their own landed in Soviet-controlled territory, permission to leave simply because they expressed a desire to do so went against the grain of the Soviet system. Thus, for a couple of months our fate hung in the balance. Alex and I were spending weeks on end in the waiting lines at the passport division of the Kaunas NKVD, getting the bureaucratic runaround. (Alex was applying for exit permits on behalf of his wife and himself. I acted for Mother, Iza, and myself.) Sometime in December, the basic policy decision must have been made—the powers that be chose to let go of the petit bourgeois elements who failed to appreciate the benefits of the Soviet Lithuanian brand of socialism. I'm convinced that in doing so, the authorities were guided by a mundane consideration: for the Soviet Intourist, several hundred American railroad tickets on the Kaunas–Vladivostok route represented a massive infusion of U.S. currency. After a protracted bottleneck, things began to move. Though somewhat hopeful, we were not complacent. Even if most of the applicants were allowed to leave, it was not a foregone conclusion that the five Erlichs would be in that number.

In the meantime, Alex and I had become semipermanent fixtures in the dismal building dominated by a somewhat autocratic virago. At some point the formidable lady took notice of me. She seemed favorably impressed with my fluency in Russian. My brother's Russian was at least as good as mine, but on this occasion, in an uncharacteristic act of cunning, he did a rather effective impersonation of a halting and barely coherent Russian speaker and thus did not attract special attention. At some point I was called out of a waiting line and ushered into a small room occupied by a nondescript, fair-haired man whose Russian was unmistakably of the Muscovite variety. He greeted me amiably and offered me a chair. (Since I did not get the name he mumbled, I shall refer to him as "Ivanov.") What followed was an extended and memorable conversation.

Mr. Ivanov launched into it by inquiring about my attitude toward the changes currently occurring in Lithuania. While I no longer had the option of following my brother's example, I chose to impersonate a budding pedant, totally uninterested in politics. "I really know very little about these things," I muttered. "But you must have some notions about what's going on," remarked my interlocutor, "you are a literate man (*vy gramotny chelovek*). You hold a master's degree from the Free Polish University in Warsaw." (The man had clearly done his homework.) I emitted a feeble petit bourgeois noise to the effect that what was happening was probably "good for workers." This clearly was not good enough for Mr. Ivanov. He assumed that as a "literate man" I was apt to profit from basic instruction in politics. He grabbed a piece of paper and drew two circles; one of them, he explained, represented the international working class, the other—international bourgeoisie. "They are engaged in a life-and-death struggle. Where are you?" Trying to eschew commitment, I located myself in the no-man's-land between the two circles only to be advised that there was no room there. "You've got to choose sides." When I moved in the general direction of the international working class, the young man concluded that I was sympathetic toward "what we are doing." As no firm denial was forthcoming, Mr. Ivanov broached a more pointed question: "If you generally approve of what we are doing, why do you want to go to America?" "My wife's aunt lives in Hollywood," I replied, "and she is very eager to join her long-lost relative." Actually, Iza did have an aunt in Hollywood—she was a dentist rather than a film star—a fact which had absolutely nothing to do with our interest in the United States. Mr. Ivanov found such a reason for wanting to emigrate to the United States rather trivial and seemed mildly disgusted by my knuckling under to my wife's unreasonable wish. But he was not altogether discouraged. "Provided you get to this America of yours," he wondered, "would you mind, after you settle there, keeping in touch with our people?" Rather sheepishly, I wondered, "What would be the purpose of these contacts?"

My inquiry was countered by a question: "What do you propose to do when you come to the United States?" My answer—"I propose to continue my study of Slavic philology at an American university"—was straightforward and truthful, but I chose to give it a somewhat retrograde twist by declaring a special interest in Old Church Slavonic, which in its Russified form became the vehicle of Russian Orthodox liturgy. (As indicated earlier, it was the only subject in which I earned a C at the Free Polish University in Warsaw.) This phony emphasis did not have its intended effect. Mr. Ivanov remained hopeful. "Fine!" he exclaimed, "You'll be meeting American professors and American students. You'll be talking to them." "Yes, about Old Church Slavonic," I muttered without much conviction. "Not all the time, not all the time!" insisted the Muscovite, in what was one of the few intelligent statements he made in the course of the two-hour interview. I had to concede the point. "You might be talking about Soviet films," continued Ivanov. "Possibly," I allowed, and took the plunge. "Are you really so interested in what American professors and students think about Soviet movies to expect me to make contact with your representatives after landing on American soil?" My interviewer was visibly angered. "Don't you tell me," he snorted, "what we should or should not be interested in."

We reached something of a conversational impasse. I realized that turning down Ivanov's "suggestion" could have serious consequences for Mother, Iza, and me. At the same time, to sign up with the appalling institution was inconceivable. Moreover, it occurred to me that were I to do so without any intention to follow up on my "commitment," I would be subject to blackmail just because Father was in their hands. The only course of action I could envision was to refuse the "offer" without revealing the degree of my revulsion from it. Ivanov was not ready to give up. "Do you think there is something unsavory about my proposal?" he inquired. "No," I lied, "there is nothing unsavory about it. But I feel uneasy about entering upon my arrival in a new land into a relationship with a foreign power. No, I'm afraid, this is not for me." Though my rationale was less than coherent and my delivery less than forceful, it became clear to Ivanov that my refusal was final. His manner promptly changed from false amiability to outright hostility. He glared at me. "I have known all along that you are lying when you claimed to be our friend." (Incidentally, I never said I was.) "You are, in fact, our enemy." As I attempted to protest, the Muscovite delivered himself of a remarkable statement: "We know all about you. We shared the files of the Polish secret police with the Gestapo. Your dossier is in our hands." This sounded ominous, but not entirely plausible: I did not think I had been prominent enough to rate a "dossier." Ivanov proceeded to build up suspense and presumably increase my anxiety by articulating very slowly, while fiddling with his pipe: "We know . . . that you were . . . one of the leaders . . . of the Zionist youth movement in Warsaw."

Though I had not been very worried, I breathed a sigh of relief: Ivanov was bluffing. He did not have a clue as to what kind of Erlich I was. (The name Erlich, with or without an *h* after the *e*, was quite common in Warsaw.) I permitted myself to laugh out loud. My interrogator was livid. When he regained his self-control, he said through clenched teeth: "If you refuse to cooperate with us, you'd better sign a statement to this effect." For obvious reasons, I was not enthused over the prospect but after some ineffectual wrangling was prepared to face the inevitable. Ivanov produced a large sheet of paper and began to dictate in a peremptory fashion. "I refuse to cooperate with NKVD of the USSR because . . . Why don't you write?" he interrupted himself brusquely. "I want to hear the rest of the sentence," I explained. "OK! here it is," he offered. "I refuse to cooperate with NKVD of the USSR because I am an enemy of the Soviet Union." "No!" I exclaimed. "I'm not going to sign this. This is untrue!" Ivanov was willing to rephrase my alleged rationale: "I refuse to cooperate because I'm a believer in the capitalist system." This time my disclaimer was as sincere as it was emphatic. (Though by January 1941 I was a dubious Marxist, I was still a socialist.) The man whom I dubbed in my mind a poor man's Gletkin—I meant, of course, the relentless interrogator in A. Koestler's *Darkness at Noon*—was visibly sweating. "I refuse to cooperate . . . because I am an American patriot." This, to be sure, was a less lethal formulation. But, emboldened by my opponent's setback, I chose to be logical. "Someday I may become an American patriot," I quibbled, "but how can I be a patriot of a country I have yet to see?" "So what do you want to say?" asked Ivanov with some exasperation. "If it's absolutely necessary," I replied, "I'm willing to say: I refuse to cooperate with NKVD of USSR. Period."

When I looked at my interlocutor, I was surprised to see anger give way to what looked like genuine sadness. "You are a literate man," he remonstrated, "and yet you propose something like this?" "What's wrong?" I wondered. "This," Ivanov declared emphatically, "is not a complete sentence." "Why?" I was being logical again. "'I' is a subject, 'refuse' is a predicate, 'with NKVD' is an indirect complement." My syntactic analysis proved unconvincing. The poor man's Gletkin kept muttering: "This is an incomplete sentence. You must give reasons—ideo-logical

reasons, psycho-logical reasons, or physi-o-logical reasons."
(Ivanov's strenuous way of pronouncing big words clearly be-
trayed a man who, to paraphrase his favorite expression, was only
half literate.) I stood my ground: "'Ideological reasons' is wrong,
'psychological reasons' is vague, and 'physiological reasons' is
absurd."

Ivanov seemed to be at the end of his tether. He glared. "OK,
sign your damned incomplete sentence, but let me tell you: your
mother, your wife, and you are not going to get exit permits."
This somewhat hesitant threat—issuing exit visas was clearly
beyond my interlocutor's jurisdiction—was followed by what
was, by my count, the second intelligent statement made by
Ivanov in the course of the "interview": "Even if you get your
papers, a great deal can happen between here and Vladivostok."
This warning was ominously plausible, but it sounded more
wishful than confident. Ivanov reached for a truly unassailable
fallback position: "Suppose you somehow manage to get to
America. Do you think you'll be safe there?" "I hope so," I muttered. "You are wrong," he announced. "There is a powerful
Communist Party in the United States; it won't take long until
this party is the government of the United States. And then,"
concluded the Muscovite, looking me straight in the eye, "the
American working class will remember those who refused to
help us in the hour of need." I tried to look shattered but probably did not succeed. There was no more to be said. I got up and
left the room. This time there was no handshake.

Four days later Mother, Iza, and I received our exit permits.
As I was hoping, the matter was beyond Ivanov's control. Otherwise, the one nonpolitical moral that could be drawn from this
encounter is that in a stressful situation, it is preferable to deal
with a jerk.

On January 25, 1941, Mother, Iza, and I boarded a grimy and
incredibly overcrowded train to Moscow. After a brief layover in
the Soviet capital, we were scheduled to embark on the world's
longest train journey, the Moscow–Vladivostok Trans-Siberian
Express.

Our first exposure to Moscow was unrelievedly grim. The rigors of the Russian winter blended ominously with the pervasive oppressiveness of the political atmosphere. Tourist attractions were few and often of dubious attractiveness. With the Kremlin barred to visitors, only the impressive cathedral of St. Basil reminded one of the architectural glories of old Muscovy. The chief landmark at Red Square was the immensely depressing Lenin mausoleum. Thousands of shabbily dressed pilgrims were slowly filing past the mummified leader under the watchful eyes of stone-faced guards. A more recent showpiece, the vaunted Moscow subway, seemed at the time more spectacular than functional. Several incongruously sumptuous stations appeared—in retrospect, perhaps unfairly—to cater to the totalitarian regime's need for self-aggrandizement rather than to the actual needs of the capital's denizens. A visit to the Tretyakovsky Art Museum did little to dispel the gloom. A guided tour of the museum which we joined briefly brought home the appalling deterioration of Russian art under Stalin, the posterlike crudeness and sycophantic monotony of the socialist realist pageants. This orgy of edifying kitsch, dominated by the highly idealized representations of the leader communing with heroic steelworkers or radiantly smiling model *kolkhozniki,* was described by our guide, whose worn, intelligent face suggested that he knew better, as a "triumph of socialist realism over formalism." Ironically, he invoked the stock formula as he was nervously waving the stragglers away from a few stranded relics of Russian avant-garde art, presumably unworthy of our attention.

After some hesitation, Mother decided to call her younger brother, Yasha, a professor of mathematics at Moscow State University whom she had not seen for twenty-three years. She identified herself on the phone as "a friend of Sonia's" who was passing through and had regards for Yasha from his sister. Mother thought that direct contact with foreigners might be politically unhealthy for him, and he would feel less pressure to show up at the Intourist hotel where we were staying if the matter at hand was merely touching base with "Sonia's friend." An hour later,

Yasha was knocking at the door of our room. Having embraced Mother warmly, he inquired, "Why did you play this game?" (Incidentally, the "game" did not work; Yasha recognized Mother.) "I wanted to make it easier for you," said Mother, "not to show up if it was truly inconvenient." "I don't think they can do much more to me than they have already done," announced Yasha, blithely disregarding the possibility that our room was bugged. "Basya [Yasha's physician wife, a stalwart party member] is in a [forced labor] camp. I doubt if they are going to bother with a nonparty mathematician."

Iza and I took to Yasha immediately. For one thing, he looked familiar. His physical resemblance to Grandfather was all too apparent. For another thing, and more important, he exuded intelligence, integrity, and a keen sense of irony. After a brief visit at our hotel, he whisked Mother away to his home. Perhaps he did not want to get involved with too many foreigners. More likely, he wanted to have Mother, after a twenty-three year interval, pretty much to himself. She told us later that she met at Yasha's house an attractive and keen-eyed teenager. It was my cousin Viktoria, whom Iza and I had the pleasure to meet fifty years later.

For the three of us, the visit with Yasha provided another occasion for a political disagreement that had been festering ever since the outbreak of the war. (The visible surge of Mother's Russian identity made her more "patriotic" and more hopeful about the benign evolution of the Soviet regime than the evidence seemed to warrant.) While Mother did not fail to appreciate Yasha's quiet courage—she realized that not every Soviet academic would have behaved this way under the circumstances— she sought to salvage from the encounter the notion that things in the Soviet Union were not as bad as we had assumed. Also, though she spent considerably more time with Yasha than Iza and I did, we felt, rightly or wrongly, that she was not ready to acknowledge the degree of her brother's alienation from the Soviet ethos. Let me interpolate at this point. Before the revolution, Yasha was a strong Bolshevik sympathizer and, for a while,

I believe, a party member. Characteristically, he left the party shortly after the Bolsheviks came to power. By January 1941, he seemed to be thoroughly disenchanted. The unmistakable ring of irony which underpinned his every reference to "them" suggested profound estrangement rather than mere disagreement.

By Soviet standards, the ride on the Trans-Siberian Express was almost luxurious. There were four passengers to each compartment—our fellow traveler was someone Iza and I had known back in Warsaw. N. Horwitz was five or six years older than I. An advanced student of architecture at the University of Warsaw, he had been the principal spokesman for a small but vocal Trotskyite faction. Having spent half a year under the Soviet occupation, he became, if possible, even more anti-Soviet than I, a perspective which he was eager to share with us. As I think back to a conversation with him, I'm reminded of Susan Sontag's highly controversial remarks at a 1981 rally in New York, called to protest the imposition of martial law in Poland. As some readers will recall, Ms. Sontag declared, to the visible dismay of many of those present, that when all is said and done, *Reader's Digest* had proved a more reliable source of information about Soviet communism than *The Nation*. My Trotskyite friend's pronouncement was equally "outrageous." "Remember," said Horwitz, "before the war we were arguing about which newspaper was closer to the truth about the Soviet Union—the Bundist *Folkstsaytung* or *Robotnik* (*The Worker*), the organ of the Polish Socialist Party. We were barking up the wrong tree. You know who knew the score about the Soviet Union? *Czerwoniak!*" (*The Red Courier,* a low-grade, sensationalist right-wing sheet).

Needless to say, this thoroughly subversive epiphany was conveyed to us, in Polish, while no one else was present. Such occasions were few and far between. In the daytime, we were accompanied by a personable young man; he was assigned to our contingent as an Intourist representative. (There was little doubt in our minds as to his other institutional affiliation.) Our "guide" was none too bright and clearly devoid of any sense of humor. At some point in our long and monotonous journey, I was moved, rather unwisely, to tell an unsophisticated political joke about two ancien régime ladies visiting the Moscow Zoo in the early days of the revolution. As they were gazing upon a camel, one woman said to the other, "Look, Anna Ivanovna, what the Bolsheviks have done to a horse!" Just as I was launched, I felt a twinge of uneasiness. Rather than being risqué, this was an anti-anti-Bolshevik joke, and I certainly did not mean to pander. However, the tenor of the story was far from clear to our "guide." At first, he froze as he realized that I was telling a political joke that contained a reference to the "Bolsheviks." After a few minutes' delay, he emitted a wary "ha, ha."

Otherwise we steered clear of politics. Our Intourist man had a pleasant singing voice. I am indebted to him for a few contemporary Soviet songs. My profound revulsion for Stalinist culture did not prevent me from mildly enjoying some of the period's more singable tunes. The lyrics ranged from innocuous to egregious. The popular 1936 song "Vast is My Land," which acquired the status of an unofficial anthem, combined a fetching tune with a brazenly mendacious text. It took truly Stalinist gall to intone, at the dawn of the Great Purge: "I do not know any other country/where man could breathe so freely."

The first week of our trip was managed reasonably well. Food in the dining room was more than adequate. As the train was plunging into deepest Siberia, it started running out of everything, including hot water. But that failed to dampen our spirits. As we were approaching Vladivostok, it really looked as if, miraculously, we were going to leave behind the land of the NKVD.

Though billed as an express, our train stopped at a fair number of stations. But getting off, just to stretch, was actively discouraged. It seems that on a previous occasion, in early January, I believe, several passengers, Polish Jewish refugees like ourselves, managed to strike up a brief conversation with a few locals who conveyed in hasty Yiddish that "things are not so hot." Further contacts with the local population were effectively cut off. Actually, as we were rattling through Siberia, no such prohibitions were necessary. When we stopped at the major Siberian city of Irkutsk, half a minute at the station was enough to propel me back into the safety of our compartment. To say that I nearly froze would have been a misnomer. My prime sensation was feeling incredibly hot inside.

As we were traversing for days on end the vast, interminable snow-covered plains, I was thinking of "The Road to Russia," the appendix to the Faustian drama of the great Polish romantic Adam Mickiewicz, *Forefathers' Eve* (*Dziady*): "A land empty, white, and open." Toward the very end of our journey, the overwhelming monotony of the unchanging scenery gave way to a spectacular landmark; for many hours our train was circling the famous Baikal, the world's largest lake. Unfortunately, much of the effect was lost on us—since some of the cruising around Baikal took place at night. Whatever we managed to glimpse of it was an awesome sight. We were told, incidentally, that this part of our trip created a serious problem for some of our fellow travelers—a sizable group of Hasidim from central Poland. During their afternoon prayers, they were supposed to face west. But as the train kept going round and round the enormous lake, it became extremely difficult to tell the east from the west.

Vladivostok was frigid and unredeemably bleak. We were subjected to a rather rude personal search. I was somewhat uneasy—during my brief association with the Vilna Institute for Jewish Research (Yivo), which was in the process of relocating to New York, I took some notes in Yiddish on a Polish tract in literary theory. Before our departure from Kaunas, Iza had skillfully sewn the notes into my overcoat. What worried me was less the prospect of having to surrender the fruits of my Yivo-based labors than the possibility of having my scribblings mistaken for a secret code. Felicitously, the notes survived. We were brusquely dispatched and conveyed to a large fisherman's boat that was supposed to ferry us and a number of fellow refugees to Japan.

The crossing turned out to be an ordeal. The Sea of Japan was stormy, and most passengers promptly got sick. I don't know how the three of us managed not to succumb. (Mother, I must say, was quite a trouper.) Our misery was compounded by an incredible congestion—over a hundred passengers had been squeezed into a boat whose normal capacity was about thirty. Our first exposure to Japanese culture was not encouraging. The crew must have been traumatized by the challenge. They ran around the boat, in a kind of angry frenzy, pushing passengers and emitting noises that sounded like animal grunts and were probably a singularly rude version of Japanese.

The voyage was mercifully brief. When we were about to disembark, I was singled out once more by the authorities. (I must have had a special appeal to secret police.) As we were lining up for visa control, I was called out into a cubicle and addressed by two diminutive-looking officials who proceeded to talk to me in a language which at first I found impossible to identify, let alone understand. After some reflection, I concluded that my interlocutors thought they were speaking Russian. (The Russian words which they were mangling were virtually unrecognizable.) After a while I began to get the drift of the questions. The two gentlemen were trying to elicit some information about the Soviet Union. The first question I was able to decode went something like, "Were people in Moscow poorly dressed?" The truthful answer would have been "yes," but, since I did not want to give too much aid and comfort to Hitler's ally, I muttered, "so-so." My interviewers seemed to want to know what I had seen while in Moscow, only to find out that I had been to the Tretyakovsky Art Museum and the Yiddish theater. With their curiosity about my experiences visibly waning, they wondered about something which was of greater interest to them: "How about troop movements?" When it turned out that I had not observed any, it must have occurred to the two operatives that they were wasting their time. With the impeded dialogue over, I joined Mother and Iza in the waiting line.

The disembarkation in the toylike port of Tsuruga was a welcome contrast with the country we left behind. We were propelled, or *hineingeworfen,* to use Heidegger's phrase, from harsh Russian winter into an exuberantly bright Japanese spring. The country of transit was yet to prove less than hospitable. But on

that brilliant February day, it was an exhilarating spectacle—
what with cherry trees in full bloom and young women in their
gaudy kimonos, we stepped out of Siberia into a stage set of
Madame Butterfly.

We were met by a representative of an American Jewish organization assisting refugees, the Joint Distribution Committee, which in February 1941 was still allowed to operate in the
territory of Japan.

After a glimpse of Kobe[2] and stunning ancient Kyoto, we
were guided to Yokohama, the most British-looking Japanese
city. Its main advantage to us was its proximity to Tokyo, which
housed all the foreign consulates. After a brief search, we established a beachhead in a house owned by an elderly Russian
woman who was supporting herself by renting rooms on a bed-
and-breakfast basis. Our landlady claimed to be a Russian count-
ess who had fallen on hard times. We had serious doubts—there
was nothing aristocratic about her demeanor or for that matter
about her Russian. But we felt lucky to be able to communicate
in a language we could handle.

Early on, we realized that our stay in Japan would have to be
more extended than we had anticipated. Most of the Bundist activists who crossed to Japan were able to pick up their U.S. visas
in Tokyo and proceed to San Francisco. Such was the case with
Alex and his family, who reached Japan two weeks after we did.
It appeared, though, that Iza and I needed an additional document in support of our visa application. By the time we secured
it, the "objective situation," as a Marxist would say, had changed.
The U.S. consulates around the world had been instructed to dis-
continue until further notice issuing emergency visas to applicants who had close relatives under either the German or the
Soviet occupation. Iza, Mother, and I belonged to both categories.
I suspect that this injunction had something to do with "offers"
made by the NKVD to a few "literate" applicants for exit permits, such as myself. I knew of at least one instance when a
person who "signed up" would later inform the U.S. Consulate
in Stockholm that he had done so under pressure but had no in-

tention of following up on this pledge. The U.S. authorities may well have concluded that among people trapped in this predicament, those who had close relatives in Soviet territory were especially vulnerable to blackmail. Be that as it may, the three of us came dangerously close to getting stuck in Japan, which, most notably after Pearl Harbor, would have been an unwelcome prospect. Fortunately, the Polish ambassador, Count Romer, whose aristocratic lineaments were more authentic than our landlady's, proved to be a man of empathy and courtesy. He seemed to be quite taken with Mother. In any case, he promised to help and was as good as his word. Ultimately, he was able to provide us with three Canadian visas.

In the meantime, the political climate in Japan had become distinctly inhospitable. We could not follow the rhetoric of the anti-Western demonstrations in the streets of Japan's major cities, but their tenor was unmistakable.

While living increasingly on borrowed time, Iza and I tried to lead quasi-normal lives, learning enough Japanese to get by in a grocery by counting up to fifteen and producing a suitably singsongy *arigato gozaimasu* (thank you), and, in spite of our limited financial and linguistic resources, to do a bit of sightseeing. We found Tokyo, which we visited several times on business, a rather remarkable blend of the Western and the indigenous, and we were very duly overwhelmed by the monumental Kamakura Buddha.

Our experience of the "system" was minimal, but one evening at our boardinghouse dramatized the fact that we were in danger of getting stranded in one of the world's most encompassing police states. Mother, Iza, and I were not the only tenants of Mme. Rumyantseva. One of the rooms in the fairly ample house was occupied by another "displaced person," a Polish journalist, a converted Jew who, embarrassingly enough, spoke Polish with a rather blatant Jewish accent. Mr. K. was bright, reasonably well-informed—and argumentative. In the middle of the evening, our trio got involved in a somewhat heated political discussion. The topic, if I'm not mistaken, was Zionism. Our general outlook at the time was anti-Zionist. Mr. K. was far from a Zionist, but he enjoyed being difficult and chose to sound like one for the argument's sake. In the process, some of the voices—especially mine, I am afraid—were raised, and the four of us managed to produce a fair amount of noise. As we later found out from our landlady, her maid was reporting regularly to the secret police; her boyfriend apparently was a full-time informer. Hearing a noisy argument, the maid concluded that some people had infiltrated the house and staged an unauthorized political meeting. The boyfriend was duly alerted—he spent most of the night waiting for the conspirators to leave. Finally, he abandoned his post in dejection, for no one had left the house.

On the Other Shore

A Tale of Two Leaders

In August 1941, with three Canadian visas in hand, we left Yokohama on the large passenger boat *Heian Maru* bound for Vancouver. It turned out to be the last Japanese ship to sail for North America prior to Pearl Harbor. Had we missed that boat, we would have, figuratively speaking, missed the boat and most likely have been interned in Shanghai as enemy aliens. To put it differently, this was another narrow escape.

Its narrowness was pointed up by a rather unnerving episode that occurred in the middle of our journey. As the tension between Tojo Japan and the British Commonwealth was mounting, the Canadian government chose to freeze the Japanese assets under its jurisdiction. This decision, promulgated several days after our departure, directly affected the status of the silk cargo that the *Heian Maru* was supposed to discharge in Vancouver. Thus, the ship was stopped in the open sea by orders from Tokyo. We spent nearly a full day waiting for further instructions. One of the options, clearly, was returning to the base—a worrisome prospect for a fairly large group of Polish Jewish refugees. It was hard not to notice the difference in reactions to this contingency between displaced people like us and the few British subjects or U.S. nationals, who appeared unruffled. Finally, there was a reprieve: *Heian Maru* was allowed to proceed on the condition that it would stop short of Vancouver. The new destination was Seattle. Those of us who were bound for Canada would be transported to Vancouver by small passenger boats bearing such names as *Queen Elizabeth* and *Princess Margaret.*

The rest of the passage was uneventful. What stuck in my mind for some reason was the tedious speechifying of a smug Jewish lawyer from Warsaw—Father had known the type only too well!—to the effect that all the problems we were facing could be reduced to the ongoing conflict between individualism and collectivism.

After a twelve-day journey, the *Heian Maru* docked in Seattle. We spent several hours aboard waiting for transportation. (Since we had no U.S. visas, getting off the boat was out of the question.) Little did I know that, more than seven years later, I would be returning to the scenic city we were now viewing from a distance to take up my first academic appointment. In the meantime, we were subjected to a dismal visit. As we were straining toward the Seattle scenery, a shriveled-up elderly woman showed up on deck. She turned out to represent the Seattle branch of the association of Polish Catholic Women, the so-called Society of St. Zita. Moving from one group of Polish Jewish refugees to another, she was scrutinizing our faces only to register, in Polish, an emphatic disappointment. "Hey, I was told there are Poles on this ship, but it's not really true. You are a Jew; you, too, are a Jew. I can always tell a Jew," she added proudly. (The word for "Jew" used by the old biddy was the mildly pejorative and condescending *Zydek,* literally, a "little Jew.") One of these so labeled, whose sound Bundist credentials were not matched by intelligence, drew himself up to his full height and announced irrelevantly: "I am a member of the Warsaw City Council." Our visitor was not impressed; she left in a huff. The brief encounter with a segment of Seattle's Polish community was less than heartwarming.

And then there was Vancouver. We loved the scenery—the snowcapped mountains, the lush vegetation of Stanley Park. Once again we experienced a vivid contrast—this time one between the increasingly pinched and mean tenor of Japan's everyday life and a sense of cornucopia, of affluence, solidity, and caloric richness epitomized by the chocolate milk shake. Also, to one raised on Dickens, there was something old-fashionedly and reassuringly British about Vancouver. We were in no hurry to leave a haven at once so cozy and so spectacular. But the reception committee, though not inhospitable, urged us to move on: "Montreal, with its large Jewish community," they opined, "is a more logical destination for people like you." That Vancouver was not a major center of Jewish culture was attested to by the quality of Yiddish attempted by one of our advisers. "Ikh hob gechanged my mind," he averred.

Our Vancouver host had a point. Montreal's Jewish community proved active and actively welcoming. The scenic multicultural city played host to vital branches of the organization that had brought us to North America, the Jewish Labor Committee, and of the Workmen's Circle, founded at the turn of the century by transplanted young Bundists. There were many Jewish labor activists in Montreal who were willing, indeed eager, to help out Henryk Erlich's family. We landed for several months in a comfortable apartment in Outremont, temporarily vacated by the Jewish trade union leader sometimes referred to as Montreal's David Dubinsky. I recall a friendly welcome rally organized by the Jewish Labor Committee. Mother and I spoke briefly in a literate but somewhat halting Yiddish. (With the exception of two of my finest hours that were still ahead of me, my Yiddish was never quite fluent.) The occasion was marred by the fatuous performance of our former fellow traveler N.S., the self-advertising member of the Warsaw City Council, who chose to speak on behalf of our group. His rhetoric was shrill, his metaphors—or rather similes—hopelessly mixed. In describing the plight of Polish Jewry on the eve of the war, he worked himself into a frenzy, stigmatizing the role of the Jewish bourgeoisie. "Toads that crawl like mice!" he cried scornfully.

In addition to a vigorous Jewish labor movement, Montreal in 1941 could boast a lively Jewish literary milieu. Shortly after our arrival, we were introduced to Ms. Ida Mazo (Massey), a prolific Yiddish poet; she specialized in children's verse and was devoted to the cause of Yiddish. In her sui generis literary salon she featured several established Jewish poets such as M. Ravitch. Iza and I promptly became close to the son of our vivacious hostess. He was about ten years younger than I and was visibly drawn to both of us. Actually, I had something to learn from him. It was Irving who introduced us to what seemed at the time his favorite volume of verse—A. E. Housman's *The Shropshire Lad*. I still remember the lines, "When I was one and twenty/I heard a wise man say. . . ."

Our contacts with Montreal's larger community were very limited and less congenial. The French majority was nursing more or less legitimate grievances. On the whole, it seemed more anti-British than anti-Nazi. Its overall attitude toward the confrontation between the "free world" and Hitler's Germany hewed dangerously close to neutrality. This attitude was only one of the reasons why we did not take to Montreal in spite of its appealing scenery. (Also, though bilingual, in 1941 to 1942 it was much more provincial than it has been during the last quarter of the century.) In any case, we viewed our stay in Montreal as temporary. Our actual objective was New York. Alex and Rachel, after a brief bout with San Francisco, were already there, taking active part in establishing a Bundist headquarters-in-exile and working diligently on an affidavit in support of regular U.S. visas for Mother, Iza, and me.

In early October 1941, Alex forwarded to us the first—and as it turned out, the only—letter from Father. Shortly after his release from the Moscow prison, he sent through the diplomatic pouch two letters—one addressed to the party comrades in New York and another to the family. As I quote the latter extensively, I propose to set aside for a while the story of my wartime travails in Canada and the United States and pause before what became known as "the Erlich-Alter case"—the twists and turns in the fate of two intrepid socialist leaders, trapped in Stalin's Russia.

"Sophie, my love, my dearest children," wrote Father from Moscow on September 27, 1941,

I embrace you all together and each of you separately. I can hardly believe that I write to you today. There were moments when this seemed to me unthinkable. I was reviewing then in my mind my entire family life. I tried to imagine your life without me. I was brimful of tenderest love for all of you and of boundless gratitude for what you had given me. . . .

There were other, more trying moments when I was getting ready for the worst (I never thought of death as the worst option)— and I was trying to bestir myself and to mobilize all the powers of resistance I could summon. I thought then mostly of you, my dear boys, of your honest eyes and noble hearts, and of the importance of bequeathing to you an unsullied name. This strengthened my conviction that I would endure. . . .

But what is most improbable is not that I am writing to you, but the sudden and dramatic change in my situation. From the cell of those condemned to death [*smertniki*] to the "Metropol" hotel suite and to solicitous care, from a contemptible accusation against me and Victor to a red-carpet treatment—this is simply fantastic, fairy-tale stuff. But enough of this. You'll get some details from Emanuel [Nowogrodzky, secretary general of the American representation of the Bund in New York].

The main elements of the story were indeed conveyed to us by the Bund headquarters: Father had never been sent to Vilna. After two weeks in Brest-Litovsk, he was transferred to Moscow's notorious Lubyanka. Victor Alter, who was arrested at the end of September in Kovel (Western Volhynia), landed in the same prison. Both leaders were confronted by charges of consistently "counterrevolutionary" and anti-Soviet activities at the behest of the Polish secret police and, more broadly, of the international bourgeoisie and, more specifically, of conspiring on behalf of the Bund's Central Committee to subvert the Soviet system. They stood firm under unbearable pressure—hunger, solitary confinement, interminable nightly interrogations—and steadfastly denied the egregious accusations in writing. Faced with the combination of brutality and ignorance, Father produced what amounted to a short history of the Bund in interwar Poland, with special emphasis on the Bund's actual attitudes toward the Soviet Union and the Communist International. More than fifty years later, when my cousin Viktoria Y. Dubnova, who lives in Moscow, gained access to the KGB archive that contained the Erlich-Alter file and was permitted to copy by hand the materials pertaining to the investigations which took place from 1939 to 1941, I marveled at the dignity, cogency, and courage which marked Father's attempt to enlighten his NKVD interrogators. While rejecting the slanderous charges and insisting that the Bund appreciated the achievements of the Russian Revolution, Father admitted to criticisms of some individual policies of the Soviet government and of the Comintern and spoke forthrightly about the divisive role of the Communists in the international labor movement and, more specifically, in Poland's Jewish trade unions. Clearly, a major objective of these careful formulations was to counter the lethal accusations that were being leveled not only at Father and Alter but also at other Bundist activists languishing at the time in Soviet jails. But since Father was far from certain that he would survive his ordeal, he was also determined to leave behind a written record of the Bund in independent Poland, free from Stalinist lies and slanders.

In the summer of 1941, the two leaders stood trial before a military tribunal. Both were condemned to death—a verdict that was promptly commuted to ten years of forced labor. But by that time, the Nazi armies were advancing rapidly toward the heart of the Soviet Union, and Stalin had concluded an agreement with the Polish government-in-exile whereby all Polish nationals arrested and interned on the Soviet territory were to be released. Thus, as Father wrote in his letter, he was propelled along with V. Alter from a death cell to a fancy Intourist hotel. As for the red-carpet treatment he was referring to, shortly after their release, Father and Alter entertained in their Metropol suite an eminent visitor. NKVD colonel A. P. Volkovysky, an assistant to Lavrenty Beria, head of Soviet secret police, apologized to the former prisoners for their treatment and asked them to consider the two years spent in jail and the verdicts a grievous "mistake." In addition to the apology, Colonel Volkovsky was bringing a startling offer. "He proposed that Erlich and Alter assume leading roles in a new organization aiming to mobilize the Jewish public opinion in the world, most notably in the United States, on behalf of the Soviet war effort, the Jewish Anti-Fascist Committee."[1]

We were not surprised to hear that in spite of their recent ordeal, which left little room for illusions about the Stalin regime, Father and Alter were prepared to take active part in the new venture provided they were given an opportunity to shape its structure and objectives. Naturally they saw Hitler as the main—and lethal—enemy. What was less clear to me, and what remains somewhat puzzling in retrospect, was Stalin's seeming readiness to entrust two Jewish socialists with leadership of an organization formed under his aegis, the more so since he must have remembered Henryk Erlich's walkout in concert with the Mensheviks on the historic meeting of the Petrograd Soviet of Workers and Soldiers' Deputies in protest against the October coup. Was it the critical situation on the front in the fall of 1941, when Russia's fate literally hung in the balance, that induced Stalin to consider, albeit for a moment, the possibility of co-opting the worldwide prestige and the international connections of Henryk Erlich and Victor Alter in order to bolster the desperate resistance to the Nazi juggernaut?

Be this as it may, the contacts made in Moscow were to be pursued in Kuybyshev—a bleak town in central Russia to which all foreign embassies were evacuated in October 1941 in the face of a direct German threat to Moscow. Erlich and Alter left for Kuybyshev as wards of the Polish embassy, with which they had established cordial relations. The Polish ambassador, Professor Stanislaw Kot, a liberal politician and a respected cultural historian, was a thoughtful and honorable man. For weeks on end, the two Bund leaders worked in tandem with Professor Kot at identifying Polish citizens incarcerated in the Soviet Union and expediting their release. There was something admirable and more than a bit unnerving about the spectacle of two brave and inwardly free men engaged in a feverish activity under the watchful eye of one of the twentieth century's most repressive police states.

Eager as we were to share Father's hope to come in the near future to New York as the head of the Jewish Anti-Fascist Committee—Victor Alter would proceed to London—we were less than sanguine. More than two months after we had heard Father's voice, our apprehensions were borne out. The Bund headquarters in New York received a chilling report from Lucjan Blit, an incisive Bundist activist, a leader of the Bund's youth movement in Warsaw, who since late October had been sharing a room with Father and Alter in Kuybyshev's dingy "Grand Hotel."

As he was to recall in London in January 1949, he was fully cognizant of his older comrades' movements during the five weeks that they spent together. "A tall man around thirty-five—one Khazanovich—came to our room several times. He was unquestionably a Jew. He would show up ostensibly in connection with matters involving the Anti-Fascist Committee. On each visit he used to report to us that no reply had yet arrived from Moscow."[2] Blit was referring here to the memorandum drafted in October by Erlich and Alter and addressed to Stalin. This carefully phrased statement stipulated that "the work of the Jewish Anti-Fascist Committee would be conducted by a presidium consisting of three members, H. Erlich, Chairman, V. Alter, Secretary, and [the third place was left open for a prominently Jewish public figure, presumably the renowned Yiddish actor Solomon Mikhoels]." Among the objectives of the new organization the memorandum listed "a campaign aiming at obtaining maximum assistance from the United States to the Soviet Union" and raised "the question of organizing a legion recruited from citizens of the U.S. and other countries that would participate directly within the ranks of the Red Army in the struggle against Nazi aggression."[3]

On December 3, while Father and Alter were temporarily away, Khazanovich called and asked Blit to inform his comrades that someone had arrived from Moscow carrying a reply. "We were sitting and drinking tea," wrote Blit. "It was 12:30 at night when one of the hotel employees . . . came up to our table and said in Russian, 'Citizen Alter, you are wanted on the telephone.' He returned immediately and said: 'Henryk, get your coat. We must leave at once.' They were certain they would be back in an hour. They never returned."[4]

Stanislaw Kot promptly intervened. A. Vyshinsky, the former prosecutor in the infamous "Moscow trials" who in 1941 was deputy minister of foreign affairs, stated that the Bund leaders had been arrested "on direct orders from Moscow." He declared subsequently that the matter did not concern the Polish ambassador since Erlich and Alter were "Soviet citizens." This egregious assertion did not discourage Professor Kot's further efforts on behalf of his distinguished countrymen. When leaving his post in July 1942, he raised the matter with Vyshinsky once again; he asked for a "souvenir" from Russia: "Give me Erlich and Alter." Vyshinsky's reply was ominous: "Future Poland will get along without them."[5]

Over the course of 1942, various Western organizations and personalities, including Eleanor Roosevelt and Wendell Wilkie, sought to approach the Soviet authorities with inquiries about the fate of H. Erlich and V. Alter. The most persistent on their behalf were the American trade union movement and the head of the AFL-CIO, William Green. The answer was deafening silence. On January 23, 1943, a number of prominent labor leaders headed by William Green and Philip Murray and distinguished intellectuals, such as Albert Einstein, sent a cable to the Soviet government requesting freedom for H. Erlich and V. Alter. A month later, this government was finally ready to respond. On February 23, 1943, Maxim Litvinov, the Soviet ambassador to the United States, wrote to William Green:

I am informed by Mr. Molotov, People's Commissar of Foreign Affairs, of the receipt by him of a telegram signed by you concerning two Soviet citizens Alter and Erlich. I am instructed by Mr. Molotov to inform you of the following facts:
    For active subversive work against the Soviet Union and assis-

tance to Polish intelligence organs . . . Erlich and Alter were sentenced to death in August 1941. [No mention is made here of the sentence having been commuted to ten years of forced labor.]

At the request of the Polish government Erlich and Alter were released in September 1941. However, after they were set free, at the time of the most desperate battles of the Soviet troops against the advancing Hitlerite army, they resumed their hostile activities including appeals to the Soviet troops to stop the bloodshed and immediately conclude peace with Germany. For this they were re-arrested and in December 1942 sentenced once more to capital punishment by the Military Collegium of the Supreme Court. The sentence has been carried out with regard to both of them.[6]

Two months later, Litvinov sent William Green another letter in which he offered an emendation. This time the sentence and the executions were said to have occurred in December 1941 rather than December 1942.

The news of the double murder produced a considerable stir in the West. There were forthright declarations of outrage on the part of the labor organizations on both sides of the Atlantic. There were editorials expressing surprise and/or indignation. In the United States, the condemnation of Stalin's foul crime was nearly universal. Predictably, the Communist *Daily Worker* slavishly toed the party line, repeating the monstrous accusations and branding the protestors as "red-baiters." The left-leaning *PM* deplored the executions of Erlich and Alter but weakened the condemnation by crippling qualifications. In some quarters, the lingering illusions about the nature of the Soviet regime as well as the fear of jeopardizing the alliance with a power that had just inflicted a major defeat on the common enemy militated against plain speaking.

This muffling effect was somewhat apparent during an otherwise impressive event that capped the protest campaign—a mass rally held in Manhattan, at Mecca Temple, on March 30, 1943. This time the combative mayor of New York, Fiorello La Guardia, was less than forceful: "We don't understand why they were liquidated. It is hard to understand. And, so we say, some of us who are real and sincere friends, to the government of Soviet Russia, we say, 'We are sorry. We are so sorry. Don't do it again.'"[7]

The labor leaders did not mince their words. David Dubinsky declared: "We have a right and a great moral duty to voice our protest, to shout out against an issue even if it is committed by an ally."[8] The distinguished liberal theologian Reinhold Niebuhr did not hesitate to speak of a "judicial murder" and offered a clear-eyed conclusion: "Russia intended to serve notice on the world, in spite of all our protests, that she was not going to tolerate anti-Communist opinion in Poland."[9]

The protests against the "judicial murder" revealed a cleavage within the noncommunist Left. There were those who were reluctant to jettison the notion of the essentially "progressive" nature of the Soviet system, who were not ready to see the Stalin regime for what it was—a ruthless and cunning enemy of freedom.

Some of these differences spilled into our home. Though all of our visitors could be relied upon to register shock and outrage over M. Litvinov's belated reply, at times these emotions were tempered by unwarranted longer-range hopefulness. Such was certainly the case with an old and respected acquaintance, the veteran Menshevik Fyodor Ilyich Dan. He had recently split off from the Menshevik émigré mainstream, represented by the journal the *Socialist Courier,* and launched a tiny left-wing faction. Since its stance entailed an implicit acceptance of the October revolution and a belief in the imminent democratization of the Soviet regime, I was inclined to label this embattled band "repentant Mensheviks." Much to my dismay, Mother, who on the eve of and during the war moved visibly to the "left," chose to join F. Dan's group.

I remember vividly F. Dan's visit that occurred shortly after the grim news had reached New York. A portly and bald man of about seventy, he spoke, as usual, with authority and precision. (Frankly, I had always thought of his personality as a bit of a dry stick, in contradiction to his wise and deeply humane wife, Lidya Osipovna.) He expressed his shock over the murder of two esteemed comrades but managed to construe it as the last outrage of its kind, as the death rattle of a decaying dictatorship. This explosion of wishful thinking was more than I was prepared to countenance. I do not remember what I said, but I am afraid it was rather rude. Mother, to whom Fyodor Ilyich was somewhat of a guru, was deeply scandalized. Alex, who had little use for Dan's optimism, seems to have found my reaction inappropriate. He clearly felt that this was no way (for a "punk" of twenty-eight) to talk to an old Marxist. In retrospect, considering the enormity of the crimes that the "decaying" system managed to commit during the following decade, I cannot bring myself to rue my irreverence.

In winding up his impassioned speech at Mecca Temple on behalf of the bereaved Bund family, S. Mendelson envisioned the moment when "thousands upon thousands of Jewish workers will make a pilgrimage to the monuments, and with heads bowed, in quiet concentration, intone the song which had so often accompanied Erlich and Alter in life, 'Di Shvue' ['The Oath,' the Bundist anthem]."[10] By March 30, 1943, when these words were spoken, the ranks of the "Jewish workers" were being decimated in Poland's ghettoes. Soon the Nazi murder machine was to preclude the possibility of such mass outpouring of grief and outrage as was envisioned by the Bund's eloquent spokesman. Yet forty-five years after the world had heard about the fate of Erlich and Alter, the city in which they lived and fought the good fight did witness a moving and spontaneous tribute to their memory and their legacy. On April 17, 1988, a monument was unveiled in the section of Warsaw's Jewish cemetery on Okopowa Street that contained the graves of two Bund leaders who had died before the war. The inscription on the new tombstone in Polish and Yiddish read: "Leaders of the Bund, Henryk Erlich, b. 1882, and Wiktor Alter, b. 1890. Executed in the Soviet Union."

Needless to say, this forthright acknowledgment of a long-suppressed truth owed nothing to the regime installed by the martial law coup in 1981. Short of an outright ban, the Polish authorities did all they could to hinder and discredit the commemoration. The only mention of the impending event in the official press was a scurrilous reference to some unspecified "cemetery hyenas" in the organ of the Polish Communist Party *Trybuna Ludu* (*Tribune of the People*). The installation and the unveiling of the monument to H. Erlich and V. Alter were due to the resourcefulness and the determination of Dr. Marek Edelman, the sole survivor of the Warsaw ghetto uprising of 1943 and a staunch Bundist, and to the active support of his Solidarity associates. The organizing committee of forty-six prominent public figures linked to Solidarity, for example, Z. Bujak, J. Kuron, J. J. Lipski, A. Michnik, and A. Wajda, called "everybody to celebrate the memory of two outstanding representatives of the Jewish community in the Second Republic of Poland, Victor Alter and Henryk Erlich."[11] The committee's call was heeded on a scale that exceeded by far the expectations of the few guests from abroad. (For medical reasons I was unable to journey to Warsaw, but Iza and our two sons were there.) To quote our son Mark, who upon his return to the States published a fine reportage in the Jewish liberal monthly *Tikkun,* "By noon on a cloudless day over three thousand people jammed shoulder to shoulder into the overgrown grounds of the Jewish cemetery on Okopowa street. As dozens of arm-banded marshals from the Independent Students' Union kept order, the crowd listened to speeches and heard messages from all over the world."[12]

Marek Edelman outlined succinctly the lives of the two men and pulled no punches in bringing out the political significance of their deaths: "All champions of freedom and justice, all foes of terror, totalitarianism, and autocracy who had found themselves within the reach of the Soviet regime were murdered by that regime."[13] S. Nunberg offered a heartfelt tribute to the fallen leaders on behalf of the American representation of the Bund in New York. Albert Shanker, vice president of the AFL-CIO, brought expressions of solidarity from the American trade unions. Zbigniew Bujak, a young and charismatic Solidarity spokesman, averred that he had only recently learned the story of the two Bund leaders. "We had to find a connection to history," he reminded his audience. "And Erlich and Alter are our past." There were messages from François Mitterand; Willy Brandt; Archbishop Jean-Marie Lustiger of Paris; the German Greens; a veteran Polish socialist in London, Adam Ciolkosz; Lord Plumb, president of the European Parliament; and my own, read by my wife, Iza. A masterful reading of a stirring poem by Zbigniew Herbert, celebrating courage and self-sacrifice, concluded the program. Yet an occasion such as this would not have been complete without the strains of the Bundist "The Oath." Somehow across the crowded cemetery grounds, the voices of the few survivors of the glorious tradition sought each other out and blended in pledging once more, in the words of the song, "boundless fidelity to the Bund."

The telling tribute to Poland's leading Jewish socialists, staged in their homeland, was symptomatic of the political ferment that had gripped the Polish "People's Democracy" and that was to change the face of Poland. (Less than a year later, the first nearly free parliamentary election was marked by a stinging defeat of the Communist Party and a surge of the Solidarity-supported candidates.) At the same time, the Soviet Union was undergoing major changes initiated by Mikhail Gorbachev. One of the implications of glasnost was an increasing readiness on the part of the authorities to own up to the crimes of the Stalin era—a process which was bound to affect the status of such men as H. Erlich and V. Alter.

On August 13, 1990, Boris Yeltsin signed the decree "On the Rehabilitation of Victims of Political Repression." On February 8, 1991, I was advised by the office of the Procurator of the USSR that "the repressions vis-à-vis Hersh V. Erlich were found unlawful" and that he was rehabilitated.

All along I viewed the clearing of the names of the murdered leaders, besmirched by a despicable accusation, as an elementary duty of any postcommunist Russian government. Yet what mattered to me more than the official "rehabilitation" of Erlich and Alter, who did not need any vindication in the court of the world's public opinion, was reliable and full information about their fate.

This was the burden of the letter that I sent to Boris Yeltsin on April 3, 1992. Having cited the known facts of the Erlich-Alter case, I expressed my concern with "ferreting out the full truth about the murder of my father and his associate" and with "bringing this information to the attention of the Russian public."

My letter was never answered. But the opening of some of the KGB archives in 1992 and the making of their contents available to the relatives of the victims of Stalin's terror furthered significantly the first of the objectives I had outlined. A major role in "ferreting out the truth" was played by my Moscow-based cousin Viktoria Yakovlevna Dubnova. By dint of unswerving perseverance, Viktoria managed to secure access to the Erlich-Alter file. (Back in 1941 she had met Father during his visit at her house shortly after his release from prison; he must have made a strong impression on the bright and sensitive teenager.) Having gained admission, she spent many days in a dingy and crowded room copying by hand as much of the file as she could. In this arduous endeavor she was assisted by her granddaughter and by a budding American Sovietologist, a stepson of my older son Henry, who was doing research in Moscow. This resourceful team managed to copy a large part of Father's cogent account of the Polish Bund's activities written in response to the malignant and ignorant Lubyanka interrogations of 1939 to 1941.

But it is the materials bearing on the second arrest that were an eye-opener. The records of the Kuybyshev prison showed that December 1941 saw neither the death sentences nor the executions. The two leaders were incarcerated in the Kuybyshev NKVD jail and placed in solitary confinement, to be known only as number 41 and number 42. No charges were proffered, no interrogations held. The records indicate that despite their insistent requests, Father and Alter were never apprised of the reasons for their second arrest. Both lodged strong protests with the prison authorities and with the Kuybyshev NKVD. V. Alter, the more impetuous of the two, wrote on April 20, 1942, that if no answer were forthcoming in four days, he might have recourse to "drastic measures."

As a result, Alter was watched closely at all times. In July 1942, the supervision was intensified. The head of the internal prison was directed "to remove urgently from prisoner #41 all items (pens, metal buckles) which he is not supposed to have in the cell." Thus, he was prevented from carrying out his threat. It is Father—clearly, he was not supervised quite so closely— who chose the route contemplated by V. Alter. Viktoria's principal finding was that rather than being executed in December 1941, Father took his own life on May 14, 1942. (He must have realized by that time that he would never come out of jail alive.) Comrade Budenko reported from Kuybyshev to lieutenant of state security Mansapov that "at 20:00 h. on 14 May it was discovered in a cell of the Kuibyshev Internal Prison, that the prisoner of Section 4, Directorate NKVD Erlich Gersh Volf Moiseevich had hanged himself on the window bars."[14] The two prison officers responsible for number 42 were mildly punished for insufficient vigilance. Head of the Internal Prison Sadeev was held under arrest for two days and the operational commissioner Grebennikov for five days for inadequate surveillance of the prisoner. "Vigilance" vis-à-vis Alter was redoubled. According to the record, number 41 was shot dead on February 17, 1943.

The materials copied by my cousin contain a document that clearly provided the basis for Litvinov's grossly misleading communication. It records the sentencing of both Father and Victor Alter by the Military Collegium of the USSR Supreme Court on December 23, 1941, and a prompt implementation of the verdicts. At the bottom of the page there is a note signed by V. Molotov and addressed to L. Beria: "Comrade Stalin has approved this text and I have sent an appropriate reply to Green, Wilkie, and others via Comrade Litvinov."[15]

Let me note that February 14, 1943, the date of the "text," preceded by three days V. Alter's actual execution. More important, the word "text" is a giveaway. Clearly, what "Comrade Stalin approved" were not the acts whose date and scope are misrepresented here but the official version of the events, a version to be communicated to the outside world. Moreover, the timing of this doubly mendacious announcement was far from fortuitous. It coincided with the final defeat of Von Paulus's army in Stalingrad. As the London-based journal *East European Jewish Affairs* suggested, "at such moments of triumph any criticism of Soviet behavior would have been expected to be low-key."[16] Russia's improved military situation might well have had something to do with the date of the execution that actually occurred. Through 1942, Stalin may have hesitated to commit anything as irreversible as a murder, let alone to notify about it the West, whose material support was absolutely essential to Russia's survival.

I recall with appreciation that Viktoria was quite circumspect about bringing me up-to-date on Father's actual fate. It would seem that no information culled from a KGB archive file could have been more devastating than what for nearly fifty years we had assumed to be the truth. And yet the news brought by my cousin during one of her annual visits was profoundly upsetting. When I thought of the despair that after a five-month ordeal must have driven Father to suicide, I felt chilled to the bone. Still there was a measure of satisfaction to be derived from the grim finding. By defying his jailers' "vigilance"—and refusing to wait for the firing squad—Father achieved a measure of control over his life.

In a compelling poem, Stanley Kunitz wrote, "In a murderous time / The heart breaks and breaks/And lives by breaking."[17] The price that my family paid for living "in a murderous time" was exorbitantly high; it was emblematic of the plight of East European Jewry, trapped between two lethal totalitarian regimes. Let me repeat: In December 1941, my grandfather Simon Dubnov was shot by a Nazi thug during the liquidation of the Riga ghetto. In May 1942, my father committed suicide in Stalin's jail.

The bulk of Father's family perished in the Holocaust. Some were rescued from the nightmare. My paternal grandparents were fortunate enough to die in their beds before the Armageddon. My uncle, a Zionist M.P., and his wife managed to get to Palestine on the eve of the war. Their two sons ultimately made their

way to Israel and the United States. My oldest and favorite
cousin and his wife landed in Paris in time. The rest of the
Lublin-based branch of the family was destroyed by the Nazi
murder machine. I mourn them all—aunts, uncles, cousins—
but I remember with special affection (and rage) my youngest
aunt, warm and lively Manya; her handsome, "Aryan"-looking
husband, George; and their daughter, everyone's favorite, sunny,
bubbling, trusting Stephanie (Stefcia).

Let me return, however falteringly, after an extended visit in the
slaughterhouse of the "real twentieth century" to the trivialities of
a "normal" life, the risk-free if financially precarious existence
of a survivor, temporarily stranded in Montreal in 1941 and 1942.

Shortly after our arrival in Canada, Iza managed to get a job
as a statistician in a major department store. (On the eve of the
war, she had followed someone's wise advice to take a course in
statistics.) I had more trouble finding marginally gainful em-
ployment. My modest academic credentials cut little ice in
Montreal. The active guidance I was offered by a well-meaning
if unexciting old-timer associated with the Workmen's Circle
had little to do with either my skills, such as they were, or my
long-term aspirations. Mr. Shatan, whose demonic name (*Szatan*
in Polish means "Satan") was remarkably incongruous, admired
Father and was all too eager to be of assistance. A seasoned and
dedicated public accountant, Shatan was convinced that accounting was the most appropriate career for a promising young
man. Though I was not entirely sure of this, I was prepared to
follow his lead for the short term. Through Shatan's good offices
I landed a job at $10 a week as a very junior accountant. My only
task was adding up columns of figures—the calculator, apparently, was not in general use—a task that I performed passably
if not outstandingly. For all I knew, I was not worth any more
than $10. But even in Montreal of 1942, it was a very modest
salary. At some point I decided to ask for a raise. I probably had
in mind $12 a week. In any case, I made an appointment with
my boss—a suave young man who had the reputation of a "par-
lor pink." He listened with feigned sympathy to my hemming

and hawing to the effect that I was having difficulty making ends meet. (I may not have put it quite as idiomatically as that, but somehow I managed to convey a comparable message.) Having toyed thoughtfully with his pipe, Mr. Shafer averred, "I fully understand your problem, Victor, but the firm cannot absorb a raise at this time." I didn't mean to confront my boss with an ultimatum, but somehow, possibly due to the inadequacy of my English, I talked myself out of the job. After getting home, I called my mentor and informed him about this contingency. He was not fazed by it. "You must find another job."

"Yes," I muttered, "but how do I do this?"

"Advertise," he said confidently.

"But what should I advertise for?" I wondered. "I do not know anything."

"Advertise," he insisted.

Feeling a total fraud, I followed his advice and advertised for a position in accounting or bookkeeping. To my dismay, I was promptly offered a job as the head bookkeeper at a small jewelry firm.

Thus began what was probably the most nerve-racking month of my life. (This, let me add, is a rather strong statement since in 1944 and 1945 I was to spend some time in combat.) I was more or less conversant with invoices, but I had no clue as to the handling of drafts. After a couple of weeks of my sojourn at Mr. Brown's firm, the accountant who would show up regularly to examine the books made his monthly appearance. I think back to his visit as one of my most despicable moments. Predictably, the examiner was not impressed. "Mr. Erlich," he said, "these books don't look too good to me." I muttered something to the effect that my predecessor—a young woman whom I met briefly on my first day—had done a sloppy job, and the two of us shared a sexist snigger at the expense of the allegedly incompetent female who actually, whatever her flaws, must have been more competent than I. In addition to hating myself for this move, I wondered anxiously what I was going to say a month later when I would have to assume full responsibility for the state of the books.

Once again fate intervened to grant me a last-minute reprieve or, if you will, another narrow escape. Before the accountant's next visit, our U.S. immigration visas came through. Alex, who was as assiduous at helping others as he was "impractical" on his own behalf, scored a coup. An eminent American Jewish trade unionist, B. Hardman-Salutsky, provided the needed affidavit for Mother, Iza, and me. I went into Mr. Brown's office to tell him that I had to leave for New York in order to rejoin the rest of my family. My boss, a pompous youngish man, who clearly had no inkling as to what a disaster I had been, professed to be saddened by the news. "You are a young man, Victor," he said portentously, "and this is a young firm. I thought you would grow with this firm." Without sharing with Mr. Brown my actual feelings about the prospect of growing with his firm, I bade him a hasty farewell.

In mid-October 1942, we got off the train at Penn Station. More than three years after leaving Warsaw, we were finally landing in New York. Alex was there, of course, pale and visibly moved. Among those who came to welcome us to the United States was our former Warsaw neighbor, the imperious Esther Iwińska, who some twenty years earlier upbraided me for my unmanly behavior, an overreaction to the imminent death of John Chesterfield. Though not given to sentimental effusions, she was clearly as happy to see us as we were happy to see her. I recall that, true to her proclivity for laying down the law, she delivered herself on this occasion of a dogmatic assertion: "America is ruled by old women." Her documentation was rather scant. Under the aegis of this sweeping generalization, my American period was launched.

After scenic but rather provincial Montreal of 1942, New York was overwhelmingly exciting and occasionally unnerving. Iza was unambivalently taken with the Big Apple; she was to remain for the rest of her life its ardent fan. I could not help but be impressed by the city's multicultural dynamism and beguiled by Washington Square and Rockefeller Center. I was less enthused over the bleakness of the area in which we landed. Assuming that we would want to be together, Alex lined up an apartment at the corner of Amsterdam Avenue and 104th Street. Iza was somewhat taken aback by this fait accompli. I too felt that he should have consulted us prior to the decision but, rightly or wrongly, chose not to rock the boat. This was not merely reluctance to hurt the feelings of a wounded family. It was also thinking ahead. My stay in New York was apt to be brief. As an immigrant, I registered shortly after our arrival under the Selective Services Act and expected to be drafted fairly soon. Iza was pregnant; I thought she might well need some logistic support before long.

One of the immediately apparent advantages of New York over Montreal was that I no longer had to depend on the guidance of an elderly public accountant. In 1942, New York was home to a number of Jewish cultural institutions. Among them was *Yiddishe Entsiklopedie,* a general encyclopedia in Yiddish. (Back in the 1940s, my Yiddish was at its most operative; I am speaking of a decent command of literary and political Yiddish—in contradistinction to many American Jews of my age, I was never capable of small talk in Yiddish.) I was offered a job as an all-around junior staff member. Volume B was in preparation. Thus, I had to become in short order an authority on all kinds of items (place names, names of personalities, terms) that begin with *B*—or, to be exact, with ב in Yiddish.

One of the pleasures of this wide-ranging assignment was working under the aegis of a remarkable man, an old acquaintance and an erstwhile political ally of my parents, the Russian Jewish socialist leader Raphael Abramovitch. In the halcyon days of the first revolution of 1917, Abramovitch, an able writer and a compelling speaker, played a major role in the Russian Bund and in the Menshevik movement. Forced into emigration, he became one of the key figures in the Menshevik émigré community and an editor of its organ *The Socialist Courier* (*Sotsialisticheskiy Vestnik*), which, first in Berlin, then in Paris, and finally in New York was the most reliable source of information about, and of insight into, the political and cultural developments in the Soviet Union. As I mentioned earlier, by the time the "Foreign Delegation" of the Mensheviks reached New York, its left-wing minority had split off the mainstream to launch a journal of its own, the *New Path,* which exuded unwarranted optimism about the imminent democratic evolution of the Soviet Union. During that period, Abramovitch was incontestably the principal spokesman for the orthodox Menshevik position. Actually, his unremitting hostility to the Stalin regime was exacerbated by personal tragedy: Abramovitch's son Mark, an idealistic young socialist who went to Spain in order to fight on the side of the republic, was ambushed and killed by the NKVD. The family ordeal contributed to a brand of anti-Bolshevism that not only Mother but also Alex found too extreme. By and large, I could live with it.

To be sure, there was nothing political about my work at *Yiddishe Entsiklopedie* or, for that matter, about R. Abramovitch's editorial responsibilities. Trained as an engineer who spent most of his life in Social Democratic politics and journalism, he was something of a polymath and thus an appropriate role model for a junior generalist. In handling some of the entries, I was able to draw on my special interest in Polish and Russian literatures. Otherwise I ranged literally from "Bath" (town of) to "Baths" (Roman, Turkish) to "Byron." Actually, the latter entry was assigned to a specialist, but Abramovitch urged me to revise it rather drastically. In his preoccupation with the anecdotal or, to put it differently, scandalous aspect of Byron's biography, the expert somehow managed to lose track of the fact that Byron was a major poet.

Another long entry that required my active intervention dealt, strangely enough, with "Lighting," that is, primarily electricity. (The Yiddish term is *Balaykhtung.*) When Abramovitch suggested that I rewrite a piece authored by a specialist, I remonstrated, "But I don't know anything about the subject." "You don't have to tell me that," replied my editor. "But you can write and he can't. The information is there, but it is poorly presented. And in case of doubt, there are a couple of reliable encyclopedias you can consult." The job proved doable; after some research, I managed to produce a viable entry. In one respect the experience proved quite instructive. Only a month after completing the assignment, I found myself as ignorant of the subject as I had been before tackling it. The information I had crammed in order to do the article flowed through me without leaving any significant residue. This, I suppose, is the inevitable fate of having acquired knowledge that is not anchored in one's brain.

As I was grappling with such contingencies, the sweltering New York summer was upon me. It brought an important event: Iza gave birth to our first son. We called him Henry Anthony.

Henry was born on June 4, 1943, at the Beth Israel hospital, at the edge of Union Square. Iza's labor pains were exacerbated by unnecessary last-minute stress. When the contractions escalated, the nurse called a callow-looking young doctor who was visibly uneasy about his role. "I have never done this before," he muttered. "You've got to start sometime," she callously replied. "And she looks healthy." Having overheard this less-than-reassuring exchange, Iza began to curse rather pungently. Her profanity was lost on the hospital personnel—she was cursing in Polish.

The actual delivery went smoothly enough. Several hours later, I was standing in front of a glass door along with another new father—we were being shown two infants. Though I did not expect the newborns to be pretty, I was taken aback by the appearance of one of them, who struck me as singularly homely, and could not refrain from asking with audible apprehension: "Is this my baby?" "No, it's mine," the man standing next to me said mournfully. Though I felt like a heel, I was greatly relieved. By comparison, Henry looked gorgeous.

I must have been both exhilarated and mildly traumatized by the combination of unbearable heat with the happy shock of fatherhood. When I emerged from Beth Israel into steaming Union Square, I realized that I had lost my wallet, which contained all my identification and a smidgen of cash. Since I was prevented from hanging around the hospital, I chose to do a bit of politicking in the neighborhood and visited the editorial offices of the Social-Democratic weekly the *New Leader.* The avuncular editor, Sol Levitas, who turned out to be a Menshevik from

Odessa, received me cordially, owing, no doubt, to the fact that I was Henryk Erlich's son. (Levitas was keenly aware of the Erlich-Alter case. He had devoted to it back in February a hard-hitting editorial.) I also met at the *New Leader* a bright and highly articulate young man who was at the time Levitas's assistant; his name was Daniel Bell. He was to grow into an influential and prolific American sociologist. I found both men congenial.

The *New Leader* was primarily concerned with foreign policy and was quite knowledgeable about it. Its stance was consistently and vehemently anti-Soviet. Predictably, Mother took a dim view of the weekly, and Alex was quite critical of it. Though I was inclined to agree that the *New Leader* was too much of a one-issue publication, I found the issue important enough to contribute two articles to the weekly in the subsequent five years.

That Sol Levitas had become an anticommunist liberal rather than a socialist became clear to me on a somewhat later occasion. It was probably in 1945 or 1946 that Alex and I attended a meeting of the Menshevik club in New York. I felt considerable affinity for these gatherings but did not make a habit of attending them. This, however, was a special occasion; the featured speaker was one of the most distinguished representatives of a fine tradition. Irakli Tseretelli, a leading Georgian Menshevik, was one of the most widely respected Social Democratic spokesmen in 1917, a man of dignity and grace. I found him singularly appealing, not least because of his much-commented-on physical resemblance to Father.

Tseretelli articulated cogently and lucidly the traditional Menshevik position. In outlining the society of the future, he envisioned a transitional period of "mixed economy" in which the public and private sectors would exist side by side. During the discussion, Sol Levitas rose to his feet. "You assume that the temporary coexistence of the public and private sectors must necessarily usher in the prevalence of the former. But what is the guarantee," he continued, "that in this competition the private sector would not gain the upper hand?" Tseretelli's answer was curt, with his Georgian accent audibly underscored by his underlying scorn: "If you postulate such an outcome, Comrade Levitas, your socialism is built on sand." I was not altogether surprised to see my brother break into frenzied one-man applause. Though I had high regard for Alex's political intelligence and his analytical skills, I could not resist what for a dues-paying Bundist was a heretical thought: socialism is ultimately a matter of faith.

But enough of Menshevik politics. Let me return to the personal. In June 1943, our kibbutz at the corner of Columbus Avenue and 106th Street—we had moved in the meantime— acquired a new inmate. The family dynamics changed. My lively and articulate two-and-a-half-year-old niece Mimi (Mirele) was no longer the only child in our midst. Though she must have had some negative feelings about being partly dethroned, she exhibited a keen and ostensibly benign interest in her cousin, whom she labeled *beybele* ("little baby"; since my sister-in-law was an ardent Yiddishist, Mimi's first language was Yiddish).

As the summer wore on, it became clear that my initial acquaintance with *beybele* would have to be brief. By June, the U.S. Army was ready for me; because of my first-born I was granted a reprieve. In early September, I had to present myself for what turned out to be a nearly two-year stint with the U.S. infantry.

"You're in the Army Now"

M y feelings were somewhat mixed. In 1943, the U.S. Army was a logical place to be—after all, the war with Germany was *our* war. (Alex felt deeply frustrated when, because of his asthma, he was found ineligible for military service. Faced with increasingly grim news from Eastern Europe, he was in dire need of a severe trial, a need which was only imperfectly satisfied by having to carry the heavy volumes requested by the more demanding readers at the Slavonic Division of the New York Public Library.) At the same time, I had an inkling that I was not going to relish the army way of life.

My apprehensions were to be fully borne out. Owing to the quirks of the U.S. Army's personnel policy, I was to wind up in the incongruous role of a combat infantryman.

The induction center, Camp Upton, in New York, gave me a fair preview of my impending transformation. Having subjected myself to the mandatory GI haircut and donned the khaki uniform, I looked somewhat displaced and forlorn. The long, slow-moving lines of soldiers waiting for various tests and medical procedures validated the description of the army modus operandi as "hurry up and wait." As the rookies were waiting, the "old-timers," who must have been at Camp Upton for more than five days, muttered ominously, "Watch for the hook."[1]

The next setting was the site of my basic infantry training, Camp Fannin, in eastern Texas. The three months I spent there were both stressful and ego-deflating. They involved such exertions as net climbing, crossing a creek on a wobbly plank, carrying an M1 rifle "at port arms," and creeping and crawling under fire. My performance was consistently dismal.

At some point, my physical ineptitude became a threat to my immediate environment. Our periodic rifle-cleaning exercise—we were enjoined to take good care of the weapons entrusted to us—entailed taking them apart and putting them together in a hurry as the sergeant urged us to "fall out into the company street carrying them pieces at port arms." I chose to simplify the procedure. Instead of breaking my M1 rifle down into small pieces that I would not have been able to assemble in haste, I tended to deal only with three major components. Yet on one occasion this strategy did not quite work. As we were "falling out into the company street," I had an uneasy feeling that my weapon was put together imperfectly. Sure enough, when we were ordered to shift the "piece" from the "port arms" position (holding the rifle in a diagonal position) to "right shoulder arms" and then to "present arms," my rifle disassembled or "deconstructed" itself in the air, with the heaviest component flying in the general direction of the commanding officer's face. Fortunately, our platoon sergeant had enough agility and presence of mind to grab the butt before it did any damage to the lieutenant. I'm afraid I'm unable to reconstruct the streams of obscenity emitted simultaneously by the two protagonists. The CO must have been too stunned by his last-minute rescue to bear down on the culprit. As I heard later from Private Klein, a slick young man who had landed the soft job of a company clerk, as soon as the company was dismissed, the lieutenant hastened to the office and pulled out my file. He must have been trying to find out if it contained any hint at mental problems. (The other possibility, of course, to use the army lingo, was that I was "bucking for Section 8," in other words, pretending to be crazy in the hope of getting a discharge.) I understand that this research proved inconclusive. The fact of the matter is that our CO asked to be transferred to another unit. While I am not convinced that my performance was solely responsible for this decision, I received a few kudos from my comrades-in-arms.

Though they did think of me as a weirdo, the cocky Texan CO was intensely disliked for his arrogance and his addiction to "chicken shit," that is, fussing over formalities such as a "proper" salute, which, it was generally felt, marked him as a callow bully who had not yet seen combat.

One of my blatant failings as a prospective rifleman was a disastrous aim. With one eye half-closed, I had considerable trouble keeping the other eye open. The fact that I was probably one of the worst shots in the U.S. Army, indeed in the free world, was amply demonstrated toward the very end of our training cycle. We had to spend a week on the rifle range firing away at our respective targets. When we were done, the platoon sergeants would go down to scrutinize the targets within their purviews. Depending on their findings, the trainees would be classified as marksmen, sharpshooters, or experts. Needless to say, I did not fit any of these categories. In fact, when my sarge returned from reviewing two targets in my general area, he was so shaken as to become incoherent. The only noises he was able to make were mumbles like "I never . . . ," "I'll be damned," or "I'll be a horse's ass." Somewhat concerned over his mental state, I urged him to make himself clearer. He finally articulated the incredible—my target was simon-pure, the other target showed more hits than seemed physically possible. Profoundly embarrassed, I muttered, "I guess I didn't make it, Sarge." I was promptly silenced—we must have been in competition with other platoons. "Shush, Erlich," exclaimed Sarge. "Everybody passed, everybody passed!" It was thus that I graduated from the infantry basic training program.

A few weeks before the end of the cycle—it must have been January 1944—I had an unexpected political experience. I owed it to my barracks neighbor, an uncommonly gloomy young man who occupied a bunk beneath mine. He was clearly Jewish—his name was Cohen. He seemed better educated than most of my barracks inmates. Cohen was not too well disposed toward me, and not without reason. Before one of the periodic inspections of our barracks, where the key issue was whether one's bed was made up according to regulations, he asked me to help him with his bed (for some reason he was behind his schedule). However, because of my ineptitude, I was lagging behind still further and couldn't be of assistance. He muttered something to the effect that I was one of the least helpful people he had ever met. I was taken aback—this did not jibe with my self-image; but I realized that in some situations incompetence was incompatible with helpfulness.

Though not much love was lost between us, one day Cohen took me aside and told me in a confidential whisper of a discussion group dealing with current events that met regularly in the nearest town, Tyler. "You might be interested in dropping in on a meeting when you have a chance." Since my occasional weekend forays into Tyler lacked an agenda, I was sufficiently interested to proceed to the address imparted to me by my bunkmate when I left Camp Fannin on my next weekend pass. I located with some difficulty an apartment where some fifteen to twenty fellow trainees were harangued by a fluent speaker on the politics of the war. It soon became apparent to me that the tenor of his remarks was consistently and emphatically pro-Soviet. What proved a giveaway was not his fulsome—and not unwarranted—praise of the defenders of Stalingrad but an insistent implication that the Soviet Union was the world's only genuine anti-Nazi entity, a claim which rested on an idealized version of Soviet politics and a profound distrust of the intentions of the Anglo-American alliance. The latter stood accused here of unconscionable foot-dragging regarding the "second front in Europe"—the meeting occurred several months prior to the landing in Normandy—which allegedly smacked of "bad faith," if not of outright sabotage of the Red Army's heroic efforts.

I could not refrain from injecting a dissonant note into the discussion. I permitted myself to recall the Molotov-Ribbentrop agreement in August 1939 as well as the fact that it was Hitler rather than Stalin who broke it in 1941. The indoctrinator responded angrily; it was Poland's fault, he maintained, that the Soviet Union was forced to conclude a nonaggression pact with Germany. The fascist Polish government had previously turned down the Soviet security guarantees and had thus torpedoed collective resistance to Hitler. I held no brief for the prewar Polish regime, but I tried to call the attention of those present to the fact that the conditions urged on Poland during the abortive negotiations included establishing Soviet military bases all over the country, a demand which the history of Polish-Russian relations had rendered, to put it mildly, problematic.

Needless to say, my contribution was not well received. The invitation to attend the meetings of the Tyler "discussion group" was not renewed. Nor was I particularly interested in returning.

A few days later, I had occasion to mention the brief encounter in Tyler to a person whom I expected to show some interest in the conclave. His name was Sergeant Valtin. When I first met this tall, dark, and somewhat sinister-looking man in the course of my training, his name rang a bell. Some months before my induction, I had read a book by the renegade German Communist Jan Valtin, *Out of the Night.* Though lacking the literary skills and sophistication of a Koestler or a Silone, Valtin's work, one of the early statements of disenchantment with communism to appear in the United States, told an absorbing story. The author of *Out of the Night* sounded like a tough operative rather than an intellectual. To meet Sergeant Valtin was to have this impression strongly confirmed. His martial skills were considerable; he was one of the best shots in our company. I suspect that Valtin would have taken scarce interest in me had he not been aware, as he clearly was, of the Erlich-Alter case. His experience with the German Communist Party had made him a fierce and a fairly knowledgeable anticommunist.

Valtin listened to my description of the "discussion group" very attentively, but it promptly became clear to me that his brand of anticommunism was different from mine. "Could you mention any names?" he inquired. "Such information would be very useful to us." I duly noted the "us." The fact of the matter is that the only name I was sure of was that of my bunkmate, and I was not inclined to share this information with Valtin. If my memory does not fail me, that was our last conversation.

In the meantime, my infantry training program was drawing

to its close. Just before our "graduation," I agreed to impersonate myself in a skit as a "trainee of the year"—an all-around sad
sack who was doing everything wrong. My readiness to laugh at
myself was duly appreciated; some of my comrades-in-arms
found it a redeeming feature.

It would seem that in view of my demonstrable and realisti-
cally enacted ineptitude as a rifleman and of some linguistic
skills I possessed, I might be offered a more suitable assignment.
But that was not to be. By the time I "graduated," Camp Ritchie,
the training center for military intelligence personnel, was over-
subscribed. The same was true of another bruited-about option,
ASTP (Army Special Training Program), set up on various U.S.
campuses to enable some basic infantry training alumni to hone
their knowledge of one of the "strategic" foreign languages.
Though I did not need any additional training in Russian, I
would have been glad to submit to it at an American university.
Yet I was out of luck. By January 1944, this program was in the
throes of retrenchment. Thus, in light of my appalling performance, I was classified as a plain "doughboy." Infantry, it seemed,
was prepared to absorb any number of misfits.

I was transferred to another infantry camp in Texas. Camp
Howze was located a few miles south of the Oklahoma border,
in that Red River Valley immortalized in song. The nearest
town, Gainesville, made Tyler look like a metropolis. Sometime
in spring, Iza paid me a visit. I managed a pass and we spent two
weekend nights in an incredibly bleak and cheap Gainesville
hotel. I have two memories of this heartwarming occasion,
vividly illustrating the genius loci. On the first day, we went
for a long walk and inadvertently crossed into Oklahoma. I recall that in search of a place where we could quench our thirst,
we drifted into a tavern filled with tough-looking, bourbon-
swilling hombres in ten-gallon hats and cowboy boots. This was
not exactly what we were looking for and hardly a suitable place
for a woman. We did not linger. My more dramatic recollection
has me running down the main street of Gainesville at the un-
godly hour of 5:30 A.M. I had to take a 6:00 A.M. bus back to

Camp Howze in order to be able to shout "Here!" when my name would be called at reveille. Though there were hardly any people in the street, I was not alone. I was treated to a remarkable spectacle of some ten oversize cockroaches marching down the street in a T formation—an awesome sight which reminded me of a Texan joke whose elaborate plot I had forgotten but whose punch line was "everything is bigger in Texas, ma'am."

The eight months I spent at Camp Howze were compounded by boredom, which entailed such unstrenuous chores as "policing the area," that is, picking up cigarette butts off the company street, and a stressful rehash of combat infantry training—some more creeping and crawling under fire, forced marches, and the like. The repeated demonstrations of my ineptitude were not lost on our congenial platoon sergeant, a reasonably bright and friendly young man who had "attended college" (a euphemism for not having graduated). He felt that I was grotesquely misassigned and that I could be of greater use to the army in one of its more specialized branches, earmarked as "limited service." Yet such a reassignment required being disqualified for combat duty on either physical or mental grounds.

"So how about taking a physical?" inquired Sarge.

"I'm afraid there is not much wrong with me," I ventured.

"Do you want to get out of this fucking outfit?" wondered my leader.

"I wouldn't mind it," I admitted.

"So let's give it a fucking try. Take your butt down to the fucking center."

I followed this injunction and predictably failed. I was classified 1A.

When I reported this setback to the sergeant, he announced, "So, your only chance is the psychoneurological test." Once again I could not refrain from a pessimistic prognosis. I am not sure how I put it—my English was still far from idiomatic—but I must have intended something like, "I hate to sound presumptuous, but I'm afraid there is nothing ostensibly wrong with my mental condition." My young adviser fell back on his

standard question: "Do you want to get out of this fucking outfit? So get your butt down . . ." and so forth.

The procedures I was subjected to were none too sophisticated. First I was given a questionnaire that contained queries
that I could not help but answer in the negative—for example,
"Are you or have you ever been attracted to members of the same
sex?" or "Do you wake up screaming?"

There was one rather involute question to which I did not respond altogether negatively. It was something like, "Does it ever
happen to you that you see in the street someone you know and
without any apparent reason you cross the street to make your-
self invisible?" This time I could honestly answer yes. True,
"without any apparent reason" did not quite apply.

Obviously, my replies were not to my advantage. After a long
wait, I was ushered into the office of a dour-looking, bespectacled
psychiatrist. Having pondered the questionnaire I had filled out,
he looked at me with little enthusiasm and hit my right leg
under the knee with the side of his hand. My reaction was "normal." I did not break his glasses. The man at the desk said with
some feeling, "Get the hell out of here." I returned to the barracks a defeated man. Clearly I was destined to impersonate a
combat infantryman.

By the summer of 1944, the overseas duties of the Camp
Howze inmates had crystallized. We had been assigned to the
103rd Division, part of the Seventh Army, led by General Patch,
a less flamboyant and a less controversial figure than General
Patton. Much of France had been liberated—we were supposed
to take positions west of Alsace-Lorraine, in the Vosges area, and
push into Germany.

Strangely enough, I have no distinct recollection of traveling
from Camp Howze to our port of embarkation, Camp Shanks,
New York, or, for that matter, of our passage to Marseille. What
sticks in my mind is the uneasy week we spent in Camp Shanks,
a week marked by tension and unmistakable outbursts of xenophobia. Though we had been trained for combat, the notion that
most of us were about to face a formidable and canny enemy

proved profoundly unsettling. I'm saying "most of us" since a few optimists in our midst clung to the hope of winding up as military police in liberated Paris—a mission which would entail such hardships as ogling winsome Parisiennes. Yet, on the whole, anxiety loomed larger than hopefulness. It soon became clear to me that the imminence of combat, the possibility of getting killed "over there," triggered a degree of animosity toward a "foreigner" speaking English with an unmistakable continental accent. I do not wish to generalize on the basis of a very small sample. As far as my comrades-in-arms were concerned, hostility toward the Japanese was all too apparent. The European conflict was something we were committed to winning, but at bottom it was "my" business rather than theirs.

The animosity toward me which I sensed in Camp Shanks found expression in a crude, though fairly innocuous, practical joke. A couple of days before embarkation, I was offered a canteen filled with what was described as Coca-Cola with a touch of bourbon. In fact, the ratio between the two ingredients was just the reverse. I was knocked out cold and came to on someone else's bunk. (No one was willing to tell me how I got there.)

After landing in Marseille, which was our staging area, we spent a miserable week shivering in wet tents. It rained without respite. The high point of the week, if it could be called that, was the assembly, held under a downpour, where a demonstrably illiterate captain who hailed from Georgia—he was addicted to such phrases as "boys, that's all they are to it"—delivered a less-than-inspirational speech. The burden of his message was that we were actually going into combat. Since he was clearly quaking in his boots, this announcement came out roughly as "bboys, th-this is it." The lingering illusions about ogling French girls were shattered. The morale of the troops at that moment was not exactly high, but it could not have been any lower than that of our leader.

In order to reach our initial positions in the Vosges area, we had to be transported from Marseille in trucks and jeeps across the villages of already liberated southern and central France.

(Our itinerary bypassed the urban areas.) Because of my residual knowledge of French, I landed a relatively privileged position. Rather than traveling in a crowded truck, I made the journey in a jeep, having been assigned as a would-be interpreter to the dour lieutenant colonel who was in charge of the convoy. The expectation was that we would be warmly welcomed by grateful locals and prepared to respond in a more or less coherent French. As it turned out, my limited linguistic skills were scarcely tested. To the visible dismay of my traveling companion, the villages through which we were passing were virtually deserted. As we realized somewhat later, enthusiasm for Americans on our trajectory was not unalloyed. Some of the areas that we were traversing had been strafed by our air force while still under the German occupation, and "collateral damage" left some residue of bitterness. More important, since our journey coincided with the harvest, most of the villagers were fully occupied in the fields.

Thus, instead of cheering throngs, we would find in every hamlet a weird-looking individual making incoherent noises while waving the French flag. Visibly disappointed by the scope and the nature of the welcome, my superior would inquire impatiently, "Erlich, who is this man?"

"Sir," I would answer invariably, "I believe he is a village idiot."

"What is he saying?" the officer persisted warily.

"Roughly speaking, sir," I would report, "he is saying hi."

"Say hi to him," I would be instructed. This, I'm sorry to say, was the extent of the interpreting I was called upon to do on that trip.

Some of the village idiots made valiant attempts to sing "La Marseillaise." Needless to say, my traveling companion would fail to recognize the tune. "What is he singing?" he would wonder. "Sir," I would reply, "he is trying to sing the French national anthem." Fortunately, I was not required to reciprocate.

Having lingered briefly at our destination, we began a steady advance toward Alsace, firing, to use the army lingo, "in the general direction of the enemy." Since at the time the Germans were in full retreat, the "enemy" was beyond the range of our vision.

Along with my comrades-in-arms, I fired my M1 rifle dutifully, knowing full well that, were the enemy in sight, he would have had little to fear from me. I am referring not to my moral qualms but to my amply demonstrated inability to hit a target.

By late December, a powerful German counteroffensive stopped us in our tracks. A hibernation more than two months long in a small Alsatian town, Buchsweiler, was marked by boredom and consistent blackouts. (Though the enemy was some distance away, the situation, as they say in the army, was "tactical.") Only a few moments stand out in memory. I recall a cozy celebration of Christmas, where we sang "Silent Night" in English and German—the pro-French locals were primarily German speakers—and an embarrassing moment during the January maneuvers. A flashlight which Iza somehow managed to send me became a source of anxiety for our CO and of potential trouble for me. I had a bad cold, and each time I would reach for a handkerchief, my pocket would light up. Whenever this would happen, a messenger from the CO would be upon me hissing, "What do you think you're doing?" I came dangerously close to being charged with sending signals to the enemy. Things quieted down considerably when I had the bright if belated idea of putting the handkerchief and the flashlight in different pockets.

While episodes such as this did little to enhance my standing with the platoon, I proved useful to the outfit in strictly civilian contexts. Since I did not smoke, I could put my generous cigarette ration (Lucky Strikes, Philip Morris, etc.) at the platoon's disposal for trading purposes. There were two items the "boys" were keenly interested in: chickens and "schnapps," a generic term used for the god-awful homemade brew which I found totally impotable but which my comrades-in-arms were willing to consume in considerable quantities. (A typical GI would drink anything that could be construed as alcohol.) All this tended to enhance my prestige, the more so since, in addition to providing the desirable commodity, I did most of the negotiating.

By the middle of March we were ready to move out of Buchsweiler. Our spring offensive was about to begin. Just before "jumping off," my conversational French was put to a severe test. After over two months of laying about, the part of the farm occupied by our platoon looked like a pigsty. I went up to our sergeant, the same congenial young man who a year earlier urged me not to spare any effort to get out of "this fucking outfit," invoked what became known as "the Eisenhower policy" of being nice to friendly locals, and suggested that we clean up the joint a bit before taking off. While this suggestion predictably released some lingering xenophobia, the sarge was his usual reasonable self. "You have a point, Erlich," he allowed. "But to do even a half-assed job, we need a broom. Now you are a smooth man [meaning—you speak French]. Why don't you go to the farmer's wife and ask her for a broom?"

Thus I was launched. But as I was approaching my objective, I realized with a jolt that I did not know the French for "broom." (Brooms did not loom too large in Victor Hugo.) Thus, when confronted by a pleasingly plump woman, I was reduced to a rough French equivalent of "Could you please give me something by means of which we could remove things we don't need?" The farmer's wife, of course, was totally flabbergasted. With verbal communication in shambles, I had recourse to enacting clumsily the process of sweeping the floor. A broom (*un balai!*) was promptly produced to the accompaniment of French for "Why didn't you say so?"

The first day of our campaign was exhausting almost beyond endurance. In order to bring some food to a unit which was cut off, we had to climb a steep hill on the French-German border, carrying, in addition to full field equipment, heavy boxes of K rations. When we returned to the valley after discharging this strenuous mission, we faced a brand-new experience, that of riding a tank as "infantry elements" of the hastily assembled task force. The ride was exceedingly uncomfortable; the jammed tank could accommodate only one of my feet. (I don't remember what I did with the other one.) The tank ride turned out to be mercifully brief. As we were rolling down the highway into Germany, we were stopped not by armed resistance but by a carefully contrived roadblock that extended for about a quarter mile. It consisted of a number of horse-driven carts and a few freewheeling horses. Clearly, we had to get off our tank; driving into horses was not an option. Our objective was to get the horses and the carts off the road using persuasion and mild physical pressure. The order of the day as enunciated by our spirited company commander, a brusque but not altogether uncongenial Texan, was unequivocal: "Push the fucking horses!" Personally, I found the project rather daunting. I gave a piebald horse in front of me a perfunctory shove. Predictably, the indoctrinated animal would not budge. As I was fumbling with it ineffectually, I sighted a brown briefcase lying in the hay which filled the back of one of the carts. Needless to say, I felt more at home with briefcases than with horses. Also, for a moment I entertained a highly implausible notion that this briefcase might contain an important document (Goebbels's diary?). Yet as soon as I grabbed the bedraggled object, the CO was upon me. "Drop the fucking briefcase," he said with feeling, "and push the fucking horse." I dropped the briefcase reluctantly. The other command was not so easily implemented. The confrontation between me and the horse which I was enjoined to push became a stalemate.

As I was grappling with the awkward challenge, it occurred to me that while the tank could not bypass the roadblock, there was no reason why some of the "infantry elements" of the task force could not do so. I soon found myself, along with some likeminded men, who must have grown tired of pushing the f——
horses, at the head of our unit. The senior member of this motley group was an uncommonly informal and pleasant lieutenant colonel. Bouncing down the road with his carbine, he called our attention to some hostile activity up on the wooded hill overlooking the highway. "Boys," he remarked casually, "there are some German snipers up there." As I was to find out very soon, his point was well taken, but it was not entirely clear what we were supposed to do about it. In the meantime, I kept advancing on my own and soon realized that I had gotten too far ahead of my platoon. My impulse was to resume contact with it by

backtracking a bit. Mindful of the officer's observation, I tried some creeping and crawling but found those activities excruciatingly slow. To expedite matters, I got up, ran across the highway on the diagonal, and hit the road. After all, I thought, this should not take more than a few seconds. My reasoning could not have been more faulty. It does not take more than a few seconds to make a target of oneself, and the sniper "up there" was clearly a much better shot than I. I did not experience severe pain—the immediate sensation was not much worse than a pinprick—but, as I lay there, I felt increasingly wet: I was losing a significant amount of blood.

Fortunately, the rescue was not long in coming. (I suspect that, had it arrived ten or fifteen minutes later than it did, I would be in no position now to reminisce about it.) Some members of my platoon were catching up with me. Among the voices of those coming my way I could discern the familiar baritone of one of the friendliest men in our company, Sergeant Gregory. This extroverted Midwesterner had taken a keen interest in me. For some reason he was irresistibly drawn to all things European, be it German lieder or Continental higher education. (At some point back in Buchsweiler, he had interviewed me in depth about my background and my academic training.) His first reaction to my plight was, "Hey, boys, I guess one of us got hit by a fucking sniper!" A few seconds later his rich voice boomed right over my head: "Hey, let's pick him up real quick! He has an M.A. from the University of Warsaw!" Even in my enfeebled condition, I could appreciate the irrelevance of the reason invoked by Sergeant Gregory for picking me up "real quick." It may have taken me a while longer to ponder the unexpected fringe benefits of an academic degree.

I was picked up with dispatch and placed in an ambulance that took me to the nearest U.S. military hospital. (I believe it was in Saarbrücken.) The trip was very stressful—every bump on the road caused excruciating pain. I had been shot through the chest—one of the bullets was still lodged there—and I was admitted for emergency surgery. Yet my main problem upon admission was extreme difficulty in breathing. One of the few images that stayed with me was that of two young medics looking at me with concern and muttering, "Try to breathe, try to breathe." The fact of the matter is that breathing was very hard work whose success was far from assured. I had lost some blood, and my encounter with the sniper occurred at the end of an extremely exhausting sequence. There were moments when I was tempted to throw in the towel—not trying to breathe seemed the easier and less demanding course of action. But the dominant feeling was that my survival was literally up to me. I know this sounds a bit corny, but it appears to be true. Somehow I managed a moment of existential lucidity, of considering soberly what I was in danger of losing. I thought of Iza's laughing hazel eyes, of placid little Henry, of my wounded family—and decided to give breathing another try.

Having weathered surgery, I was transported—another acutely uncomfortable but considerably longer trip—to Dijon and admitted to the largest and probably best-equipped American military hospital on the Continent. Shortly after my arrival in Dijon, I was operated on again. The chest surgeon in charge, one of the gloomiest men I ever met, was apparently a highly skilled professional. My steady recovery was expedited and, for all I know, made possible by incredible amounts of penicillin that had to be injected several times a day. Once again I was lucky: penicillin had been invented only four years earlier, and I was not allergic to it.

Otherwise days were long and dreary. The only uplift was provided by occasional visits from a pretty and vivacious nurse. Everyone was in love with Lieutenant R. and vied for her attention. The nights were difficult. Instead of sleeping pills I was given a shot of whiskey—a treatment that made some of my fellow patients openly envious. On one occasion I could barely decode a whispered question from the nearest bed: "How much?" My neighbor was clearly offering me a deal.

Shortly after I had become an ambulatory case, I was asked to do some arduous interpreting. Apparently my surgeon had acquired in Dijon the reputation of something of a medical miracle man. He was indeed a remarkable craftsman who handled successfully cases more difficult than mine, including one that involved the removal of a bullet lodged at the edge of a heart muscle. At some point, an ancient-looking Frenchman who turned out to have been an army chest surgeon during the First World War showed up to inform himself about his younger confrere's triumphs, and I was enrolled as a would-be interpreter. The task exceeded by far my linguistic resources. My command of medical terminology, whether French or English, was very limited. I did more gesturing than verbalizing. I suspect all I managed to convey to the venerable visitor was that some of the cases were very difficult and yet we had survived.

I was still in the hospital, though much recovered, on VE-day. It was wonderful to hear that the war was over and that we had won, though frustrating to have to spend the day—and the night!—in the hospital rather than in the streets, drinking milk instead of Burgundy.

A couple of weeks later, I bade farewell to Dijon and left France on a hospital ship bound for Charleston, South Carolina. I recall the journey with some pleasure. Since the population of the ship, drawn as it was from all branches of the army, came considerably closer than the 103rd Division to being a cross section of humanity, finding a kindred spirit proved much easier. I had good conversations aboard the boat with a gentle and sensitive fellow patient who was an apprentice painter or a budding art historian. After disembarking, we spent some time together walking down the magnolia-lined streets of Charleston. During one of these leisurely walks, I became aware that I was dragging my right leg. There was no physical reason for my doing so. Clearly, it was entirely a matter of unwitting empathy with my new friend's injury. As we were passing a stately mansion, a winsome young woman appeared in the door and graciously invited the two stragglers in for a cup of tea. We promptly accepted— it was a decorous and genteel occasion. It occurred to me that I would not have been a beneficiary of Southern hospitality had

I not been in the company of a fair-haired and thoroughly WASPy-looking young man.

The next day, I was transferred to Memphis, Tennessee, where I landed at a large army medical center, Kennedy General Hospital. My mood upon arrival combined optimism about my condition with a measure of pessimism regarding my prospects. Since I had largely recovered, I was under the impression that the army might be reluctant to dispense with my absolutely essential services and send me to the still active Pacific theater. My apprehensions turned out to be totally groundless. I overestimated the pace of my recovery: I was still having a bit of trouble using my right arm. Thus, after a battery of tests, I was offered a straightforward medical discharge and the status of a disabled veteran.

Though my bout with the German sniper could easily have been lethal, I emerged relatively unscathed. Moreover, there were some fringe benefits: a modest addition to my prospective income in the form of a disability pension and a foreshortening of my period of service. Had VE-day found me totally unimpaired, I probably would have been retained for a while, because of my residual German, by the American military.

Since I was lucky enough to have been seriously wounded, by June 1945, I was done with the war. I was ready to go home to rejoin Iza, little Henry, and the rest of my New York–based family. It was high time to keep the promise given to my NKVD interrogator and resume my graduate study of Slavic philology (if not of Old Church Slavonic). My odyssey was over and so was the string of narrow escapes. What lay ahead was the "normal" existence of a budding Polish Jewish academic felicitously displaced into the United States.

Back to School

Russian Formalism with Roman Jakobson

In September 1945, I landed at one of the major centers of Slavic studies in the United States. Philosophy Hall, which housed Columbia's Department of Slavic Languages, was located at the heart of a large and formidable-looking campus. After an eight-year interval, it was good to be back at school.

This time my objective was a Ph.D. in Slavic literatures. (I was given some credit for my Warsaw M.A.). Moreover, my focus had changed. I chose to specialize in Russian literature with a strong secondary emphasis in Polish literature. I never thought of this shift of emphasis as an abandonment of Polish literature. Throughout my career, I would periodically offer a course in Polish romanticism. One of my most effective essays, which appeared in my second book, *The Double Image* (1964), dealt with the Polish romantic poet and playwright Zygmunt Krasinski. Yet for once I was guided in part by pragmatic considerations. As Slavic studies were taking hold at the American universities, the market for Russian literature promised to be considerably larger than for other Slavic literatures. No less important, ever since my early infatuation with Gogol's Ukrainian tales, I have had a special relationship with the Russian classics. Moreover, during my nonacademic interlude, I was increasingly drawn to Russian modernism or, to put it differently, to Russian poetry and criticism of the first quarter of the twentieth century.

My affinity for twentieth-century Russian literary scholarship was significantly enhanced by the impact of one of its most distinguished representatives. Once again my luck held. My graduate studies heavily overlapped with the presence on the Columbia faculty of Roman Jakobson, a preeminent Slavic and general linguist of our time, an influential literary theorist, a charismatic teacher, and a commanding figure. During the years 1945 through 1948, I took as many courses offered by this incredibly versatile scholar as I possibly could, be they comparative Slavic philology or an introduction to general linguistics, a seminar in early Czech culture or in Russian oral ballads (*byliny*), as well as studies of the structures of the Russian noun and the Russian verb. What with a wealth of psychological and anthropological considerations brought to bear on semantic analysis of the Russian inflectional system or the Russian verbal aspects, the latter courses proved more provocative than the urbane but unexciting survey of Soviet literature taught by our departmental chairman, Ernest J. Simmons.

Part of the appeal of Jakobson's dissection of Russian grammar was rhetorical; it was couched in a Russian that was at once eloquent and richly idiomatic. I knew some "downtown" Russian Jewish *intelligenty* who would repair to Morningside Drive in order to savor Jakobson's superlative delivery. One of them, a friend of Mother's, delivered herself of an apt pun, which, like all puns, virtually defies translation. Now, the Russian title of the verb course was *Struktura Russkogo Glagola.* While in modern Russian *glagol* means "verb," in early Russian, in fact, as late as the elevated style of the Pushkin era, it could mean "word" (*verbum*). This is how it is used in a famous Pushkin poem, where a prophet is enjoined to go down into the world to "set the people's hearts on fire by the [divine] Word" (*glagolom zhech serdtsa lyudey*). Mrs. B. quipped that Jakobson manages to "set people's hearts on fire" by talking about the verb (*glagol*).

To say that Jakobson the lecturer was unquestionably at his best when he spoke in his native language is not to suggest that he failed to communicate in English. Already at the early stage of his American period—he came to this country during the war—he had a solid command of English linguistic terminology. Yet quite a few words of common usage would elude him. I recall that in a course that often featured the English vernacular, he depended heavily on an elderly amateur linguist, Judah Yoffe, who would attend the class religiously, always sitting in the first row. Jakobson's lively presentation was punctured time and again by questions, addressed with some urgency to the white-haired Russian Jewish auditor: "Judah, what is x in English?" Judah would provide an English equivalent with dispatch.

I felt privileged to gain access to so many facets of Jakobson's erudition and sensibility. So potent was his charisma that I briefly toyed with the possibility of changing my emphasis to Slavic linguistics. In retrospect, I am glad I resisted this temptation. Literary criticism is where I belong. Clearly, I was running the risk of confusing the scope of linguistics as a discipline with the range of the most creative and broad-gauged linguist I have ever known.

Though I did not become a linguist, my massive exposure to Jakobson furthered an active involvement with what was one of his distinctive strengths, notably poetics—or, more specifically, with a linguistically oriented theory of poetry which lay at the core of a school of literary criticism that became for a number of years my major intellectual concern.

As indicated earlier, already back in Warsaw I began to move away from the Marxian approach to literature in search of what a New Critic would call a more "intrinsic" perspective on imaginative literature. The scribblings I managed to smuggle out of the Soviet Union were detailed notes in Yiddish on a form-and-style-oriented Polish tract in literary theory. Perhaps more important, sometime in 1937 I attended a couple of meetings of the vital Polish Literary Club at the University of Warsaw, which was demonstrably drawn to structural analysis of verse and of artistic prose. I was especially impressed by the brilliant young scholar of versification Franciszek Siedlecki, author of the innovative *Studies in Polish Metrics,* as well as the sophisticated if somewhat Talmudic David Hopensztand and his discussion of point of view in the prose of an influential contemporary Polish writer. Siedlecki and Hopensztand were to perish during the war. The only surviving key member of the circle whom I met again in Warsaw in 1960 was the articulate Stefan Zólkiewski, who was to play a visible role in postwar Poland's cultural life as a cross between an influential—and relatively open-minded—"official" literary critic and an establishment bon vivant.

The political ambience in the circle was decidedly leftist. Yet its dominant methodology was not Marxist. Both Siedlecki and Hopensztand were taking their cues from a remarkable school of Russian literary scholarship which originated in the second decade of the twentieth century, a school of which Roman Jakobson was one of the architects and which became the subject of my dissertation and my first book, so-called Russian formalism.

Let me pause before this remarkable pleiad, made up of unorthodox literary scholars and linguists such as Boris Eikhenbaum, Roman Jakobson, Viktor Shklovsky, and Yury Tynyanov. The formalists viewed literature not as a reflection of society or a battleground of ideas but as a verbal art or, to put it differently, as a unique mode of discourse, characterized by the "orientation toward the medium."[1] "The subject of literary scholarship," said Jakobson in an early study, "is not literature in its totality, but literariness, i.e., that which makes of a given work a work of literature."[2] In literary art, maintained the formalists, especially in poetry, language is not simply a vehicle of communication. From a mere tag, a proxy for the object, the word becomes here an object in its own right, an autonomous source of pleasure as multiple "devices" at the poet's disposal—meter, rhythm, euphony, imagery—converge on the verbal sign to reveal its complex texture. Artistic prose, conceded the formalists, lacks the tight organization of language that characterizes verse; it works in larger verbal blocks. Yet the difference is not one of kind but of degree. The events or motifs that constitute the basic story material or, in formalist parlance, add up to the "fable" (*fabula*) are not simply related; they are mediated through narrative devices and organized into a plot for maximum aesthetic effect. Viktor Shklovsky, whose sweeping generalizations and clever bons mots helped shape the formalist approach to narrative fiction, in a characteristic overstatement proclaimed the archetypal novel-parody, Laurence Sterne's *Tristram Shandy,* "the most typical novel in world literature."[3] The most typical because the most literary, the most keenly aware of itself as a novel and of the inherent conventions of the genre.

These basic assumptions were tested in acute if occasionally abstruse studies of rhythm, style, and composition as well as the numerous shifts in Russian literary history. Through the good offices of Boris Eikhenbaum and Yury Tynyanov, Pushkin's place in the evolutionary scheme of Russian literature was significantly altered. Seen this time from the vantage point of style and genre rather than theme and worldview, the great poet appeared not as a demiurge of nineteenth-century Russian poetry but as an heir to the pioneering efforts of the classicistic era. In B. Eikhenbaum's pathbreaking essay "How Gogol's 'The Overcoat' Is Made," the famous story became an apotheosis of the grotesque, an intricate piece of expressive stylization rather than a moving plea for the "little man."[4] To the same resourceful and perceptive literary historian who was to develop into the leading Tolstoy scholar of our time, the moral crises of the young Tolstoy appeared primarily as a struggle for a new style, a challenge to romantic clichés grown stale.[5]

Many of these reinterpretations were as vulnerable as they were provocative. The essential lopsidedness of some of the original formalist assumptions was exacerbated by the strident polemical style that seemed de rigueur in the first years of the revolution. In a strenuous effort to make themselves heard among the clatter of competing manifestos, the formalists found extravagant overstatement necessary. In their early studies, Jakobson and Shklovsky played down the links between literature and society and denied the relevance of any extraliterary considerations. In a spirited plug for Russian futurism, Shklovsky did not hesitate to proclaim: "Art was always free of life and its color never reflected the color of the flag which waved over the fortress of the city."[6] And Jakobson in his first study, dealing with the leading Russian avant-garde poet V. Khlebnikov, went so far as to maintain that "to incriminate the poet with ideas and feelings [presumably expressed in his work] is just as absurd as the behavior of the medieval public which would beat up the actor who played Judas."[7]

Eventually, in recognition of the inadequacy of their initial premises and in the face of a concerted attack on the part of the Marxist-Leninists, the formalists made a last-minute attempt to combine rigorous formal analysis with some hasty sociologizing. But this makeshift synthesis came too late. By 1929 or at least 1930, the methodological debate in the Soviet Union was abruptly discontinued. Formalism was suppressed as rank heresy and in a curiously circular reasoning branded as "false because it was reactionary and reactionary because it was false." Throughout the Stalin era, "formalism" remained a multipurpose term of abuse. But, as more recent developments clearly indicate, the substantive influence of formalist theorizing and literary-historical research on serious students of literature in Russia could not be undone by bureaucratic fiat.

If in Russia the maturation of the formalist movement was cut short by extrascholarly pressures, a judicious restatement of the basic formalist tenets proved possible in another Slavic country. Dmitry Čiževsky, Roman Jakobson, Jan Mukařovsky, and René Wellek, the theorists of so-called Czech structuralism, grouped around the Prague Linguistic Circle founded in 1926, sought to salvage the seminal insights of Russian formalism without emulating its youthful excesses. This time the watchword was, in Jakobson's phrase, "autonomy of the esthetic function rather than separatism of art."[8] Within the modified structuralist framework, "literariness" was no longer the only pertinent aspect of literature nor for that matter merely one of its many components but a strategic property informing and permeating the entire work, a principle of dynamic integration, a *Gestaltqualität,* to borrow a term from another field. By the same token, the work of literature was not simply "a sum-total of devices employed in it," as Shklovsky had mechanistically phrased it, but a multidimensional verbal structure, held together by the aesthetic purpose.

The advantages of the new perspective are evident in Jakobson's and Mukařovsky's explorations of Czech romantic poetry and in Dmitry Čiževsky's illuminating encounter with that touchstone of Russian criticism, Gogol's "The Overcoat," in an essay forging a plausible link between the story's verbal texture and its moral universe. Unfortunately, Prague structuralism was allotted little time for testing its hypotheses. The intellectual climate of postwar Czechoslovakia was less than hospitable to any departures from Marxism-Leninism. But its fertile legacy spells sophisticated awareness of context, function, and pattern.

In fleshing out this story, the Slavonic Division of the New York Public Library proved invaluable. It was no less precious to be able to commune at length with one of the leading representatives of the vital movement. In his Columbia days, Jakobson, especially when his scholarly libido was engaged, could be a generous and remarkably informal thesis adviser. I recall a characteristic sequence. We met at Schrafft's on Broadway, several blocks from Columbia's Philosophy Hall. Jakobson was being extremely informative and at times compellingly gossipy. At midnight we were unceremoniously kicked out—Schrafft's was closing. Since there was still a lot of ground to cover, we adjourned to a Jewish deli that stayed open until the wee hours. We did not conclude our conversation until 2:00 A.M. (Alex, who was the leading worrier in the family, was about to alert the police.)

What Jakobson was most effective at conveying was the ambience of the movement, the air of intellectual excitement that permeated its early conclaves or, to quote Viktor Shklovsky, "evenings at the Briks'": Osip Brik, a staunch admirer and friend of Vladimir Mayakovsky, was keenly interested in the problems of verse language. It was his unorthodox effort to tackle poetic euphony that became the focus of lively discussions at his Petrograd home. Brik's clever and irresistibly attractive wife, Lili, who became part of Russian literary history as the main love object of Mayakovsky and the inspiration of some of the most explosive love poems in the language, watched with mildly amused surprise the philologists' passionate interest in such technical aspects of verse analysis as the repetition of consonantal clusters, dealt with in Osip Brik's "hieroglyphs." But she could and did share fully in the intoxication with the modern poetic idiom that pervaded the gatherings. "Verses were then," wrote Lili Brik many years later, "our only passion. We gulped them down like drunkards. I knew all of Volodya's [Mayakovsky's] poems by heart and Osip went completely wild over them."[9] During my evenings with Jakobson, it became apparent to me that the "intoxication with verses," notably with the most resonant futurist poet, was an essential aspect of the formalist ethos.

I could not help but be beguiled by the sense of Jakobson's passionate engagement with the creative ferment of a hectic decade, even if I was not fully attuned to his enduring romance with the futurist brand of the Russian poetic avant-garde. Though I admired, and still do, the electrifying power of Mayakovsky's talent, I was out of sympathy with his Soviet flag-waving poems—which, in all fairness, Jakobson found distinctly inferior to "Volodya's" love poetry—and had some difficulty with the notion of the seminal but often hermetic V. Khlebnikov as the century's greatest Russian poet. Moreover, I found the extremist temper of futurism less than congenial.

This is not to deny that in telling the formalist-structuralist story I was demonstrably influenced by my thesis adviser's attitude toward some of the protagonists. Thus, while I wrote with considerable respect about the eminent comparatist Viktor Zhirmunsky, a moderate sympathizer with the formalist movement, my characterization of him as an "academic par excellence" may have sounded, against the backdrop of the more venturesome and more bohemian formalist project, restrained if not ambivalent.

When many years later—in 1967, to be exact—I met Zhirmunsky at a comparative literature congress in Belgrade, he proved quite satisfied with this description: "You were right to say that I was more academic than Jakobson or Shklovsky. I don't regret this."

Jakobson's tangled feelings toward Shklovsky may have colored my presentation of formalism's spirited spokesman. Over the years, the warm friendship between "Vitya" and "Roma" had been strained, finally to the point of rupture. Early on there was a whiff of sexual rivalry. (For a while Jakobson and Shklovsky were wooing the same woman, Lili Brik's perky sister Elsa.) The relationship was further impaired by Shklovsky's hedged act of contrition: in 1930, as Soviet culture was being whipped into uniformity, the formalist standard-bearer was forced to offer under unbearable pressure a public "apology for a scientific error," while trying to salvage some formalist insights. Finally, by 1940 there was an overt disagreement about Mayakovsky, with Shklovsky hewing much closer than Jakobson to the official perspective on their favorite poet, posthumously canonized in the Soviet Union, in Stalin's phrase, as the "most talented poet of the Soviet era." Hinting broadly at Jakobson's having landed in the United States, Shklovsky wrote, in sorrow rather than in anger, "You've missed the point, Roman. You've missed it by an entire ocean."

If my thesis adviser's slant on his former comrade-in-arms in 1947 to 1948 may account in part for the degree of ambivalence I display in my book toward Shklovsky, some of it was unquestionably self-generated. I fully appreciated Shklovsky's historic role as an effective phrasemaker of an important movement, and I delighted in the wit and pithiness of such dicta as "[Isaac] Babel's principal device is to speak in the same tone of voice of the stars above and of gonorrhea."[10] And yet at times I would find his enfant terrible–ism more irritating than amusing. Did I sense on occasion that his more "outrageous" pronouncements such as, "Art was always free from life," were not merely a historically explicable overreaction to the critical status quo but also a preview of latter-day fallacies? I hesitate to credit myself with an inordinate degree of prescience. Suffice it to say that some of the developments in French structuralist, let alone poststructuralist, literary theory have dramatized the pitfalls of the new dispensation. I have in mind the tendency to turn the insistence on the centrality of language to literature, indeed to culture, into enthroning language as the only reality and treating literature as a self-referential or, in Roland Barthes's phrase, "tautological" activity.

By the spring of 1948, most of my dissertation research was done. After passing my qualifying Ph.D. examinations, I was offered an assistant professorship at the University of Washington in Seattle. About the same time, Jakobson accepted an invitation from Harvard to occupy a prestigious chair of Slavic philology. As our ways were parting, he was hoping that I would present him with part 1 of my opus, dealing with the history of Russian formalism. As it happened, all I could produce was a rather long chapter 1, devoted to prehistory, the antecedents of the formalist movement. Quite predictably, Jakobson thoroughly approved of the piece—it bore a strong imprint of the seminar he had taught on the roots of formalism—but was somewhat disappointed by the scope of my presentation.[11] His overall verdict was vintage Jakobson: "I like what you have written, but I don't like what you have not written."

With Jakobson "defecting" to Harvard, my departmental chairman, Ernest J. Simmons, became perforce my thesis supervisor. During my first two years at the University of Washington, I would send him the emerging chapters. The situation was a bit delicate. Simmons was not particularly knowledgeable about my subject and clearly out of sympathy with it. There was also his unconcealed animosity toward Jakobson. To begin with, not much love had been lost between the two protagonists. By the time my chapters began to come Simmons's way, his animus was exacerbated by Jakobson's rather peremptory departure for a Slavic stronghold in which, I understand, Simmons was actively interested. His negative feelings toward the erstwhile colleague spilled rather embarrassingly into his sparse substantive comments on the margins of my dissertation. A typical stricture was: "Do you always have to use honorific adjectives when referring to Roman Jakobson?" Yet it would be unfair to imply that Simmons's contributions were altogether unhelpful. The punctuation system, especially the use of commas, which I tended to follow was Continental rather than American. Simmons's guidance in this realm was eminently constructive.

By the fall of 1950, I was ready to dispatch to Professor

Simmons a longish dissertation. A few months later, I had to fly to New York to defend it. This proved a rather elaborate occasion. Though Simmons was not too closely attuned to my efforts, he apparently found them creditable enough to invite to my defense an array of eminent Columbia humanists. I am not sure whether he wanted to impress me with the caliber of the men he could assemble around the table or impress his colleagues by the quality of the dissertations submitted to the Slavic Department. Be that as it may, the gathering looked formidable. Since I devoted a paragraph to the distinguished Russian-Polish classicist T. Zieliński, Simmons featured the renowned Gilbert Highet. A brief reference to Hegel led my chairman to draw into the committee Columbia's leading Hegel scholar. A mention of Flaubert must have justified the presence of the flamboyant scholar of French literature W. Frohock. Finally, there was Lionel Trilling. He looked distant and weary. When his turn came, he said, "It's a very fine dissertation," and relapsed into withdrawal. (If I'm not mistaken, he took a brief nap while Manfred Kridl, professor of Polish literature, spoke at inordinate length.)

On the whole, the defense went well. In spite of his animosity toward Jakobson, Simmons clearly was pleased with my performance. Actually, I felt at one point that Simmons might not have been the only member of the dissertation committee to be irked by the fulsome praise I had heaped on Jakobson. Frohock's main contribution to the discussion was a quip: "Few dissertations have an epic hero. This dissertation has got one. His name is Roman Jakobson."

Throughout my stay at Columbia, my principal association was with the Slavic Department. Yet my interest in Russian literature and culture led me to spend some time at one of the first strongholds of Sovietology in the United States, Columbia's Russian Institute. In 1946 and 1947, I attended two graduate seminars taught by Ernest J. Simmons, titled respectively "Literature and Social Change" and "Soviet Literary Theory." As we were sitting around the table, the former Camp Fannin inmate was reminded rather uncomfortably of the Tyler, Texas, "discussion group." I was dismayed by the uncritical treatment accorded such Soviet shibboleths as "socialist realism," an increasingly meaningless term, once defined by a Polish wag as "that brand of naturalism which is currently favored by the Central Committee." The unmistakably pro-Soviet tenor of the proceedings was somewhat muted but not significantly altered by Simmons's guarded, circumspect manner. (His characteristic response to my strictures was, "You have a point, Victor, but you are pressing it a mite too hard.") My fellow students were, on the whole, unambiguously committed. Some of them were to achieve considerable prominence as teacher-scholars of modern Russian literature. Eventually their politics and their perspectives on Soviet culture changed dramatically, especially as evidenced by Rufus Mathewson's perceptive dissection of Soviet mentality. But back in 1946 and 1947, I was clearly out of step and once again a troublemaker. I recall a portly young man who was at the time teaching Russian history at Sarah Lawrence. He struck me, rightly or wrongly, as a bit of a Communist apparatchik. After my typically "subversive" contribution, he seemed to survey the troops and send a mute signal to one of the like-minded: "It's your turn to go after Erlich."

For several decades after my graduation from Columbia, Roman Jakobson remained a significant presence in my life. He was unstintingly supportive when I needed a recommendation from a senior scholar and warmly appreciative of whatever contributions I had occasion to make toward celebrating his towering achievement. On October 16, 1956, he wrote to me in praise of the essay on "Gogol and Kafka" which I had just submitted to a Festschrift in honor of his sixtieth birthday: "I was deeply touched by your beautiful contribution to the volume. In my opinion, it is one of the best literary contributions."

Jakobson's personal life was quite complex. He was married three times. I never had a chance to meet his first wife, who, I understand, was Russian Jewish, but I knew quite well the other two—a remarkably attractive Czech folklorist Svatya (Svatova)

Pirkova and his ardent Polish disciple, and a fine literary scholar in her own right, Krystyna Pomorska. But this was only part of the story. Since Jakobson was cross-eyed, I hesitate to claim that he had a roving eye. Suffice it to say that he was enormously responsive.

I saw quite a bit of him during the academic year 1953 to 1954, which Iza and I spent in Cambridge, Massachusetts. (I was granted a leave by the University of Washington, having received a so-called Ford Fellowship, designed to enable promising young academics dwelling in "the provinces" to spend a year in the vicinity of a major university library.) One conversation with Roman Osipovich was especially memorable. Actually, "conversation" is hardly the right word. When we met for lunch at the Harvard Faculty Club, Jakobson was uncharacteristically, indeed somewhat worrisomely, taciturn. I found myself in an unfamiliar role of trying to entertain Jakobson, to keep the exchange going. It became apparent that there was only one thing Jakobson could talk about. He took his time about broaching it. He had just suffered a major emotional setback or, to put it differently, sustained a narcissistic blow. He had "proposed" to a young woman, a Ph.D. candidate with whom he was deeply infatuated, and was rejected. I must admit to having been somewhat puzzled by my former teacher's "proposition." To quote a protagonist in Gogol's *The Inspector General,* a coy matron mindlessly wooed by the incomparable Khlestakov, he was "in a certain sense married." What mattered was that, however realistic his "offer," it was turned down.

Having indicated that much, Jakobson fell silent for a few minutes. When he was ready to speak again, he made a startling comment: "I guess the game is over. I guess I'm washed up." I expressed astonishment and disbelief. Clearly, at fifty-eight Roman Osipovich was at the peak of his intellectual powers. But he persisted in his defeatism: "In order to do scholarship I have to be emotionally engaged. I cannot do real work unless I've got something going on the other track."

As it happened, Jakobson had several productive decades

ahead of him (he died in 1992). In the spring of 1954, he spoke
out of the depths of a momentary depression. I was not really
worried. But I was struck, if not altogether surprised, by the intensity of his commitment to a profoundly libidinized view of
the life of the mind.

Another episode provided further evidence of a strongly held
sense of priorities. Some five years after our sojourn in Cambridge, I received a flattering invitation from UCLA, which was
then in the process of rebuilding a full-fledged Slavic Department. When consulted by the dean, Jakobson urged my candi-
dacy for the departmental chairmanship. I was gratified by the
fine offer but was not ready to move. I had always had considerable trouble taking Los Angeles seriously as a city; it struck me
upon a brief visit as disconnected and garish. (As far as I know,
Los Angeles is the only American city where the local branch of
Sears has the shape of a mosque.) Having gratefully turned down
the first UCLA offer, I received two years later a more attractive
one, this time with a whiff of Hollywood-like hype. A visit
clearly was called for. At some point Dean Dodd took me, both
literally and figuratively, to the top of the hill. Having driven me
to a plateau with a spectacular view of Los Angeles, he mused,
"There is no reason to assume that this will not be the best Slavic
Department in the nation, indeed the free world." I duly admired the view, but did not actually say yes, which did not prevent Dean Dodd from inquiring, "Who do you think should be
number two?" I told Dean Dodd how much I appreciated his
confidence and promised to sleep on his generous offer. Having
done so, I still did not feel like trading Seattle for Los Angeles.
I sought to make my second no as effusive as possible.

Though I did not hear from Jakobson directly, somehow the
three-thousand-mile distance between Cambridge and Seattle
did not prevent me from acquiring a clear sense of his disapproval
over my decision. He enjoyed "seizing" potentially important positions in U.S. Slavic studies by placing strategically his prized
disciples. He was also convinced that UCLA would have been for
me the right career move. (As far as he was concerned, Seattle had

done its bit.) Unquestionably, he was miffed. Yet about a year later he was prepared to accept my invitation, on behalf of three university departments, to visit Seattle and offer yet another version of his seminal lecture "Linguistics and Poetics."

I had the pleasure of serving both as his impresario and his host. As Iza, Roman Osipovich, and I were sitting around our kitchen, a very winsome neighbor dropped by to borrow some eggs. After she left, our guest, rather to my surprise, took Iza aside. "An attractive woman," he muttered. Iza agreed. "Is this by any chance the reason," he continued in a strictly confidential tone, "why Victor turned down those offers?" The clear implication here was, "if so, I'd understand."

In some respects, Jakobson was a typical Continental mentor. He was strongly inclined to micromanage the careers of his favorite students. He also expected them to follow his lead where academic politics were concerned. On one occasion I found myself unable to do so. What was at issue was whether to take part in the international congress of Slavicists, scheduled to be held in Moscow, in the fall of 1958, the first gathering of this kind since the war. Jakobson was very actively involved in the preparations for this congress. He saw it as a major event, an occasion for a significant "dialogue" between the Western and the Soviet Slavicists. He wanted the American delegation, which he was to lead, to be as strong as possible.

Yet some of the American and West European Slavicists were none too eager to attend a Moscow-sponsored event. The memories of the brutal suppression of the 1956 Hungarian uprising were still vivid. The Berkeley contingent, which included the dean of Western literary Sovietologists, Gleb Struve, and the eminent Polish literary scholar Waclaw Lednicki, chose not to go to Moscow. So did Harvard's Russian historian Mikhail Karpovich and its authority on Polish literature Wiktor Weintraub. (I had valued Wiktor highly ever since my year at Widener Library.) I had grave doubts. When I expressed them to Jakobson, he felt, as he put it in his letter, "unjustifiably offended." We talked at some length on the phone, and Jakobson was at his most persuasive. On

March 2, 1947, he was under the impression that "the whole misunderstanding had been dissipated." A week later, I felt compelled to disabuse him at some length. "I am afraid," I wrote, "that you will be once more disappointed by what I have to say. But may I urge you not to feel 'offended' or 'shocked'? Our tactical differences over the advisability of taking part in the Moscow congress do not involve any fundamental values; they are entirely due to somewhat divergent estimates of the situation."

I proceeded to maintain that a real "dialogue between the Western and Eastern Slavicists was not likely to develop in the chilling atmosphere of Moscow" and urged the relevance of protest, explaining that "it is in part the lack of vigorous *official* gestures, let alone actions, which makes some of us feel that it may devolve on the Western *intellectual* to make use of whatever opportunities for protest come our way." Before closing, I conceded that there was a great deal to be said for going to Moscow. "Either course of action is honorable. . . . It is a tribute to your persuasiveness that I was swayed twice. But on balance I find the role of a nonparticipant a more congenial one."

There was a protracted silence at the other end of the line.

Let me mention for the record another occasion on which Jakobson was not altogether happy with me. Shortly after coming to Yale in 1962, I was invited by an eminent member of Yale's English Department, one of the leading New Critics, W. K. Wimsatt, to take part in an annual event over which he was presiding, the English Institute at Columbia. I was asked to contribute to a panel on poetics a paper on Jakobson's best-known structural analyses of individual poems, his short studies of two sonnets, Baudelaire's "Les Chats" and Shakespeare's "Th' expense of Spirit in a Waste of Shame."

My treatment of the two touchstones was consistently respectful and at times admiring but not altogether uncritical. I found Jakobson's analyses an impressive demonstration, indeed a celebration, of the shaping powers of language and of the poems' adeptness at dramatizing this power by revealing and proliferating the multifarious verbal patterns. Yet I could not help but agree with I. A. Richards's stricture, in an otherwise emphatically positive assessment of the Jakobsonian dissection of the Shakespeare sonnet, that only some of the patterns detected in a poem by a linguist's keen eye are aesthetically "operative" or, to put it differently, germane to the poem's overall thrust. I did not presume to offer on the run a satisfactory basis for distinguishing between the patterns that are "operative" and those that are not, but I was strongly suggesting that such a distinction could not be made on strictly linguistic grounds.

My chairman seemed to be genuinely pleased with my presentation. Helen Vendler, who spoke with her usual incisiveness, thought it not critical enough. Not unexpectedly, Jakobson took umbrage at my mild demurrers. He was not very good at taking criticism, no matter how respectful, on the part of former disciples. A mutual acquaintance, based at the time in Cambridge, heard him mutter somberly after reading my paper, "He doesn't understand."

I have said enough to demonstrate what should have been obvious, notably that the "epic hero" of my dissertation "was human, all too human." But whenever I think back on our many encounters, the memories of occasional frictions and minor disagreements are dwarfed by an abiding sense of intellectual gratitude. I feel indebted to Jakobson for his invaluable guidance and unfailing, if occasionally a bit intrusive, support, for all he taught me about language and about what he called in his pioneering study "language in its esthetic function," that is, poetry. No less important, I am profoundly grateful to him for having conveyed to me so vividly the sense of scholarship as high intellectual drama.

Born in Moscow in 1896, Jakobson belonged to a remarkable generation of avant-garde artists and scholars that included Velimir Khlebnikov, Osip Mandelstam, Vladimir Mayakovsky, Boris Pasternak, and Vladimir Tatlin. I was fortunate to know him as well as I did. Time and again I felt in his teaching and his conversation the vivifying breath of the creative afflatus of a fertile era.

Academic Pioneering in the Pacific Northwest

In August 1948, our New York period came to a close. Iza, little Henry, and I were girding our loins for a transcontinental trip. Seattle was beckoning. Even though it was the first North American city I had a chance to glimpse, en route to Canada back in 1941, the only things I knew about it, as we were leaving the Big Apple, were that it was very scenic and that it was nearly as far from New York as one could be within the continental limits of the United States.

For Iza and me, leaving New York was not a simple matter. Iza's feelings were very mixed. She was not quite done with her work toward an M.A. in psychology at the New School for Social Research, which in the mid- and late 1940s was a remarkably stimulating place. When, during my Columbia days, Iza and I would get together in the evenings at Schrafft's, Iza could easily counter my talk about Jakobson with vivid reports about the charismatic art historian Meyer Schapiro and the subtle and sophisticated Viennese psychoanalyst Ernst Kris. From my perspective, going all the way to Seattle was both appealing and wrenching. I was eager to plunge into America and switch from being a "mature" graduate student to junior faculty status, but it was not easy to say good-bye to Mother, to Alex and his family, and to the larger Bundist *mishpokhe* (family) with whom we had shared so many stages of our odyssey.

Actually, after my discharge from the army, my association with the Bundist émigré community became somewhat tenuous.

Even before the war, my connection with the movement was less organic than was Alex's. Now, having landed in New York as survivors of a national and personal disaster, we were facing a drastically restricted field of activity.

What with his acute political intelligence, my brother was not unaware of the dim prospects for a Jewish socialist movement in postwar America. Yet his dominant political emotion was, to quote our anthem, "The Oath," "boundless fidelity to the Bund." Needless to say, I, too, felt profoundly indebted to our tradition. But I was less inclined than was Alex to let my political stance in the New World be shaped by loyalty to the past. For one thing, I had persistent and gnawing doubts about the relevance of the Bundist project to the American realities. For another, though I remained wedded to the fundamental socialist values, I was no longer an orthodox socialist, let alone a Marxist. I felt sympathetic toward, if not exactly enthusiastic about, postwar Social Democratic "revisionism" which scaled the vision of a classless society down to a compassionate version of the welfare state. Thus, whenever I took part in the policy debates at the plenary sessions of the New York Bundists, I sounded like a rightwing Menshevik trying to speak Yiddish.

I sensed for some time that my less-than-wholehearted engagement was a matter of some disappointment to the leadership of the so-called coordination committee of the Bundist diaspora, most notably to its chairman, the thoughtful and relentlessly mainstream Kraków activist Emanuel Szerer with whom I had worked closely on the eve of the war in getting out the Bundist Polish-language biweekly *Nowe Zycie* (*A New Life*). It is not without some hesitation, I suspect, that in the summer of 1948 he decided to mark Iza's and my departure from New York by a farewell get-together. I recall this evening not only with affection but also with some measure of accomplishment. It happened to be my finest hour in Yiddish. Throughout the years, my command of political Yiddish was viable if not outstanding. Back in 1945 I had contrived a canned fifty-minute speech in Yiddish on the socialist movement in Europe that I had unveiled at various branches of the Workmen's Circle in New York State and New Jersey. Interestingly enough, my elderly audiences responded to the medium—the fact that I spoke Yiddish—rather than the message. The assessments of the former ranged from benign appreciation ("It's nice, a young man speaks Yiddish") to the sharply critical ("Which language do you really speak?").

This time I was in uncommonly good form. I was moved by E. Szerer's warmly retrospective speech and responded as effectively as I ever did in Yiddish. Proof positive that I did well was praise of both the substance of my remarks and of their delivery that I received from the best authority on the subject, the formidable Jewish scholarly polymath and founder of the Yivo Institute of Jewish Research, Dr. Max Weinreich, who was gracious enough to attend the occasion.

At the end of August, after a long journey that had its anxious moment—at the Chicago railway station we briefly lost sight of Henry, who was spellbound by a shop window—we reached our destination.

Back in 1948, downtown Seattle still had a somewhat raw, frontier-town quality. The scenery was predictably and variously spectacular: two rugged mountain ranges, two major peaks (Mount Rainier and Mount Baker), a lovely lake, a bay. True, some of these riches were all too often screened out by the insistent drizzle. Whenever clouds would lift, to quote a rather corny song, "one could see forever." On the relatively few days when Seattle's solid Fujiyama, Mount Rainier, would emerge, the locals would mutter, "the mountain is on."

The Pacific Northwestern lifestyle was robustly outdoor-oriented. After spending two weeks in Seattle—school had not yet started—Henry wondered, "How long are we going to stay here, in the country?"

By that time, I had my hands full. The outfit that I was joining, the Far Eastern and Slavic Department, was a rather unusual hybrid. Its core was provided by a colorful and vigorous China program. The University of Washington turned out to be one of the most vital centers of Far Eastern studies in the United States. It was presided over with considerable panache by the articulate and resourceful English-born and -bred "China hand" George E. Taylor, who on social occasions could be easily provoked into spirited renditions of Gilbert and Sullivan operettas. (His personal dynamism reminded someone of the Italian saying *Englese Americanisato diabole incarnato*—"An Americanized Englishman is a devil incarnate.") Taylor's enterprise brought to the University of Washington a fine array of Sinologists, such as the intense political scientist Franz Michael, the scholarly cultural historian Ernst Wilhelm, and the distinguished linguist Li-Fang-Kuei, as well as promising young interpreters of Japanese history, culture, and politics. As I realized early on, in the face of the inexorable rise of Chinese communism, the China field in the United States tended to be politically polarized. Where Harvard's leading Far Eastern pundits such as John K. Fairbanks were not immune to the sanguine "liberal" perspective on Chinese Communists as "agrarian reformers," Fairbanks's Seattle counterparts, while not wedded to the Kuomintang, considered it considerably less of a threat to the American national interests than Mao and his cohorts.

The Russian program was a fairly recent appendage to Far Eastern studies, clearly a beneficiary of George Taylor's aggressively nonparochial outlook, epitomized by his often stated conviction, "The world is round." (Seen from Seattle, Russia could be viewed as the westernmost extension of the Far East.) For a while now the department had played host to a Russian language program, comprised of several middle-aged Russian émigrés. The most colorful member of the team was the jolly, round-faced Anna Levitskaya, whose main pedagogical technique was teaching students to sing Russian "old favorites." There was also a rather bizarre and insistently versatile figure who sought to range over Russian-language teaching, history, and, unfortunately, literature. The scope of Ivar Spector's pedagogical and publishing endeavors was not matched by their quality. His *College Russian* was probably one of the least useful texts of its kind. His surveys of nineteenth-century Russian literature and of Russian history were unmistakably amateurish. At some point, a course in Russian history that Spector was offering was seriously undercut by the History Department's decision to deny academic credit to students who chose to attend it. Since there was no one to speak on behalf of Russian literature, Spector went on teaching courses on the Russian novel, marked by flamboyance, verging on histrionics, and excessive self-reference. I was told that in speaking of the early Soviet novel *The Road to Calvary* by Alexis Tolstoy, which featured the First World War and the Russian Revolution, the lecturer would digress into his own alleged experiences in the Tsarist military to the extent of exhibiting to the class his thoroughly healed bodily injuries.

Dealing with war themes would provoke this vivid performer into belated bursts of Russian patriotism. In one of his digressions he would be drawn into heavily accented eulogies of the Russian Red Army's valor, which he would contrast with alleged British cravenness. "Remember Singapore?" he would exclaim. "The Japanese bring big guns. They fire. What do you think the British do? Do they fight? No, the British don't fight. They shurrender. And now look at Stalingrad. The Germans bring big guns. They fire. What do the Russians do? Do they shurrender? No, the Russians don't shurrender. They eat shnow."

My first task was to beef up our literature offerings with advanced courses and seminars in Russian poetry and criticism, which I was prepared and eager to teach. My next move was to introduce some historical Slavic linguistics. (I was only too mindful of, even if not entirely sold on, the Jakobson notion of the symbiotic relationship between literary scholarship and the science of language.) This move included requiring of Slavic majors a course in which I had failed to excel back in Warsaw: Old Church Slavonic. I had no difficulty injecting the course into the curriculum. But back in 1950 and 1951, I was a very inexperienced administrator. I managed to "sell" the requirement without increasing our staff or, to put it bureaucratically, securing an additional budgetary position. Thus I had considerable trouble answering the question: Who is going to teach the new course?

Clearly, at least for the following academic year, I was stuck with it. Though my performance in Warsaw was less than stellar, I knew more about the subject than anyone else on the University of Washington faculty. Actually, the course, though not one of my best, was not a total loss. The genuine interest in the rather recondite subject exuded by the six or seven desperate souls who enrolled proved somewhat contagious. But I vowed that next time, the job would be done by a properly trained linguist. It was time to seek advice from Roman Jakobson.

Roman Jakobson was clearly glad to hear from me and thoroughly approved of my quest for a Slavic linguist. His suggestion, though, was uncharacteristically hesitant. "Maybe Bob Stimson," he said after a moment's reflection. "Why maybe?" I inquired. Jakobson's recommendations were usually considerably more emphatic. "He is a bit nervous," averred my mentor. As I probed further, it became clear that Stimson tended to stutter. Otherwise, Jakobson assured me, he is very able and knowledgeable. Within a holding environment, his stutter should not be much of a problem. All this made me a bit nervous, too. But time was running out. I decided to take a chance on Stimson's "slight" stutter. After all, Bob's rhetorical effectiveness was not a major consideration; his courses were not likely to draw crowds. I made an appointment with the friendly dean. I managed to persuade him that our program needed a full-time linguist and that one recommended by Roman Jakobson was apt to be a good bet. The dean authorized me to approach Stimson and offer him an assistant professorship with the annual salary of $6,000, with the proviso that if our new colleague sounded unhappy, I could go as high as $6,500.

I called Cambridge and talked for a few minutes, outlining Bob's prospective teaching duties. When I mentioned $6,000, his response was a staggered moan that could have easily been interpreted as expressing profound unhappiness. I should have known by that time that Bob's stutter was especially obtrusive on the phone. (During a largely one-sided long-distance conversation with Bob, Jakobson is known to have exclaimed, "Bob! I'm not going to pay for your silences!") But, in view of the dean's "flexibility," I felt justified mentioning a strong possibility of $6,500—only to hear the same impeded and mournful sequence, clearly unrelated to the sums I was manipulating. When Bob regained more or less articulate speech, he uttered, "ok-key." As I was hoping, the modest number of "customers" and their demonstrable motivation audibly reduced Stimson's stage fright.

When Bob visited with Iza and me, he impressed us as a versatile, if inevitably somewhat impeded, conversationalist. He revealed on that occasion considerable knowledge of Polish— interestingly enough, he stuttered less in Polish than in either English or Russian—and of detective fiction. (He was, it turned out, a member of the Baker Street Club.)

Bob Stimson's stay at the University of Washington proved fairly brief. Since his stuttering did not interfere with publication, his scholarly reputation grew. The university where he studied as an undergraduate called its native son back.

During my first two years in Seattle, I had my work cut out for me among teaching a new set of courses, building up a graduate program in Slavic, and pushing my dissertation. Yet I somehow managed an active and enjoyable social life. Like most newcomers to the University of Washington, Iza and I landed in ramshackle temporary quarters known as the "faculty village." The accommodations were rather modest, but the atmosphere was congenial and often intellectually stimulating. Since the Russian program was at the time decidedly underdeveloped and the Far Eastern core of my department, though quite substantial, thematically exotic, it was good to be able to commune on the neighborhood basis with keen young economists, mathematicians, classicists, and "English lit" people. Some of this boisterous sociability was the kind of fun I had largely missed during my graduate student days. I had never regretted having made early on a commitment which was to remain the anchor of my personal life for more than five happy decades. But in the years 1932 through 1939, I skipped the period of "playing around," of heady, short-term emotional involvements. Now, at the age of thirty-four, at our first Seattle-based New Year's Eve party, held across the street from our cottage, I was smitten by an irresistibly attractive young faculty wife, who was not unresponsive. After a while I stepped back from the brink—I was taking my marriage too seriously to drift into a full-fledged "affair." The initial glow has never subsided. Over the years, intense infatuation evolved into an enduring *amitié amoureuse* (loving affection).

To return to matters curricular, Russian studies at the University of Washington were significantly enhanced by the arrival of an intense Harvard-trained Oregonian, Donald W. Treadgold, who came to fill a new opening in Russian history. Don soon became a greatly valued colleague and a personal friend. A serious, hard-working, dedicated scholar and exemplary academic citizen, he was to develop into one of the key figures in Slavic studies in this country as editor of our association's journal *Slavic Review* and one of the pillars of the university's Far Eastern and Russian Institute. Though our backgrounds and temperaments differed considerably—Don's was a bit more austere than mine—we worked together harmoniously, enjoyed each other's company, and shared many intellectual interests and commitments.

Politically, we were to begin with on the same wavelength. In his first years in Seattle, Don was a fairly conventional liberal. But he was too incisive a scholar of modern Russian history to harbor serious illusions about the Soviet system. During presidential elections, we voted Democratic. In 1952, when we faced the choice between Eisenhower and Stevenson, we opted without hesitation for the latter. While we did not see eye to eye with the Democratic standard-bearer on every issue, we were drawn to his graceful eloquence, his insistence on "talking sense to the American people," in the face of reckless right-wing demagoguery. Not all the "American people" appreciated Stevenson's rhetoric—to the more "red-blooded" among them it appeared as "sissy" or highbrow. Actually, Stevenson was hardly an intellectual. He was simply more literate and more articulate than the garden-variety American politician.

During Stevenson's first presidential race, Don and I and a few like-minded graduate students contrived a small-scale grass-roots campaign. The general idea was this: Don and a sidekick would park at the edge of a shopping mall and attempt to harangue passersby. In order to insure an attentive core audience—middle-class shoppers are not apt to respond to street propaganda—a small group would be dropped off a couple of blocks from the target. One of the "imports" would come around at a casual, meandering pace to challenge the speaker with such questions as, "How about this mess in Washington?" (a vaguely "Republican" reference to minor scandals brewing under the Truman administration). It fell to me to impersonate a confused "independent" but Republican-leaning voter. On more successful occasions, the technique seemed to work. The crowd would swell to fifteen or twenty. A senior Sinologist colleague—I believe it was Franz Michael, who at the time favored Stevenson—took a rather dim view of our playacting. "I have a queasy feeling about this," he said, after viewing one of the episodes: "You are having too much fun. *We're going to lose!*" Another friendly passerby voiced a different concern: "The confused grassroots voter had an unmistakable foreign accent."

I scarcely need to recall that Franz Michael's apprehensions were fully borne out. Very much to the dismay of the intelligentsia, foreign-born or native, Eisenhower won by a landslide. A Viennese psychoanalyst who landed in New York told our Seattle-based friend, the distinguished child analyst Edith Buxbaum, "There must have been a fraud at the polls. Everybody I know voted for Stevenson."

If my presidential politics were consistently Democratic, I had serious foreign policy disagreements with many "liberal" colleagues. While I fully shared their revulsion from McCarthyism or, more broadly, from the know-nothing right-wing brand of anticommunism, I thought their anti-anticommunist stance philosophically wrong and politically counterproductive. In some quarters I acquired the reputation of a cold warrior. This, needless to say, was a gross simplification. Though I was in sympathy with the Truman-Acheson policy of "containing" Soviet expansionism, I had grave misgivings about some aspects of its implementation, most notably the tendency of several U.S. administrations to support any third-world regime, however corrupt or unpopular, that claimed to be anticommunist. Yet I was prepared to own up to support for our U.S. stand in Korea and the airlifts to Berlin.

Some of my "village" neighbors who combined a naive brand of liberal populism with instinctive pacifism were distinctly unhappy about the U.S. response to the North Korean aggression. One of them was Sam Tucker, a friendly but decidedly unexciting teacher of French literature. I would often run into him at the "village" garbage dump. He was invariably accompanied by his two little boys. I asked him once why he always brought them along for these inevitably somewhat smelly outings. He answered gravely, "It is a good experience for them. One meets all kinds of people."

I was not altogether surprised that when South Korea was invaded, Sam thought the U.S. response too precipitous. "Why did we rush into it?" he wondered. "We should have tried to find out more about the invaders' intentions." I resorted to what was admittedly an unsubtle simile. Supposing, I said, you and your wife, Ann, are walking down a dark street in a notoriously unsafe neighborhood. Suddenly two sinister-looking toughs jump Ann and start tearing her clothes. Would you expend your limited resources in time and energy by inquiring, "What do you actually have in mind?" Both Sam and Ann found my analogy unforgivably coarse.

On occasion, such disagreements spilled into semipublic debates. In 1950 or 1951, I engaged in dialogue on one of Seattle's radio stations with the well-spoken liberal University of Washington historian Giovanni Costigan. At a somewhat later date, I was sucked into debating an awesomely articulate radical figure, Max Shakhtman. In the early 1950s, he was a leader of one of the two Trotskyite organizations in the United States, the Workers' Party. I was told that he had come to Seattle to stave off a crisis—one of the leading local Workers' Party activists had defected. The movement needed to be "firmed up." Be that as it may, the news of his arrival galvanized some of the nonparty Seattle leftists—Shakhtman had the reputation of a consummate polemicist—who hoped that this visit might provide an occasion for a serious "debate."

The setting for the potential event was provided by a somewhat bizarre institution. The Church of the People was a motley congregation of vaguely radical old-timers, former members of Industrial Workers of the World and of the Socialist Party, and ex-Trotskyites. Though by 1950 I was only mildly left of center, I found the nostalgic integrity of the group strangely affecting: I do not remember whose idea it was to invite me to the meeting of the "church" as Shakhtman's potential opponent. I was not particularly eager to assume this role but was willing to give it a try. (The Church of the People was, of course, a misnomer. Whatever residues of the radical "old-time religion" the various members remained wedded to, their frame of reference was relentlessly secular. At the still-functioning Sunday school, "God" was a taboo word.)

The hoped-for encounter drew some sixty to seventy people, and when we gathered, it was far from clear that a debate would materialize. What was called for was a "proposition" on which Shakhtman and I would emphatically disagree. "Perhaps," said Shakhtman, *"Professor* Erlich"—his tone clearly suggested that he was using "professor" as a pejorative term—"would care to frame the proposition." It was clear to me that Soviet experience would have to be the bone of contention. "There are those," I began, "who would argue that the seizure of power in Russia by doctrinaire Marxists was bound to usher in totalitarianism. I'm not prepared to posit this." "By god," cried Shakhtman, "neither am I! It's utterly wrong!" The old-timers looked despondent. I tried again: "No, Marxism per se, even when it won by force, did not have to degenerate into Stalinism. But it is at least arguable that Marxism-Leninism was all too likely to undergo such transformation." "No!" bellowed Shakhtman. Things were looking up. "We've got a debate!"

The chairman laid down the ground rules. Each speaker was granted a half hour and a brief summing up, following a free-wheeling discussion.

My argument, which I managed to keep within the time limits, was relatively simple. The October revolution, or to be more exact, the October coup, installed a one-party dictatorship, undergirded by a ruthless police machine. Lenin's "centralist," that is, authoritarian, concept of the party, in spite of the leader's last-minute misgivings, paved the way for victory in the interparty struggle for power of the canny, unscrupulous apparatchik (Stalin) over the spellbinding orator (Trotsky). At some point, my brief account of the totalitarian deterioration of the Soviet regime became more literary than analytic. My discussion of the infamous Moscow trials, a judicial slaughter of the bulk of the architects of the October revolution, bore a strong imprint of Arthur Koestler's *Darkness at Noon,* which had impressed us greatly back in the 1940s, most notably the novel's epiphany, voiced by its protagonist Rubashov: "The means have swallowed the ends."

Shakhtman began his rebuttal sotto voce; his subdued, barely audible delivery formed a stark contrast with his overheated rhetoric: "After *Professor* Erlich's [once again the sarcasm was unmistakable] savage attack on the Russian Revolution, I would like to offer a few random remarks." He spoke for an hour and a half. Though he was extremely fluent, his total disregard of the ground rules was clearly recognized by the bulk of the audience as arrogance. My opponent was, unquestionably, a more seasoned debater than I. But I may have "won" by default.

During our exchange, Shakhtman sounded like an orthodox Trotskyite, but his political stance soon began to evolve. The man who could not find anything wrong with the Soviet Union prior to 1926, that is, before Stalin's victory over Trotsky, by the mid-1950s had moved so far to the right as to make common cause with such trade union leaders as George Meany in supporting U.S. involvement in Vietnam.

All these travails, whether academic or political, scholarly or administrative, were indoor affairs, yet the wholesome Pacific Northwest way of life was gradually making itself felt. I was as appreciative as the next Seattleite of all one could see and savor on a clear day. Walking to the campus across the university bridge whenever "the mountain was on" was invariably a bracing experience. But for a while I was quite content to treat the spectacular scenery as an energizing backdrop. I did not feel duty-bound to "do" anything about it. The notion of camping, which came up early on in conversations with fellow young parents, initially left me cold. I remembered vividly the miserable week I spent back in 1944 getting soaked in a tent in the Marseille staging area. My first reaction to the idea of camping was: Why should I stay in a tent if I don't have to? Iza was increasingly intrigued by the prospect, and so was Henry, who by then was a lively boy of eight or nine.

I should mention the fact that in the meantime, our family had expanded. In October 1949, Iza gave birth to our second son. We called him Mark, because we liked the name, and gave him the middle name Leo in honor of Iza's father, who, as we found out while still in New York, had died toward the end of the war, having walked all the way from Warsaw to Kraków in the aftermath of the Warsaw uprising. To be sure, in 1952, when I was talked into camping, Mark was too young to participate. Mother, who came to visit us to sample our Seattle way of life and to meet her new grandson, was more than willing to babysit. Our first camping experience was an unalloyed pleasure. The Olympic Peninsula is staggering in its diversity—a vast ocean beach, a scenic mountain lake, and, above all, a semitropical rain forest where on a sunny day the light is green!

As we were pitching our tent upon the hill overlooking the beach, we were vouchsafed a "thar' she blows" moment—a good-size whale was entering "our" waters. Henry was in seventh heaven!

Obviously, there had to be a sequel. For our next outing, we picked one of the finest and best-equipped West Coast camping areas—Mount Rainier National Park. Our first bout with the

Olympic Peninsula offered a distant glimpse of a whale; the second outing featured a closer encounter. Since we had been advised that we might run into a bear or two, we were not altogether surprised to see, as we were entering the parking area, a brown bear's solid bottom sticking out of a garbage can. (His mug, someone explained, had become imprisoned in a mayonnaise jar.) This time both Henry and his parents had a traveling companion. Carol, a "village" neighbor and an effective secretary of the University of Washington's Department of English, came along with her son Bruce, Henry's contemporary. (Bruce was a nice boy, though none too bright. Mother, who was visiting us again and who made this venture possible, was not altogether happy about Bruce. She thought he might drag Henry down intellectually. Iza and I chose not to worry about it.)

In the evening, three tents were pitched. Carol stayed in one, Iza and I in the other; Henry shared the "children's tent" with Bruce. Iza told him to visit with us in case of need. As Iza and I were about to go to sleep, we heard a mild scratching noise on the surface of our tent.

"Henry?" said Iza. "What's the problem?" There was no response.

"Henry, why don't you say something?" Silence.

I ventured, "Maybe it's not Henry," and peered out carefully only to make one of my pithiest statements ever recorded: "It's not Henry."

Iza promptly got the point. "What should we do?" she wondered somewhat apprehensively.

"Let's lie low," I suggested. Our visitor was clearly less interested in our company than in food. Since our tent lacked the latter, the bear walked quietly away.

A Year on the East Coast

Beyond Formalism, Isaiah Berlin

In spring of 1953, I was awarded a Ford Foundation fellowship which, in conjunction with a leave of absence from the University of Washington, enabled my family and me to spend the following academic year in Cambridge, Massachusetts. The choice of residence was far from fortuitous. Widener is one of the world's great libraries. No less important, by the early 1950s, Harvard was one of the most vital centers of Russian studies in the United States.

Shortly after our arrival in Cambridge, I began to shuttle between my cubicle at Widener and a desk at the Russian Research Center on Dunster Street. The center, of which my economist brother, Alex, was one of the early and most active devotees, had been founded in the wake of the Second World War to further interdisciplinary investigation of the Soviet Union. The population of the second floor of the center building, where I landed, epitomized the diversity of the budding Sovietologist community. My immediate neighbors were a stolid Ukrainian, Nick De Witt, and an amiable if somewhat bland apprentice economist, Norton Dodge. The edges of the "suite" were occupied respectively by the volatile young political scientist Zbigniew Brzezinski and the keen intellectual historian Leo Haimson. I had no real contact with Brzezinski until a considerably later occasion. As for Haimson, I would periodically join him for lunch at his favorite neighborhood French restaurant, Henri Quatre. I found Leo quite congenial if at times a bit abstruse.

The most dynamic presence around the center was its prime sociologist, Alex Inkeles, whose quicksilver mind was allegedly matched by his rapid-fire classroom delivery. I was told that during a discussion period in his class, a young woman's hand went up. "Do you have a question?" Alex inquired. "Yes," said the student. "Could you please speak more slowly?" Being a reasonable man, Inkeles chose to ponder the question for a while only to conclude, "I don't think so." Both Iza and I were taken with Alex's incisiveness and freewheeling intellectual curiosity. We found his wife's gentleness and fine literary sensibility equally appealing. Bernadette and Alex were to become valued personal friends.

There was no dearth of intellectual stimulation within walking distance of Harvard Square. I did not always see eye to eye with the budding master historian of Russia Richard Pipes but thought him a worthwhile and vigorous conversationalist. It was a real pleasure to get to know the man whom my New York–based cousin Ludwik Seidenman—the same relative who many years earlier had queried my feeble rationale for copying a Gogol volume—described as the most intelligent person he knew, Harvard's authority on Polish literature, Wiktor Weintraub. I found him an eminently thoughtful and gentle man, a first-rate scholar and a graceful essayist, uncommonly well informed about all that mattered in Polish culture and politics, a clear-eyed and sober exegete of Polish romanticism.

It was good to renew my contacts with Roman Jakobson (see "Back to School," page 125); it was quite an experience to meet another distinguished Slavicist and former member of the Prague Linguistic Circle, the intellectual and literary historian Dmitry Čiževsky. A Russified Ukrainian who spent much of the interwar period in Czechoslovakia and subsequently landed in Heidelberg, he was persuaded by Jakobson to relocate to Harvard. His stay in Cambridge proved temporary, but he was still there in the academic year 1953 to 1954. Čiževsky never made a full adjustment to Harvard. He did not speak English, though he knew it better than he would admit, and steadfastly refused to master it. German, which he spoke with a heavy Ukrainian accent, had been, he felt, on top of the three Slavic languages he could handle, enough of an imposition. Nevertheless, he acquired something of a constituency among the Slavic Department's graduate students. By the time I came to Cambridge, he was firmly ensconced at St. Clair's, a café off Harvard Square, where he would preside twice a week over a table, regaling his devotees with anecdotes about the Austrian loser Graf Bobbie; now and then his daughter Tanya, who was at the time a Ph.D. candidate in Slavic literatures, would translate the German stories into Russian or English.

Prior to meeting Čiževsky, I had been very much aware of his erudite and vital contributions to Slavic intellectual and literary history, such as *Hegel in Russia,* and most notably of his excellent essay on "The Overcoat," which fifteen years later I was to quote repeatedly in my *Gogol.* My occasional chats with him in the environs off Harvard Square strongly suggested that in "real life" he was uncannily attuned to his favorite writer. It is fair to say that Čiževsky was one of the most eccentric personalities in a field not exactly immune to idiosyncrasy. This remarkable scholar seemed to share Gogol's belief in the personal devil and a free-floating existential paranoia, a sense of being beleaguered by dark forces. During one of our walks in the vicinity of campus, we dropped by a cigar store. At some point Čiževsky took me aside and, pointing at the store owner, offered in a conspiratorial tone, "He is a Greek." The statement seemed plausible. Čiževsky somberly surveyed the scene. "They are all Greeks," he murmured darkly. The generalization was as vague as it was dubious. But the implication was clear: "We are surrounded." As we proceeded toward Harvard, the plot seemed to thicken. At some point we passed a rather comely young woman. "A faculty wife," muttered Čiževsky, a bit of information that sounded credible and, on the face of it, not too worrisome. Apparently, I was wrong. "She is a vampire," asserted Čiževsky. "Are you sure?" I inquired. "There is no doubt about this," insisted my guide.

A year free from teaching and committee work and given entirely to research and intellectual self-improvement was not merely eminently worthwhile; it was also at that juncture in my career quite essential. I was preparing for publication a slightly abridged version of my dissertation, the first full-length study of Russian formalism in any language. In view of the relative importance of its subject matter—formalism was a remarkably coherent manifestation of the twentieth-century turn toward structural analysis of literature—my first book was destined to become my most influential publication. Over the years it was translated into German, Italian, Spanish, Korean (a pirated version), and, quite recently, Russian.

Ultimately, the academic year 1953 to 1954 proved nearly as productive as it was enjoyable. Yet through much of the fall, my concern with Russian formalism and its aftermath was overtaken by a political addiction. The ground floor of the Russian Research Center building was dominated for several months by a good-size television set which for several months featured a spellbinding spectacle, the McCarthy-Army hearings. The main protagonists outside of McCarthy were Secretary of the Army Robert Stevens, McCarthy's clever and slippery sidekick Roy Cohn, Democratic Senator Stuart Symington, and the Dickensian attorney Joseph Welch. I don't remember how many hours I spent in front of the set, along with some like-minded center aficionados. I could not tear myself away from the drama, whose high point, as some will recall, was the cri de coeur of the old-fashioned yet at that moment singularly effective attorney: "Have you no sense of decency, sir?" I felt privileged to witness what was widely recognized as the beginning of the end of the sinister demagogue's career. The hearings, watched by millions of "ordinary Americans," graphically exposed McCarthy's brutality and unscrupulousness. For once television proved useful. McCarthy did not merely sound like a villain. He also looked like one.

With the hearings finally over, I could resume on a full-time basis my agenda—a matter of putting the finishing touches on my *Russian Formalism* as well as an early phase of moving beyond its subject. In a sense, I had already anticipated this process in my dissertation by distancing myself from the excess of "pure" formalism and embracing the methodologically mature "structuralist" revision of the initial formalist tenets. What I now felt increasingly in need of was fleshing out the implications for literary criticism of the more encompassing perspective on literature, sketched in the 1930s by the theorists of the Prague Linguistic Circle, Roman Jakobson, Jan Mukařovsky, René Wellek, and Dmitry Čiževsky.

As I look back on my major publications of the following two decades, it occurs to me that their overall tenor could be summed up by drawing on the title of a collection of essays by a fine Polish poet, the translator and critic Stanislaw Baranczak, who was to inherit Wiktor Weintraub's chair of Polish literature at Harvard. I'm speaking of Baranczak's *Ethics and Poetics*. But on second thought, I had better try to convey my emerging critical stance by quoting from the paper I presented at a 1958 comparative literature congress in Heidelberg, "Some Uses of Monologue in Prose Fiction: Narrative Manner and Worldview," where I discussed monologue as a mode of speaking to oneself about oneself in Turgenev, Dostoyevsky, and Camus. "What is attempted here," I wrote, "is a *Problemstellung*, a brief inquiry, based largely upon materials drawn from Russian prose fiction, into some psycho-ideological functions of monologue or soliloquy as a narrative mode."[1] "The problem which I am trying to outline," I went on, "is but a small facet of a larger question—that of the relationship between verbal structure and worldview, between the literary mode of expression and the attitude toward reality which it embodies, the kind of human predicament it helps dramatize. If, as a German esthetician (Emil Lucka), has put it, imaginative literature is 'the world transformed into language' (*die Welt in Sprache verwandelt*), the verbal device is the writer's most potent means of grappling with reality. In literary art, ideological battles are often fought on the plane of the opposition between metaphor and metonymy, the meter and free verse."[2]

Nearly fifteen years later, I set out to redefine Russian futurism as a central yet distinct strain within the Russian poetic avant-garde. I was guided by the proposition that no single criterion, however salient, could provide the basis for a truly viable definition of a literary "ism." No consideration, I conceded, "is more essential to such an undertaking than the attitude toward language which informs the given movement, than its explicit or implicit poetics."[3] Yet it was equally obvious to me that each school of poetry could be seen as a cluster of poetic devices and moral gestures, and that in taking measure of an "ism," close attention must be paid to what might be legitimately construed as its characteristic ethos, temper, or ambience. The ambience I was prepared to construe as distinctively futurist—"an attraction to violence," verbal or otherwise, an "outrageousness" of manner, an idolatry of the new, a "fetishism of Time"—is all too apparent in Vladimir Mayakovsky but fundamentally alien to Osip Mandelstam and Boris Pasternak.[4]

In anticipating the stance that was to inform my essays collected in *The Double Image* (1964), my introduction to Gogol (1969), and *Modernism and Revolution* (1994), I have gotten far ahead of my story. Let me return to my fertile Cambridge experience.

In the process of taking advantage of the intellectual opportunities provided by Harvard that year, I chose to audit two courses—American National Character, taught by David Riesman, the author of *The Lonely Crowd,* and Russian Intellectual History, offered by the famed visitor from Oxford, Isaiah Berlin.

The former venture proved disappointing. Riesman's lectures, thoughtful at their best, were often brief and somewhat perfunctory. The main emphasis was laid here on classroom discussion, which could have been worthwhile but most of the time was not. It tended to be nearly monopolized by an extremely long-winded and clearly somewhat disturbed individual. To my surprise, the lecturer exercised little control over the situation. At some point, I decided to make common cause with another Ford Fellowship auditor, a keen if a mite-too-earnest comparative literature scholar from UCLA who was married to Alex's pert childhood friend. We bestirred ourselves to approach Riesman and ask him why he was giving the compulsive talker so much latitude. His answer was pithy: "He needs it." Both Ralph Cohen and I thought Riesman's attitude overly therapeutic.

Isaiah Berlin's course was quite a different matter. It was consistently fascinating if rather difficult to follow. Berlin spoke even faster than Alex Inkeles, with an unmistakable Oxford accent. Harvard undergraduates clearly had some trouble keeping up with Berlin's race through the highlights of nineteenth-century Russian thought. Since by the early 1950s he had achieved a celebrity status, taking a Berlin course was clearly a thing to do—his opening course drew a crowd of about three hundred. By the end of the semester, the audience had shrunk to under one hundred. Needless to say, my attendance never faltered. I believe I got all of Berlin's major points even if I missed some of his rapidly delivered punch lines. More important, I found his portrayals of the leading nineteenth-century intelligentsia spokesmen apt and vivid and his assessments thoroughly congenial. It was difficult not to share his delight in the deeply humane and richly endowed Alexander Herzen and his frank dismay at the radical polymath Nikolay Chernyshevsky, who was to be canonized in the Soviet Union as the author of the grimly hortatory *What's To Be Done?*—possibly the most influential bad novel ever written. Lenin expressed his admiration for Chernyshevsky by borrowing the title of his novel tract for his own major polemical pamphlet. The affinity between the late-nineteenth-century "revolutionary democrat" and the Bolshevik chieftain did not escape Berlin's attention. "A bleak tradition," he boomed unhappily.

I do not recall the occasion on which I first had the pleasure of meeting Isaiah Berlin personally. I am glad to say that over the years, this acquaintance blossomed into a friendship which Iza and I found most enriching. During one of our early encounters, it became clear to me that Berlin very much enjoyed using his mother tongue, Russian. (He was a young boy when his parents settled in England, but he spent the first years of his life in Riga, at the edge of the Russian Empire.) When we first switched to Russian, I was quite impressed by his fluency and congratulated him on it. "You are too kind, you're too kind," responded Berlin in his staccato. "I speak a halting Russian." It must have occurred to me that there was a reason why I derived special pleasure from conversing with Berlin in the language of Russian: he spoke it at an almost normal speed.

Whether in English or in Russian, talking to Berlin was an unalloyed pleasure. The liveliness of his mind, his wit, and his superlative gift of gab made him, in Princess Margaret's phrase, "one of the world's best conversationalists." Like many superb talkers, he could be easily provoked into a monologue. In this respect, our meeting in London in 1969 could well have been considered paradigmatic.

Iza and I did quite a lot of traveling that year. Prior to embarking for the Middle East, I told Isaiah that at some point we expected to visit London. "Call me when you get there," urged Berlin, "and we'll have tea at the Ritz." (The family of Isaiah Berlin's delightful wife, Dame Alene, whom he had married in 1956, owned the Ritz hotel chain.) As soon as we made contact in the hotel lounge, Berlin fired off a rapid question: "What have you been up to?" It so happened that we had just visited Israel, Greece, and Turkey. Knowing of Berlin's special interest in and commitment to Israel, I chose to emphasize the former. (I had given two lectures, in Jerusalem and Tel Aviv, respectively.) This took care of our high-tea session. My brief mention of Israel triggered Berlin's extended and extremely well-informed disquisition on Israel's political parties.

Our "exchange" was undeniably one-sided, but I did not feel preempted. After all, I contributed the subject. More seriously, in talking to Berlin, one always felt included; there was an unmistakable warmth, a genuine interest in what one was "up to."

It is scarcely necessary to say that Berlin's uncanny command of language made him a singularly effective public speaker. Yet on one occasion I became aware of the rather exorbitant cost of his rhetorical virtuosity. Sometime in the mid-1960s, I had occasion to chair Sir Isaiah's public lecture on nationalism. (I had in the meantime left the University of Washington for Yale.) I called for him at the office of a distinguished Yale historian and, as we were about to start toward the lecture hall, asked him the usual "How are you?"

To my surprise, his response was both substantive and worrisome: "Terrible, absolutely terrible."

"What's wrong?" I inquired. "Are you unwell?"

"No," answered Berlin, just a bit more cheerfully, "I always feel terrible before a lecture."

I found this difficult to believe—an acute case of stage fright in a master performer? As I listened more closely than usual to the process, I realized that the seemingly effortless speaker was placing himself under considerable pressure. He spoke, as usual, without a single prop, in a rapid verbal torrent punctuated by semicolons rather than periods, as if fearing that, should he pause at any point, he might not be able to resume the flow, firing into space singularly well-chosen adjectives. To put it differently, he sounded like a man who had wired himself for a nearly uninterrupted fifty-minute delivery.

When the remarkable performance ended, it was rewarded by hearty applause. As I was about to say that Sir Isaiah would be glad to entertain some questions, I realized that the speaker was no longer with us. I briefly thanked him and the audience and tore off in search of Sir Isaiah. I found him huddled in the checkroom—he was visibly embarrassed and mumbled something like, "I'm sorry. Everybody applauded. I guess I was overcome by shyness."

Some years later, I had another occasion to preside over a Berlin lecture. I was moderating a series of lectures on Tolstoy, in conjunction with a significant anniversary. Isaiah Berlin had agreed to speak on Tolstoy's philosophy of art. (I recall that he was later harshly and unfairly critical of his talk. It may not have been the most effective Berlin lecture in my memory, but he was incapable of being unrewarding.) Once again he made a premature getaway. And yet I recall this visit with special pleasure. Iza and I prevailed upon Isaiah and his lovely wife to spend the night in our Hamden house. Our get-together was eminently congenial. At some point, Isaiah embraced the notion that he was related to Iza and began to refer to her as his cousin. The actual kinship, if any, was more distant than that. But mutual affinity was undeniable. It was a joy to have Isaiah and Dame Alene under our roof. Their subsequent thank-you notes were as gracious as they were heartwarming.

I especially cherish Berlin's letter where, after voicing his guilt over "not staying for these questions," which he attributed to "nervousness and modesty and to no other cause at all," he wrote, "In the end personal relations is all that matters. No doubt art survives, and so do intellectual attainments. Like Tolstoy I am ready to give up prospects of posthumous repute for happiness in our lifetime, to which you had historically contributed."[5]

While deeply gratified, Iza and I thought the relative clause extravagantly generous. It was all too apparent that the person who deserved full credit for Isaiah's newly found emphasis on personal relations and personal happiness was none other than Dame Alene.

Sometime in the course of my European travels (1959–60), made possible by a happy confluence of the Fulbright and Guggenheim fellowships, I was having an hour-long chat at the famed Café des Deux Magots with a savvy journalist. Melvin Lasky served for a number of years as an American editor of the London-based *Encounter,* which, along with Paris *Preuves* and I. Silone's *Tempi Presenti,* was one of the main outlets of the liberal anticommunist Congress for Cultural Freedom. Since I was in general sympathy with the congress and found *Encounter* quite worthwhile, I welcomed the opportunity to meet the journal's capable editor. He, for his part, had been thoroughly briefed about the Erlich-Alter case. As a well-connected middleman whose principal mission was bringing together eminent Western intellectuals, he "knew everybody"—in fact, in the course of the hour, he managed to drop an impressive number of names. A shrewd appreciator of gifted men and women, Lasky had something apt to say about most of the protagonists. I was struck by the phrase he reserved for the most dazzling figures in his gallery—"a bird of paradise." No one I know, insisted Lasky, fits the description better than Isaiah Berlin. I could not agree more.

Lasky's image seemed to me to capture the combination of richness and glitter that made Isaiah Berlin so engaging and indispensable a presence. But as I was pondering the nature and the sources of his appeal, I realized that his verbal dazzle might be, and on occasion had been, mistaken for a lack of substance, that to some of our contemporaries he appeared to be more of a celebrity than a major intellectual force. Thus, the keen if often controversial Christopher Hitchens, taking unfair advantage of Berlin's own self-deprecating remark, termed him "overrated." In the early 1970s, I heard the same dour opinion from an intelligent but rather humorless literary scholar. (That not much love was lost between Berlin and the stiff academic is evidenced by the fact that the latter happened to be the target of the only cutting remark I ever heard Berlin make: "There is a dead mouse inside of him.")

Whatever the motive for questioning Isaiah Berlin's importance, I found the notion of his being overrated egregiously wrong and profoundly irritating. Since Berlin did not write a single full-length book (his succinct biography of Karl Marx comes closest to meeting this description), since he was a superb talker and his most resonant work is an essay on Tolstoy's philosophy of history, "The Hedgehog and the Fox," first delivered as a lecture, an impression had prevailed that his contribution to intellectual discourse was largely oral. It took the energy and assiduity of Berlin's former student Dr. Henry Hardy, who had gone to the trouble of collecting the Oxford philosopher's scattered writings, to produce four volumes featuring, respectively, nineteenth-century Russian thought (*Russian Thinkers*), philosophical essays (*Concepts and Categories*), portraits of major challengers of the Enlightenment (*Against the Current*), and affectionate tributes to eminent contemporaries (*Personal Impressions*).

What matters more than the respectable bulk and the impressive range of Isaiah Berlin's intellectual accomplishment is the fact that he managed to tackle with subtlety and incisiveness some of the most vital moral-political themes of our time. No one has made a more eloquent and nuanced case for pluralism

than has Berlin, most notably in his "Two Concepts of Liberty."
I have in mind his insistence that "the ends of men are many, and
not all of them are in principle compatible with each other."[6] He
also wrote, "The extent of a man's or a people's liberty to choose
to live as they desire must be weighed against the claims of many
other values, of which equality and justice or happiness or security or public order are the most obvious examples."[7]

The recognition of the tensions between equally valid claims
made Berlin unalterably opposed to any doctrine that smacked
of utopianism, most notably to Marxism-Leninism, with its fan-
tasy of a perfect society or, to use the Soviet cliché, of a "radiant
future."

I found it both significant and characteristic that the Russian
intelligentsia's demonstrable vulnerability to the mystique of a
revolution that would resolve all societal conflicts did not prevent Berlin from speaking of this "dedicated" order with empathy and appreciation. For one thing, he recognized the range and
diversity of the intelligentsia legacy better than did such Western scholars as Richard Pipes or, for that matter, than did the Russian novelist Aleksandr Solzhenitsyn. While he did not mince his
words in decrying "the bleak tradition"—the grim single-track-
mindedness that anticipated Bolshevism—he eagerly embraced
as a kindred spirit a man whom a twentieth-century liberal could
admire and identify with, the true Russian pluralist Alexander
Herzen. Wary as he was of the pitfalls of spiritual maximalism,
Berlin did not refuse to be moved by the intelligentsia's moral
fervor.

Berlin's most appealing virtue, his generosity of spirit, is writ
large in the eloquent tributes to some major contemporary figures, most of whom he knew personally, ranging from Churchill
and Roosevelt to Pasternak and Akhmatova. In his fine introduction to *Personal Impressions,* Noel Annan wisely notes that
Berlin "intensely enjoys celebrating men and women whom he
admires."[8] It is this quality which makes his "Meetings with
Russian Writers" so profoundly moving. I find especially compelling Berlin's description of Pasternak's impressively idiosyn-

cratic speech—"He spoke in magnificent, slow-moving periods, with occasional rushes of words . . . lucid passages were succeeded by wild but always marvelously vivid and concrete images"⁹— and that incomparably intense, all-night encounter between Anna Akhmatova and the distinguished envoy of Western sensibility and imagination from which she had been so brutally torn away. And, there is, finally, that unsurpassed tribute:

> She did not in public, or indeed to me, in private, utter a single word against the Soviet regime, but her entire life was what Herzen once described virtually all Russian literature as being—an uninterrupted indictment of Russian reality. The widespread worship of her memory in the Soviet Union today, both as an artist and as an unsurrendering human being has, as far as I know, no parallel. The legend of her life and unyielding passive resistance to what she regarded as unworthy of her country and herself transformed her into a figure . . . not merely in Russian literature but in Russian history in our century.[10]

I am sorely tempted to go on quoting, to revisit the rolling crescendos that crown "Winston Churchill in 1940" or "The Hedgehog and the Fox." But I had better stop short of an eloge. Suffice it to say that I was fortunate to know this "bird of paradise" as well as I did. In my long life, I have sustained irretrievable losses, but I have had my share of luck. It was good to be at Columbia from 1945 to 1948. This enabled me to overlap with Roman Jakobson. It was perfect timing to be around Harvard in 1953 and 1954. Otherwise I may not have met Isaiah Berlin.

Outreach in Seattle and a Continental Interlude

Upon our return to Seattle, I found my position at the University of Washington somewhat enhanced. I had been granted tenure, and the Ph.D. program in Slavic studies toward which I had started working shortly after my arrival had been approved. These developments were due in no small measure to the fact that my slightly abridged dissertation was in the process of turning into what became my most resonant book. Moreover, I had succeeded in persuading our genial dean to authorize another appointment in Russian literature. (The dean was sensible enough to realize that the flamboyant old-timer Ivar Spector was a dubious asset to the graduate program.)

My new colleague, Yury Pavlovich Ivask, was an elderly émigré Russian man of letters—a minor but creditable poet and a graceful, freewheeling essayist. I do not quite recall why I chose to turn to Ivask in building up our staff. I had a fairly high regard for his literary sensibility—he was steeped in Russian poetry, he was available, and on paper he looked good enough to the administration. He had just earned a Ph.D. in Slavic literatures at Harvard. Jakobson and Čiževsky were his most prestigious examiners. Actually, as I found out eventually, both formidable scholars were underwhelmed by Ivask's performance during his Ph.D. examination. (It so happened that I was privy to two very disparate perspectives on that event. The only shared motif was indignation.) According to Jakobson, Ivask revealed "scandalous" ignorance of Slavic linguistics. When asked to list the major differences between Russian and Belorussian phonemes, the candidate had absolutely nothing to say. "It was appalling!" fumed Jakobson. Ivask was equally scornful. "After all," he remonstrated, "I am a literary critic! Why was I expected to know anything about that dismal subject?"

As a teacher Ivask proved a mixed bag. He was not too well equipped to offer students methodological guidance. But his best lectures, offered, to be sure, in Russian, were lively and quite astute.

Ivask seemed to enjoy talking poetry to me. Otherwise, he cut a rather lonely and somewhat incongruous figure in the Pacific Northwest. He kept muttering about his preference for Novaya Angliya (New England). His dream would eventually come true a couple of years after my move to Yale (described later), when Ivask, his eccentric wife, and their much-loved cat landed at the University of Massachusetts in Amherst.

Not unlike Pnin, one of the more appealing Nabokov characters, Ivask seemed somewhat of a misfit on an American campus. For all I know, he may have been one of Pnin's real-life prototypes. (I suspect this somewhat befuddled Russian college professor is a composite type.) Some of Ivask's dicta struck me as a bit Pninlike. I recall attending together with Ivask in the late 1950s a meeting of the Modern Language Association (MLA). I had been to such conclaves for a decade and, as we were milling around the lounge, kept running into a number of good acquaintances. A certain amount of kissing and hugging ensued. After eyeing these goings-on for a while, Ivask opined: "They like you in America." I found his use of metonymy engagingly parochial.

Shortly after landing in Seattle, Ivask delivered himself of another characteristic assertion. When told that Nina Berberova, an elderly and remarkably vital Russian woman of letters, in the wake of a conference in Chicago got into her car and drove all the way to Princeton, where she was teaching at the time, Ivask expressed total incredulity. "I don't believe this," he declared. "Russian intelligentsia don't drive."

One of the pleasures offered by a fourteen-year stint at the University of Washington was an increasingly friendly association with the Department of English, most notably with its remarkably effective and congenial chairman, Robert B. Heilman. An eminent New Critic—and a distinguished Shakespearean scholar—he combined critical acumen with administrative skills and exemplary academic values. He proved on a number of occasions—if proof indeed was needed—that an intelligent and principled conservative could be a more reliable departmental chairman at a state university than a liberal uncertain of his standards. When a philistine member of the University of Washington Board of Regents queried the visiting appointment of the fine Canadian literary critic George Woodcock because of his overt philosophical commitment to anarchism, Heilman demolished in a masterly letter the notion that this gentle and thoughtful writer might threaten the American system of government. He was no less forthright on behalf of the department's most colorful and gifted member, its poet in residence, Theodore Roethke. A craggy, robust, earthy author of some of the most delicate love poems in the language, Roethke was notoriously emotionally unbalanced. His mental breakdowns, one of which actually occurred in the classroom, would land him not infrequently in what he referred to as the "booby hatch." When another regent wondered, in view of Roethke's periodic absences, whether the State of Washington taxpayer was getting his money's worth, Heilman shot off another admirable letter. While conceding the somewhat staggered nature of Roethke's academic performance, he insisted that any U.S. university would be proud to have on its faculty one of the finest contemporary American poets.

Presiding over a large and heterogeneous department was not an easy task. When Heilman took over, University of Washington senior English faculty were decidedly a mixed bag. Back in the 1920s, one of the key figures was the influential Vernon Parrington, whose approach to literature was dominated by sociocultural concerns, with little attention paid to literary values. While Parrington was a scholar of some distinction, a second- or third-string Parringtonian was a singularly uninspiring sight. It took considerable energy and skill on Heilman's part to inject into the department he led literary sensibility and critical sophistication.

One of the welcome innovations he introduced was adding to the regular English department offerings a position in comparative literature, which was occupied through the 1950s by the thoughtful and knowledgeable Jackson Matthews. Shortly after joining the University of Washington faculty, Matthews became engaged in a mammoth project financed by the Bollingen Foundation—a deluxe edition of the complete works of Paul Valéry. At some point, editorial commitment took the Matthewses for an extended period to Paris. We were to see quite a bit of this congenial couple during our Guggenheim-supported stint with *la ville lumière* (as will be discussed subsequently). I recall a rather incongruous episode walking together with Jack Matthews down a shady block of the Rue de Rivoli. Draped in a black Byronic cape, he was guiding me through a thoroughly mundane endeavor—buying some francs on the black market. While keeping our eyes open for stealthy dealers, we were talking about Paul Valéry.

There were only so many senior appointments available to Heilman that could change the tenor and enrich the texture of his department, yet he managed to contrive an imaginative visiting program that brought to the campus a number of prominent literati. The most spellbinding among them was Dylan Thomas. In the course of the fourteen years I was destined to spend in Seattle, he gave two poetry readings. Thomas was easily the most effective poetry reader I ever encountered. I can still hear his resonant Welsh voice and his richly sensuous consonants which made his renditions of "Do not go gently into that good night" and "Poem in October" major campus events.

Thomas's appearances, which drew large and enthusiastic crowds, were followed by bibulous English Department parties to which both Iza and I were invited. One of them was especially memorable. At some point, the guest of honor became visibly attracted to Iza and demonstrably intoxicated. His clumsy attempts to play footsie with Iza indicated that he was pretty far "gone." Soon he was too inebriated for courtship. I vaguely recall an inconclusive confrontation between Thomas and a local poet. Presently he nearly collapsed and had to be ferried out of the Heilman home to a downtown Seattle hotel. I understand that the next morning, he woke up in a double bed, facing a fellow poet slowly recovering from an insidious hangover.

Among our visiting celebrities, Dylan Thomas had the most compelling stage presence, even if offstage he was not immune to pathos. I recall with pleasure the considerably less picaresque visit of Irving Howe, who did a summer stint at the University of Washington after teaching for a term at Stanford. Iza and I felt an immediate rapport with Irving. I found his blend of lucid and supple literary criticism with thoughtful radical politics quite congenial. (By the mid-1950s, Howe had abandoned his early Trotskyite commitment and was moving toward a modulated brand of democratic socialism.) I believe that we would have clicked in any setting; here, some three thousand miles from the Big Apple, this New York intellectual seemed to find our presence especially welcome. He had mixed feelings about Stanford. "They don't get Jewish jokes," he said scornfully.

Our Seattle encounter was the beginning of a warm and mutually regarding relationship. After moving to the East, we had several opportunities to commune with him and his two successive wives—Ariane, an attractive psychologist, and Ilana, a friendly, direct Israeli. When already at Yale, I had occasion to speak on Russian modernism at the seminar Irving taught at the Graduate Center of the University of New York. In retrospect, he was partly responsible for my last academic study, *Modernism and Revolution.* At some point, he had urged me to write a book about Russian literature of the 1920s. Moreover, back in the late 1970s at one of the Cape Cod parties hosted by Ariane Howe, I ran into Bill Goodman, who was at the time general editor of Harvard University Press; we got to talking about my projected book about Russian artistic prose of the twenties. A typical reader of

Partisan Review, Goodman was so much taken with my subject that after several exploratory walks during the next Cape Cod summer, he signed me up for Harvard University Press without the benefit of a single page. The project was not completed until after my retirement in 1985.

To extend the list of more or less noted writers who visited the University of Washington under Bob Heilman's aegis, I should mention James T. Farrell and Nelson Algren. Since I do not recall having met the latter, I shall confine myself to reporting a rumor. It seems that at an advanced stage of an inevitable dinner party at the Heilmans', Algren was asked a rather indelicate question about Simone de Beauvoir's performance in bed. (He was reported to have had a brief liaison with the formidable French feminist during her visit to Chicago.) Allegedly he screwed up his face and said, "She thinks all the time."

I did meet Farrell; it was a dubious pleasure. Like Dylan Thomas, he did not take long to get intoxicated. Though at a comparable stage of the party Thomas had looked like a drunken Welsh pig, the inebriated Farrell, if possible, exuded even less charm. He became aggressively drawn to a young classicist's wife. In view of the husband's mounting anxiety, the author of *Studs Lonigan* had to be whisked away. Prior to this untoward contingency, but already under the influence, Farrell launched into a loud and somewhat profane anticommunist harangue. He had just joined the American branch of the Congress for Cultural Freedom (described earlier). Since I was in some sympathy with that organization, I was sorry to have to conclude that the coarseness and partial incoherence of Farrell's argument did little to bolster his position.

All in all, I found fellow traveling with our English Department quite enjoyable and rewarding. Thus, I was pleased to hear that, when Jackson Matthews resigned his position to devote himself full-time to the Valéry project, Heilman toyed with the idea of "seducing" me into comparative literature. (I understand that he tried to talk my chairman, George Taylor, into letting go of me and that George was not too receptive.) To be sure, the decision was mine. I was gratified and not uninterested, but my primary loyalty was to the graduate program in Slavic studies that I had pioneered. Little did I know at the time that before long this loyalty was destined to be more severely taxed.

In the meantime, I was granted an extended Continental interlude. In 1957, a young Dutch linguist and an erstwhile Columbia classmate, Cornelius van Schooneveld, invited me to join him for a year as a visiting professor of Russian literature at the University of Leyden (Holland). I remembered vividly Cornelius's high-pitched voice and his total dedication to Jakobson's brand of structuralism. He had just been placed in charge of Slavic studies in Leyden, traditionally a stronghold of Slavic linguistics or, to use a more old-fashioned term, Slavic philology. In line with the Jakobson notion of a symbiotic relationship between linguistics and methodologically fertile literary scholarship, van Schooneveld promptly proceeded to build up the Leyden offerings in Russian literature. He offered a full professorship to a vivid member of the Amsterdam intelligentsia, Karel van het Reve, and a visiting position to me.

Van Schooneveld's invitation worked—I was granted a Leyden-based Fulbright lectureship for 1957 to 1958. Actually, I was hitting a jackpot. I landed at the same time a Guggenheim fellowship. It enabled me, with the university's cooperation, to stretch our European sojourn to fifteen months.

My teaching duties at Leyden were far from onerous, due entirely to the strategy adopted by my Amsterdam colleague, who was visiting the States while our appointments were being processed. Van het Reve had no intention of getting saddled with an overly demanding teaching load. His plan was simple: "You'll teach once a week, I'll teach once a week, and that will be enough for the poor bastards," that is, the students. (Karel's American English was by then quite idiomatic.) As a result, I lectured on the Russian symbolist movement only on Thursdays.

The "poor bastards" were, by American standards, unfailingly polite but rather passive. Even though I encouraged questions, those were few. On the whole, the students' English was adequate. I wondered now and then if I failed to communicate—or if they were uninterested. I was reminded of Ted Roethke's complaint about his Italian auditors—he had done some "Fulbrighting" in Rome—"the fuckers were not getting my jokes!" It was not until nearly the end that I was prepared to blame my students' passivity on excessive deference. Around Easter one of my most congenial colleagues, Irene Ginzburg, threw a party for the benefit of the advanced students. Iza and I were invited. The gathering turned out to be a spirited Russian "sing" led by a vivacious professional. Since I enjoy such occasions in an amateurish sort of way, I did not need too much encouragement to take active part in the proceedings. My students were visibly surprised to discover that the "prof" was human. Too bad there was only one session left—my new image clearly made it the liveliest of the year.

My featherlight teaching load left ample room for other pursuits: exploring the treasures of Holland's fine museums—the Rembrandts, the Vermeers, the Van Goghs—a splendid trip to Italy during the long Easter vacation, and frequent train trips to Paris. Now this was not "the first time I saw Paris." Back in 1926, I accompanied my parents on a brief visit to the city of my imagination. With *Les Misérables, Quatre-vingt-treize,* and *Notre Dame de Paris* under my belt, I had walked in a daze rediscovering familiar landmarks—Notre Dame, Saint-Chapelle, Place de la Concorde, Conciergerie, "Chez Maxime." More than thirty years later, we would land at Regent's, an inexpensive and intimate hotel on Rue Madame, in the vicinity of the Jardins de Luxembourg. It was easy to fall in love again with Paris and, after a while, to feel strangely at home on the Left Bank. As I wandered down the narrow alleys often bearing quaint or picturesque names such as "la Rue du Chat Qui Pêche" ("Cat Who Fishes Street"), I muttered to myself graceful verses by a fine Polish poet and essayist Antoni Slonimski: "Oh! How close to one's heart/Are those walls piled up by history/Fetching streets of Paris/*Chansons* of architecture."

The main asset of our hotel was its "madame," a friendly,

shrewd, well-spoken Parisienne. (I noted that in Paris, lower-middle-class people often had a remarkable command of language.) Once, after spending a week at Regent's, we sought her advice about an appropriate tip for the maids. She cited a respectable sum and added gravely, "C'est une belle tradition française" (It's a fine French tradition). We sought her guidance again when we decided to visit *une bôite de nuit* (nightclub). She delivered herself of a crisp and modulated disquisition. After mentioning one of the establishments, she paused and added, "C'est un peu special" (It's a bit "special"), the implication being that the joint in question catered to homosexuals. Having produced a fairly long list, Madame paused again. "But you probably want to hear Edith Piaf." We did.

We proceeded to the nightclub located not far from St. Germain des Prés (on Rue Jacob?). The place was crowded and the lights low. After an aperitif, the singer made her appearance. She was slight and altogether unglamorous, not to say homely. As soon as she opened her mouth, the initial impression became totally irrelevant. Her range was impressive—as the serenely sexy "La Vie en Rose" and "C'est Merveilleux" were followed by the darkly explosive and defiant "Je ne Regrette Rien." It was a memorable evening.

To be sure, our sorties into Paris were often more academically motivated. Some time in the fall of 1957, I was invited to lecture on Russian formalism at the main Paris stronghold of what was known in the United States as Russian area studies, l'École Pratique des Hautes Études. My appearance was arranged by Clemence Heller, a somewhat frenzied academic operative who seemed to owe such clout as he had at l'École Pratique to a close association with the Rockefeller Foundation. An Austrian Jew married to an American heiress, Clemence Heller tended to entertain visiting scholars in a grand style. The first time around, he treated me to an elaborate lunch at an expensive restaurant. As we were leaving, he tossed on the table rather nonchalantly a substantial-looking batch of bills. I understand that before the end of the academic year, Heller's marriage collapsed, which visibly affected his lifestyle. All he could afford on a much later occasion was a modest repast at a neighborhood bistro.

I was participating in an advanced seminar on Soviet culture taught by the controversial young French Slavicist Claude Frioux. He was destined to become a rather prominent left-wing university operative during the 1968 turmoil at the Sorbonne. Already in the 1950s, Frioux's politics were quite distinctive. He was a sui generis Communist or, to use a then current phrase, a "Eurocommunist." I'm referring to a short-lived trend in the European Communist movement, of which the Italian party was a prime example, sharply critical of the Stalinist legacy, including the post-1930 streamlining of Soviet culture. Eurocommunists were not Trotskyites, but they shared the latter's nostalgia for what was known in Paris as *les années vingt* (the 1920s) and had a weakness for the avant-garde, most notably futurism. Frioux, who earned his doctorate by writing a dissertation on Mayakovsky, could be counted upon to have a soft spot for my subject. But this was more than could be said for some members of his seminar.

By 1957, I had acquired some expertise at lecturing on formalism. Nearly a decade earlier, I had contrived a fifty-minute canned talk, which I unveiled on a number of academic occasions with ever-decreasing dependency on props. But this was different: I had to speak in French. Though my reading knowledge of French was quite good and, as they say in Paris, I could *me debrouiller*—that is, somehow manage—in a conversation, improvising a coherent intellectual sequence was beyond my ken. I needed a prepared statement. Before leaving for Paris, I scribbled it on a batch of index cards, which I inserted in my briefcase. A few hours later, Iza and I were alighting in front of our favorite hotel. But as we entered, we realized that the briefcase was gone, and so were my index cards. The situation, as they might put it in Poland, was "good but not hopeless." The text could be reconstructed. But this emphatically was not the case with a precious book that I was not supposed to have in the first place. During my previous trip to Paris, I had managed to check out of the best

Russian academic library, which served somewhat incongruously l'École des Langues Orientales Vivantes, a copy of the celebrated study of Dostoyevsky's poetics by the distinguished literary theorist Mikhail Bakhtin. Actually, the book did not circulate, but I solemnly vowed to return it in no more than two weeks. Needless to say, I was worried and embarrassed by the disappearance of my briefcase and had some trouble producing another batch of index cards. When I was entering the precincts of l'École Pratique des Hautes Études, my spirits were low. They were instantly lifted when Clemence Heller peeked into the seminar room, cried, "The briefcase has been found!" and ran on.

The story of that miraculous rescue did not emerge until after the session. In the meantime, I was both intrigued and elated. As a result, my delivery was probably more spirited than it would have been otherwise. But it was during the discussion that I needed to be in good rhetorical form. A rather grim-faced gentleman attacked me in no uncertain terms. There was nothing "Eurocommunist" about him. He was unremittingly hostile toward the OPOYAZ and clearly incensed by my treatment of the brutal suppression of formalism in 1930. I was forced to strike back, which I did, to my surprise, quite effectively. This was unquestionably my finest hour in French. When one gets mad in a language one commands imperfectly, one is apt to grow either inarticulate or, with luck, more eloquent than usual. I was lucky.

As soon as the discussion was over, I hastened to Clemence Heller's office in order to recover the briefcase and to hear from his lively assistant the amazing story. It seems that my successor in the taxi from which I emerged on Rue Madame was a weary, middle-aged secretary, a Parisienne of Russian Jewish persuasion. She must have left her own briefcase at her place of work and, as she was leaving the cab, she absentmindedly picked up the briefcase lying next to her seat, a fact that she did not fully realize until she landed dead tired in the apartment she shared with her elderly father. As she was plopping in her favorite chair with a glass of wine, the old man, who apparently was not devoid of intellectual curiosity, explored the contents of the alien briefcase only to find two distinctive items—a library book on Dostoyevsky in Russian and an issue of a Yiddish monthly (the Bundist *Unser Tsait*). He got excited and cried out, "He (she) is a Russian Jew! You must help him!" By that time the daughter had recovered sufficiently to respond to this cri de coeur. The provenance of the Russian book was easily ascertained—it bore the stamp of l'École des Langues Orientales Vivantes. The guilt-stricken librarian—he was not supposed to let me take Bakhtin to the Hague!—remembered that the man to whom the book was lent was scheduled to speak at the other center of Russian studies. (The Russian academic community in Paris was a small world.) The old man's plea was heard and the briefcase delivered to Clemence Heller's office.

A friend, aware of my narrow escapes, once claimed that I had a guardian angel. If so, on that particular occasion my guardian angel had his hands full.

During our periodic visits to Paris and our more extended Guggenheim-supported sojourn on the Left Bank in the fall of 1958, we came into contact with a remarkable Polish group located at the outskirts of Paris, in Maisons Lafitte. An hour spent on a suburban train and a healthy walk would bring one to what was a hardworking trio and the editorial office of *Kultura,* one of the most influential Central European émigré publications. The journal was launched in the wake of the Second World War and lasted for more than fifty years, owing primarily to the dedication of three tireless individuals. Jerzy Giedroyć, the founder and the immensely resourceful editor of *Kultura,* was a clear-eyed opponent of postwar Poland's Communist regime. But in contradistinction to the prevalent Polish émigré opinion, he was anti-Soviet rather than anti-Russian and in distancing himself from interwar Poland's official policy spoke with empathy about the national aspirations of the Belorussians and the Ukrainians. The continuity, indeed the very existence, of the publication, informed by Giedroyć's distinctive political vision, was insured by an absolutely essential couple—Zofia and Zygmunt Hertz. The

former was a full-time secretary to Giedroyć and, no less important, an amanuensis who cooked for the team, while the latter
took care of the distribution of the journal. The common theme,
as I saw it, was total commitment. Giedroyć and Zofia Hertz
were dedicated to the cause. Zygmunt, the least political of the
three, seemed to be dedicated to Zofia.

One of the substantial strengths of *Kultura* was Giedroyć's
ability to solicit, often under pseudonyms, contributions from
acute and independent-minded individuals based in Poland.
(When, after the collapse of the regime, their identities could be
revealed, it became clear that the journal had featured some of
the most interesting heterodox Warsaw and Kraków essayists.)
The watchword was responsiveness to everything that was vital
and creative in contemporary Polish culture. No wonder that
Kultura opened its pages to the distinguished man of letters
Czeslaw Milosz, who after a brief bout with postwar Polish diplomatic service "chose freedom," and to the brilliantly idiosyncratic
novelist Witold Gombrowicz, who had landed in Argentina on
the eve of the war.

Among the major contributors to *Kultura,* there was Gustav
Herling-Grudziński, the author of one of the best gulag mem-
oirs. Though he lived in Naples, he was a frequent visitor at
Maisons Lafitte. His part personal, part essayistic "Diary Kept at
Night" was for a number of years probably the most compelling
feature of *Kultura*'s every issue. I enjoyed meeting Herling-
Grudziński. He was articulate and tough-minded; his scorn for
the Communist regime was all too apparent. Like Giedroyć, he
was a strong personality—shortly after 1989, their alliance
foundered on an irreconcilable difference of opinion. Herling-
Grudziński was profoundly out of sympathy with the political
compromise, the so-called roundtable agreement that led to the
gradual demise of the Communist regime. Giedroyć was, on balance, in favor of the process, which ensured a bloodless transition. I had some affinity for Giedroyć's position, but I deplored
Herling-Grudziński's walkout—it impoverished *Kultura.*

One of the most appealing members of the *Kultura* circle was the art and literary critic Konstanty "Kot" (Cat) Jeleński. Engaging, versatile, and uncommonly broad-minded, he was probably the most genuinely tolerant intellectual I have ever known; Jeleński was a cultural middleman par excellence, an effective link between Giedroyć and the French literary and art world, most notably the Paris branch of the Congress for Cultural Freedom and its house organ, *Preuves*. It is through Jeleński's good offices that Iza and I got invited to a star-studded reception hosted by one of the congress operatives, held in a posh section of Paris. After a certain amount of milling around, we were intercepted by the friendly Kot. He was wondering whether we enjoyed meeting Mary McCarthy. "I don't think we've run into her," I muttered. "Oh yes, you have!" exclaimed Jeleński. "I saw you talking to her some ten minutes ago!" So this handsome, white-haired lady who chatted with us about her granddaughter was no less a figure than Mary McCarthy! When we saw her again— this time as a hostess at an "intimate" dinner party, there was nothing mellow about her manner. The subject of the conversation escapes me; all I remember was the trenchant effectiveness of a put-down, fully consonant with Mary McCarthy's reputation. And she was *very* attractive!

Finally, there was Józef Czapski, a valued contributor to *Kultura* and a member of its extended family: Czapski and his sister "Pani Maria" occupied a wing of the Maisons Lafitte mansion. I recall this tall, gaunt, Don Quixote–like figure with special affection. A gifted and versatile painter and a lucid writer, Czapski exuded total integrity, indeed purity. His *Inhuman Land*, a poignant record of his Soviet experience prior to his joining General Anders's Polish Army, while an unremitting indictment of the "inhuman" system, was drenched in compassion for the long-suffering Russian people. His Christianity was profoundly ecumenical.

It so happened that when the Nazi threat to Moscow had propelled many Russian writers to Tashkent, Czapski met Anna Akhmatova there and escorted the poet through a fogbound city from a literary get-together to her temporary residence. The encounter left a telling echo in Akhmatova's lyric cycle "Tashkent Pages":

> It could have been Istanbul or Baghdad,
> But, alas, not Warsaw and not Leningrad—
> And this bitter dissimilarity
> Was as stifling as the air of orphanhood.
>
> We were together in that mysterious fog
> As if we were walking through a no-man's-land
> And suddenly a moon diamond
> Rose over our meeting-parting.
>
> And should this night come back to you too
> On your unfathomable life path
> Know that someone's dream
> Had been haunted by this sacred moment.[1]

Once again Akhmatova hit upon le mot juste. Few of her contemporaries were endowed with so exquisite a sense of the sacred as was Józef Czapski.

From Seattle to Yale,
with Visits to Israel and Russia

Shortly after our return to Seattle, we moved to a new house. The one we had been renting proved a stopgap. It was conveniently located, but it had no view—a major drawback if one lives in Seattle. We landed in a fetching cul-de-sac. The house was more than adequate, but its main asset was a sweeping view of Lake Washington, the two mountain ranges, and, on a good day, Mount Rainier.

In line with my policy of keeping Roman Jakobson abreast of major developments in my life, I reported to him the acquisition of a panoramic view. He was not bowled over. In fact, he sounded somewhat enigmatic: "I wonder how much time you'll have for savoring this view." Clearly, he was privy to some relevant information. It did not take him long to divulge it. There was a brand-new endowed chair of Russian literature at Yale. Mr. Bensinger, the head of Brunswick Corporation (maker of bowling balls and the like), was a successful Yale alumnus who decided to endow a chair at Yale. Russian literature was not his first choice—he was leaning toward business administration. But Kingman Brewster, a singularly effective and persuasive provost, who in 1961 because of President Griswold's terminal illness was the most influential Yale administrator, was eager to strengthen Yale's Russian studies and prevailed upon the donor to benefit Russian literature.

Apparently, I was not the only candidate. Yale's Sovietologists had someone else in mind, but Brewster chose to listen to one of

Yale's most formidable scholars, "Mr. Comparative Literature" René Wellek, who favored me strongly. (Some six years earlier Wellek, who as a former member of the Prague Linguistic Circle had a considerable affinity for the subject of my first book, helped launch it by providing the first edition of *Russian Formalism* with a friendly and knowledgeable introduction.) Thus, in the fall of 1961, I was invited to Yale to speak about Pushkin. I felt honored to be introduced by Roman Jakobson and gratified to hear him describe my first book as "indispensable." The exercise went well enough. A month later, I was offered the Bensinger Chair as of fall 1962. Needless to say, it entailed a full professorship and an appropriately substantial salary.

To be sure, I was gratified and, for the first time, keenly interested in an outside offer. By 1961, as mentioned previously, I had two offers from UCLA, a strong feeler from Cornell, and an urgent invitation from Bloomington, Indiana. My former Columbia colleague, the chair of the Indiana University Slavic Department, made a brave attempt to seduce me by inviting at the same time Edward Stankiewicz and one of my favorite American scholars of Russian literature, Hugh McLean, and gravely, if not persuasively, urged me that any further contributions to the field, which he expected me to make, could occur only in Bloomington. By and large, I had not had much difficulty in saying no—courteously and appreciatively, to be sure—to either Los Angeles or Bloomington—I thought the former too garish and the latter much too small. An endowed chair at Yale was quite a different matter. But saying yes was far from easy. For one thing, there was this newly acquired and truly stunning view. For another thing, and more important, there was a strong bond of loyalty to the program that I had built from scratch. One likes to feel needed, let alone indispensable. As I was brooding over the Yale offer, two active and relatively mature graduate students generated a letter to the university administration bearing forty-five signatures—I had not realized that so many people had gone through our mill!—to the effect that Victor Erlich's departure from the University of Washington campus would be an "unmitigated disaster."

I was in a real quandary. Generally, when faced with a major decision, I am not apt to temporize. But since I was truly conflict-ridden, I clutched at a straw offered by Iza. It is fair to say that her attraction to the Yale offer was even stronger, or less impeded, than mine. While I had some problems with the University of Washington bureaucracy—my promotion was not as rapid as my tenure—on the whole, I felt strongly supported by the administration and greatly appreciated by students. Iza was distinctly unhappy with our Psychology Department's philistine response to her legitimate intellectual aspirations. Moreover, our older son, Henry, was a junior at Harvard. Whatever our final decision might be, spending at least one academic year on the East Coast seemed to Iza an appealing prospect.

With my inner conflict far from resolved, I proved more amenable to a delaying tactic than I would have been otherwise. In December 1961, I called Kingman Brewster to say that I would be glad to come to Yale for a year as a visiting professor and "come clean" before Christmas of 1962. I recall that on the day when I tampered thus with the Yale offer, while running through the University of Washington campus I bumped into the distinguished Milton Scholar Arnold Stein and quickly conveyed to him the substance of my conversation with Brewster. Arnold smiled a diabolical smile and muttered, "This sounds like saying to St. Peter, 'I'll drop in for a while and see how I like it.'"

Whatever Brewster's feelings actually were, he handled the situation with urbanity and grace. When I greeted him on the phone, "How are you, Mr. Brewster?" his prompt response was, "That depends entirely on what you are going to tell me." Having listened to my unorthodox proposal, he said, after a brief pause, "I'll convey your decision to those mainly responsible for the offer and will be in touch with you shortly." He was as good as his word. I was offered a visiting professorship of Russian literature for 1962 to 1963. (I understand that René Wellek, my main sponsor, was a bit surprised by my temporizing, but said confidently, "He'll like it here. He'll stay.")

In early September 1962, Iza, Mark (who did not object to the move), and I landed in a home some four miles from the Yale campus in residential North Haven. (The owner, a professor of classics, was on sabbatical leave in Greece.) I was offered a spacious office on campus that had previously been occupied by the formidable comparatist Erich Auerbach.

The very beginnings of my Yale career were somewhat stressful. After two weeks of teaching a graduate course on the Russian symbolist movement, I had to switch from the classroom to an operating table. Complicated emergency surgery for a serious intestinal problem proved necessary. I found myself in the hands of a strongly recommended Yale Medical School surgeon. (In fact, Dr. H. Taffel's high competence, coupled with his melancholy demeanor, reminded me of the impressively glum army surgeon whom I was lucky to encounter in Dijon.)

My recovery was as sound as had been the treatment. It did not take me long to realize that coming to Yale was the right move. (I said yes to Brewster in early December.) Yale's psychiatric community was a vast improvement over Seattle's. The Slavic Department did not reach its peak until several years later, but already in 1962 it was eminently congenial. It was a pleasure to see again my Columbia classmate Robert Jackson, who in the meantime was developing into one of our leading Dostoyevsky scholars. His love of Russian literature and his generosity of spirit promised decades of affectionate colleagueship. Another architect of Yale's Slavic Department was a Kraków-born and -bred Slavic linguist, Alex Schenker, a man of urbanity and considerable administrative skills, who was steeped in Polish culture. Over the years, Alex and I had our disagreements, but our friendship remained intact. He was a tower of strength during my medical emergency. The intricate surgery lasted more than three and a half hours. Throughout the entire anxious wait, Alex sat with Iza in the waiting room. One does not forget such things.

By the late 1960s, our department had been greatly enhanced.

Roman Jakobson had the happy notion of propelling our way a distinguished Italian Slavicist, one of the world's best authorities on early Slavic literatures, Riccardo Picchio. Riccardo combined impressive scholarship with warmth; he was a dedicated and an enthusiastic teacher. Slavic studies got a major shot in the arm when we managed to lure away from the University of Chicago Edward Stankiewicz, easily the best Slavic linguist of his generation. Ed, born and raised in Warsaw—the latter was among many things we would share—came to this country too late to be a student of Jakobson's at Columbia or Harvard, but he became, in fact, a much-valued and creative follower. A wide-ranging linguist, Stankiewicz is keenly attuned to literature. His perspective on structural analysis of poetry, while demonstrably indebted to Jakobson's, is, to my mind, often an improvement on the master's occasional schematism. Needless to say, Ed and I became fast friends.

All in all, it is no mere institutional chauvinism to insist that at its peak Yale's Slavic Department deserved to play host to some of the nation's best graduate students in our field. For a number of years now I have been glad to reserve one of the bookshelves in my study for published dissertations of our alumni. Each of these books has made a difference. Let me mention just a few: Monika Greenfield's subtle and sophisticated *Pushkin and Romantic Fashion,* Susanne Fusso's incisive and lucid study of Gogol's *Dead Souls,* Saul Morson's penetrating *Freedom and Narrative*—Bob Jackson and I share the credit for guiding this intense English major toward Russian literature!—and, last but not least, exemplary close readings of Russian lyric poetry from the Pushkin era to Brodsky by a fine poet and an incisive analyst of poetic texts, Tomas Venclova.

It was a joy to work and commune with these deeply motivated and gifted budding scholars and, more broadly, to be part of what was clearly the most gratifying period in the history of Yale's Slavic studies. No less rewarding were my occasional extended absences from the campus, made possible by a second Guggenheim and a National Institute for the Humanities Fellowship. The first significant absence occurred in 1969—our main destination was London, but one of the high points of the year was a far-flung trip which included, in addition to glimpses of Greece and Turkey, visits to Israel and the Soviet Union.

I had been meaning to visit Israel for some time now. In 1969, there were two academic pretexts. I was invited to lecture at Tel Aviv University on "Gogol and the Grotesque" and to speak under the auspices of the Russian studies program of the Hebrew University in Jerusalem on the ferment in post-Stalin Russian literature, most notably on Aleksandr Solzhenitsyn.

The fact that our initial exposure to Israel was masterminded by its academia made our visit both personally and ideologically more congenial than it might have been otherwise. As one who by 1969 had evolved from consistent anti-Zionism to an ambivalently critical, "non-Zionist" stance, I had no trouble finding common language with the Israeli intelligentsia, leaning as it was toward the "Peace Now" position. I especially enjoyed meeting the Frankels. Jonathan, raised in London, was a fine scholar of modern Jewish history who was yet to contribute an excellent introduction to an English translation of Mother's biography of Simon Dubnov. Edith, a lively and attractive woman, was an American-born and -trained Sovietologist.

My talk on Gogol, held under the auspices of the Tel Aviv University Department of Poetics and chaired by my prospective colleague, the versatile and erudite literary scholar Benjamin Hrushovsky (Harshav), did little to confirm Arthur Koestler's hasty generalization, offered in his novel *Arrival and Departure,* about the erosion among the young Israelis of the intellectual intensity which marks the Diaspora Jew. Strong commitment to literary theory, signaled by the name of the department which sponsored my lecture, was apparent during the get-together that followed it. As we were communing over tea and three kinds of cake—typical Israeli fare—my earnest young colleagues were going at the definition of the "grotesque" with a zest worthy of East European Talmudists. It was encouraging to see that the age-old tradition of relentless hairsplitting was alive and well in Tel Aviv.

My extramural response to Israel of 1969 was more positive than I had expected, but it was at times somewhat wary. The dominant impression was that of vitality. There was a bracing sight at the Wailing Wall in Jerusalem—a group of young Israelis breaking into a wild, exuberant dance. Looking at this spontaneous outburst, I could not help but feel, "They cannot get us down!" And yet, talking to many an Israeli in the street, typically a cab driver, I would bristle at the symptoms of nationalist hubris, of triumphalism, triggered by Israel's stunning military victory in the Six-Day War. It made me apprehensive about the road ahead.

We did quite a bit of traveling within Israel, but we kept returning to Jerusalem, drawn as we were by the austere beauty of the Old City. At an early stage of our visit my speaking engagement with Hebrew University earned Iza and me a prestigious invitation. It so happened that my audience included a niece of Israel's president. She had just arrived from Moscow to settle in Jerusalem and informed her uncle that one Victor Erlich had lectured on Solzhenitsyn. President Shazar, a prominent figure in the Labor Party, was formerly, under the name of Rubashov, a historian and a disciple of Simon Dubnov. Having consulted his notes, he promptly concluded that I was a grandson of Dubnov's. An invitation to the unpretentious Israeli White House followed. When tea was brought in, the friendly, heavy-set first lady—as I later found out, a prominent literary critic and a translator of *War and Peace*—exclaimed, pointing to the inevitable cake, "Eat it! It's homemade!"

As we settled in, Mr. Shazar wondered in which language we should proceed. Hebrew was summarily eliminated—neither Iza nor I could handle it. Yiddish was briefly considered—both Mr. Shazar and I could manage it, but that would have excluded Iza. We settled for Russian—the president was clearly pleased with the choice.

At first the conversation was a bit sluggish. Early on the president took me aside to elicit Iza's maiden name. Since she did not know either Jewish language, he may have wondered if Dubnov's grandson married a shiksa. He was not only reassured but visibly excited when I said "Shneerson." The fact of the matter is that this thoroughly secular politician became in his late years quite devout and strongly drawn to the Hassidic branch of Judaism whose stronghold was the Meah Sharim section of Jerusalem. For this fiercely Orthodox community, Menachem Shneerson, the so-called Lubavitcher Rabbi, to whom Iza was very distantly related, was a cult figure. Having heard the magical name, the president forgot all about my roots or, as a traditionalist Jew would say, my *ikhes*. He dashed upstairs and brought from his study a hefty volume in Hebrew about distinguished Jewish families. Its title, I believe, was *Jewish Dynasties*. The genealogical tree of the Shneersons loomed large in the book. Our genial host was clearly pleased to be able to inform Iza how many generations separated her from the founder of the Shneerson "dynasty," Zalman Shneer. I am afraid the figure has slipped my mind.

Soon after the visit to Israel, and twenty-three years after our frigid and tense stay in the forbidding Russian capital, we were, in the words of the Beatles song, "back in the USSR." We returned for a three-week visit, which included Moscow and Leningrad, this time as American tourists with academic credentials and connections.

Predictably, our first impressions were more favorable. People encountered in the streets were dressed solidly and warmly if, on the whole, none too elegantly. Back in 1941, we had been promptly identified as foreigners in spite of our threadbare clothing. In fact, my worn raincoat had elicited an embarrassing and totally undeserved enthusiasm. In 1969, even though we looked more respectable, we seemed to have "passed" on occasions. (Iza's Russian was quite fluent and mine nearly native.) Moreover, from the sightseer's point of view, the Soviet Union had become a more rewarding place. The entire Kremlin complex, which encompasses some of the world's finest church architecture, was thrown open to inspection. The Tretyakovsky Art Museum no longer attested to the "triumph of socialist realism over formalism." The most glaring specimens of Stalinist style had been removed. At the same time, nonrealistic Russian masters such as the symbolist painter M. Vrubel had reemerged from the Orwellian "memory hole." The readmission of Russian modernism to the national pantheon was clearly a timid and halfhearted affair. Retrospective exhibits of such early-twentieth-century figures as N. Roerich, B. Kustodiev, and N. Altman were being held in small, unofficial art galleries rather than in the national museum designed for the general public. Yet this public was now being shown the masterpieces of one of Europe's greatest religious painters, Andrey Rublyov, to the accompaniment of inevitable Soviet rhetoric. We overheard a dutiful teacher inform a group of grade-school children that Rublyov was the most "progressive" artist of his time.

Owing to some previous contacts, to shared interests and allegiances, and to sheer luck, we were privileged to meet and, in spite of the brevity of acquaintance, became close to a number of thoughtful and independent-minded Russian intellectuals. Such hopefulness as was engendered by our surface impressions was significantly qualified, if not altogether dispelled, in the course of remarkably candid and illuminating conversations. We emerged from these intense encounters with two salient emotions—abiding affection and admiration for the spiritual resilience of the men and women we had the good fortune to meet and an equally profound dismay at the contents of their central message.

Let me recall an extended and significant conversation with an appealing and thoroughly trustworthy colleague, a fine scholar of Russian literature in the 1920s, Galina Andreevna Belaya. But first—an essential digression.

Some two years earlier—to be exact, in the summer of 1967, as I was sitting on the porch of a Cape Cod cottage which we were renting—I saw a stranger, clearly lame, slowly making his way toward me from his car. In introducing himself he said he was "working for the government," which by that time I could recognize as a euphemism for being employed by the CIA. He did not waste any time in making the purpose of his visit clear. He had traveled to my summer hideout from his Washington, D.C., office to tell me about a Russian dissident intellectual who had just "chosen freedom." His name was Arkady Belinkov. He and his wife had taken advantage of a trip to Yugoslavia to cross into Austria and ask for asylum at the U.S. embassy in Vienna. Through the good offices of a CIA operative, the Belinkovs landed in Greenwich, Connecticut. Mr. J. had journeyed to Truro to inquire if Belinkov's presence on the East Coast and his availability for an academic appointment were of interest to Yale's Slavic Department. I did not hesitate to answer this question in the affirmative.

I had been aware of Arkady Belinkov as the author of a stunning study of Yury Tynyanov (see pages 128 and 129). The eminent formalist literary historian and theorist is dealt with in Belinkov's book primarily as a historical novelist, most notably as the author of *Death of Vazir-Mukhtar,* a fictionalized biography of a remarkable contemporary of Pushkin's, the playwright and diplomat A. Griboedov. Belinkov's monograph was a critical tour de force. Using as his central theme the plight of a heterodox Russian intellectual under the repressive regime of Nicholas I, Belinkov managed to offer a thinly veiled account of the dissidents' ordeal under Stalin. The book acquired among the cognoscenti the reputation of a muffled bombshell. The subversive message had been decoded.

Needless to say, the prospect of having on our faculty the author of *Yury Tynyanov* had considerable appeal to me, as I knew it would to my colleagues—I spent a long and arduous day journeying to Greenwich (and back to Truro) to look up the anxious and totally helpless couple at the quaintly named Pickwick Arms Hotel and to offer to Belinkov the prospect of a lectureship of modern Russian literature at Yale. To make a long and complicated story short, my task as a chairman was not simple. Securing the appointment for Belinkov was the easiest part of the job. Integrating him into the Yale community was quite a different matter. After spending fifteen years in the gulag—as a penalty for having written a prematurely anti-Nazi novel—he was a serious cardiac case. He was, predictably, a man of considerable intelligence. No less predictably, he was consumed by a rage toward the regime whose brutality he had fully experienced. I had no difficulty sharing his loathing of the Stalinist system, but we did not see eye to eye on teaching Soviet literature to American students. While I felt that such a course ought to include, though not be confined to, literary works of merit which managed to be written and published during the Soviet period, Belinkov insisted on exposing his students solely to second- and third-rate writers in order to demonstrate what literature had been reduced to under the Soviets.

We were offered scant time to resolve our differences. Some five years after coming to Yale, the Belinkovs took a fatal trip to Italy; a disastrous car collision on the Rome–Naples highway made open-heart surgery imperative. Belinkov never recovered.

But I am getting away from my story. In 1969, as we were embarking on our far-flung trip, we were entrusted by the Belinkovs with an important message as well as warm regards for a Moscow literary couple whom they trusted implicitly—Galina A. Belaya and Lev Shubin. No wonder Galina Andreevna was among the first persons I contacted after coming to Moscow. I knew that she would want to hear from and about the Belinkovs. Also, I had good reason to believe that she would give me a candid and credible appraisal of the literary scene in the Soviet Union of 1969. When I called Galina Belaya at her office at the Institute for World Literature, she was polite and clearly interested but predictably reserved. (My standing with the official Soviet establishment was not good. *Russian Formalism* was generally ignored, with the exception of a single, unambiguously hostile reference. I was told later that the copy of the book available to the VIPs was in considerable demand.) Yes, said my colleague, she was interested in meeting me. "We have a great deal to talk about," she added carefully. Not surprisingly, there was no question of my visiting her at the institute.

As for neutral ground, she hesitated between a café in her neighborhood and a bench in a park; it was obvious to me that she preferred the latter. (Sandboxes are less likely to be bugged.) We agreed to meet at Mayakovsky Square and proceed to a park. I met a handsome, vital woman. A rapport was promptly established. I found Galina Andreevna a remarkably articulate and deeply humane person. She was soon to become a valued colleague and a warm friend.

When we sat down in the section of the park dominated by young mothers and their children, Galina Andreevna proved eager for some news about the Belinkovs. She was not surprised to hear about the difficulties I had run into in trying to arrange an appropriate curriculum for Arkady and was clearly in sympathy with my position. As I had hoped, she spoke of Russian society and scholarship of the late 1960s with authority and utmost candor. My new friend did not deny that the lot of the ordinary Soviet citizen had improved significantly since Stalin's death. Yet she was more mindful of the underlying continuities, more preoccupied with the tenacity of Stalin's totalitarian legacy. The leitmotif in her tales was the routine harassment of literary intellectuals, the creeping erosion of such modest opportunities for self-expression as had become available under Khrushchev, a matter not so much of outright prohibition as of bureaucratic obtuseness and timidity. The middle-echelon hacks had interpreted the stolid bleakness of post-Khrushchev leadership as an invitation to small-mindedness and ideological retrenchment. Relatively innocuous studies, which only several years earlier would have gone past the censor easily, were being blocked by a last-minute editorial decision. An essay on the "little man" theme in early Soviet literature that raised with much circumspection the problem of the human cost of social change or a medley of pronouncements on art and literature by Ilya Ehrenburg, a respectable enough figure to rate a prestigious funeral in 1967, was shelved, after initial encouragement, to the accompaniment of timorous muttering, "We had better not. It is very interesting but this is not the right moment." It was a tribute to the compelling quality of Galina Andreevna's narrative, and to the importance of her subject, that I had not realized until I got up from our bench after nearly two hours of absorbing talk that I was about to turn into an icicle. (Moscow can be very cold in early April!) It was high time to conclude our dialogue, but not before agreeing to meet again, this time at Galina Andreevna's home. (In spite of my dubious status, my colleague insisted that Iza and I visit her before leaving for Leningrad.) Lev Shubin, my new friend's first husband, was a freelance literary critic who had just published an essay that was making an impact on the profession—an astute analysis of a remarkable oeuvre that was being rediscovered—that of Andrey Platonov. (For several decades now, Platonov has been widely recognized on both sides of the Atlantic as one of the most original Soviet prose writers.) Shubin's intellectual acumen and intransigence were as apparent as were his wife's—in fact, he seemed to hate the Soviet regime with a passion—though he lacked her indomitable vitality and energy. I was told that he suffered from chronic depression. It seems that shortly before our visit, he had a long and candid conversation with one of the leading Soviet psychiatrists. Having emerged from a long and profoundly gloomy session, the "expert" is said to have opined, "If I felt about the Soviet system the way Mr. Shubin does, I, too, would be chronically depressed."

Meeting Lev Shubin led to a totally unexpected encounter with a grand old man of Russian literature. It so happened that a personal friend of Lyova's, Klara Izrailevna, was a secretary to a distinguished man of letters—a splendid children's writer, a versatile literary critic, and an authority on the art of translation, Korney Ivanovich Chukovsky, who, at the time, was recovering from a heart attack at one of Moscow's elite hospitals. The name Korney Chukovsky meant a great deal to me and to my family. My brother, Alex, and I were raised on his delightful fables, most notably his deft and whimsical poem "The Crocodile." An influential literary critic on the eve of the First World War, he encouraged Mother's early poetic efforts and praised highly her fine wartime lyric cycle *Mother (Mat')*. When Klara Izrailevna suggested that we pay him a visit at the hospital, we seized the opportunity.

Though a man of about eighty-five, Chukovsky was animated and welcoming. He was singularly attentive to Iza and friendly enough toward me, though at first just a bit wary. Since I was described to him as an American professor of Russian literature, he must have been wondering, "What do *they* know?" He must have concluded soon, having asked me some astute questions, that I was OK. But he became nearly maudlin when it turned out that I was a son of his former protégée Sonya Dubnova. "I remember her well," he exclaimed, "a shy, blonde girl with a braid! She was so promising!" He promptly demonstrated his nostalgia for the days gone by. As we were chatting, he reached out to pick up four items—three for Mother and one for me. Lying in his hospital bed, he seemed to be surrounded by the complete works of Korney Chukovsky. All of the books were inscribed—mine pleasantly, the ones designed for Mother movingly. It was a pleasure to deliver them to the addressee when we were back in the States.

Two days later, I was sitting in a dark and dingy Moscow apartment with a sick, half-blind man over seventy. One of the finest Russian literary historians of his generation, a leading scholar of nineteenth-century Russian literature, a man of prodigious erudition and astounding civic courage, Professor Oksman was never a political activist. Yet because of a personal association with an opposition leader, he had spent a number of years in Stalin's jails and concentration camps. He reemerged into academic prominence in the 1950s only to become a decade later persona non grata for having bravely stood his ground against bureaucratic pressures and having denounced timeservers and police informers among his colleagues. Though his intellectual vitality and lucidity were not visibly impaired either by his illness or his ordeals, he was very despondent. "Like many of us," he said, "I had endured much greater horrors under Stalin than I have in recent years. And yet I am more pessimistic than I was thirty years ago. In those days a great deal of what we were going through could be ascribed to Stalin's personal characteristics. Today we have no such alibi; now we know"—he made a sweeping, melancholy gesture—"it's the system." Professor Oksman fell silent. The shadows darkened. "Let me say one thing, though," he added. "The young are not bad, not bad at all."

Significantly enough, a similar note was sounded in a remarkable memoir, which in the late 1960s was making a major impact on those who cared about the fate of Russian culture, *Hope Against Hope* by Nadezhda Mandelstam. She was cautiously hopeful about the "young," not because she expected them to recapture the initial élan of the October Revolution but because she sensed in them a recoil from Soviet ideological rigidities and pieties and a reaching for "values we thought had been abolished forever." "The birth of our new intelligentsia," she wrote, "is accompanied by a craving for poetry . . . it brings people back to life, awakens their conscience and stirs them to thought."[1] The "craving for poetry," the intense personal involvement with the destinies of Russian literature, was indeed the most meaningful link between the older and the younger intelligentsia. For men and women we encountered, be they young, old, or middle-aged, genuine literature was the focus of deepest emotional loyalties; it was literally a mode of moral survival, the last refuge from official cant, an antidote to hopelessness and despair.

In most of the homes that we had occasion to visit, we found three literary icons—Anna Akhmatova, Boris Pasternak, and Aleksandr Solzhenitsyn. When genuine rapport was established, the visitor was likely to walk away with a precious gift, a telling token of confidence, such as a haunting old photo of Akhmatova or a copy of the latest "underground" letter of Solzhenitsyn. A line from a memorable modern poem could serve as a password, an admission ticket to the embattled order of the like-minded, a realm, one might add, not altogether unlike the one conjured up in Osip Mandelstam's spellbinding 1920 poem which summons the devotees of the Word to a secret rite in the vaults of the beloved city: "We shall meet again in Petersburg/As that is where the sun's interred."[2]

As for contemporary poetry, while most of our interlocutors appreciated Evgeny Evtushenko's rhetorical panache, they thought him a dashing second-rater. The rising star of Russian poetry, they affirmed, was the young maverick, a protégé of Anna Akhmatova, Joseph Brodsky. That had been my impression, too. Having read Brodsky's "Elegy for John Donne," I was eager to meet this walking oxymoron, a Leningrad metaphysical poet.

Shortly after our arrival in Leningrad, we ran into one of our graduate students who was spending the academic year 1968 to 1969 in the Soviet Union. He had befriended Brodsky and was eager to arrange a visit. I felt grateful for the opportunity to see the poet in his habitat, which he would later describe vividly in his remarkable volume of English prose, *A Room and a Half.*

In real life, Joseph's own "half" was screened from his parents' share of the apartment by a pile of books and suitcases. Brodsky was friendly, lively, and keen. He was visibly taken with my wife, whom he kept calling "Pani Iza." Clearly, he was pro-women and pro-Polish. (Back in the 1960s, Poland had a special appeal to heterodox young Russians as a relatively open "people's democracy" where books and journals banned in the Soviet Union were occasionally available, a sui generis "window to Europe," to quote Pushkin's famous line.) In recognition of this fact, our host made a feeble attempt to speak Polish to Iza. His Polish vocabulary proved limited, but it was a good try.

Brodsky's choice of books was testimony to his high admiration for English poetry. His admiration for W. H. Auden was by then part of the record. At some point, he took a slender volume off a shelf. "Do you know Philip Larkin?" he inquired. He seemed to take pride in being probably the only Leningrader to know and own a book by this thoroughly English poet.

When Brodsky's gulag ordeal was cut short by international protests, he was allowed to go to the West. Owing to personal connections, he found himself in Ann Arbor, Michigan. After a few years he felt landlocked and headed for the East Coast and ultimately for the Village. In the meantime, his reputation was growing steadily.

Shortly after Brodsky's arrival in the United States, Yale's Slavic Department invited him to fill one of our Wednesday afternoons designated for prestigious visitors. This was not yet a poetry reading, but a get-acquainted, question-and-answer session. Predictably, our entire department, including the middle-aged Russian émigrés who comprised Yale's Russian language program, was on hand. When one of these pedagogues asked Brodsky a rather unoriginal question—"How do you like America?"—he reflected for a while and answered, "It's OK. (*Nichevo.*) It's a normal country." The language teacher was clearly hoping that Joseph would rave and felt slightly deflated. He did not realize that Brodsky had just paid his adoptive country a major compliment: "[As distinguished from my homeland,] it's a normal country."

Over the next fifteen years or so, I repeatedly played host to Joseph Brodsky at extremely well-attended poetry readings sponsored jointly by the Slavic Department and at least one of Yale's residential colleges; on one of these occasions I had the pleasure of introducing him. I must own up to somewhat mixed feelings about his reciting style. The wide thematic range of his verse was partly undercut by the monotony of the delivery—the persistent liturgical chant—though there was no denying its cumulative potency. His opening remarks were invariably arresting and at times deliberately provocative.

Some years before his untimely death at the age of fifty-five, I was spending a fair amount of time in the vicinity of Washington Square. I was teaching a graduate seminar on Russian formalism at NYU. I met Brodsky at a cozy Italian restaurant in the heart of the Village. As always, I was impressed by the keenness and originality of his mind. At the same time, I was uncomfortably aware of a somewhat reckless strain in his daily behavior. He smoked heavily through dinner and drank copiously; now and then he would swallow a nitroglycerin pill. To say that he was not taking good care of himself would be an understatement.

When he died, everyone who knew him shared the loss of a major talent and a first-rate intelligence.

Let me return just for a while to Leningrad in April of 1969 to recall two important encounters. First, there was an evening of uncommon intellectual intensity spent at the home of an accomplished literary scholar, the author of major studies of Russian lyric poetry and of psychological prose, a disciple of such leading formalists as Boris Eikhenbaum and Yury Tynyanov, Lidia Jakovlevna Ginzburg. She was visibly a guru and a role model for many searching young literati. The gathering was marked by an ardent commitment to the life of the mind and to literary values. I found myself drawn into the freewheeling discussion, venturing more categorical statements than I am generally apt to make. I was both amused and pleased when a sophisticated and attractive young woman exclaimed after I had offered one such pronouncement, "It's terrible! You sound just like Lenin!" My lack of enthusiasm for being coupled with the Bolshevik leader was easily offset by the satisfaction of hearing the name used in a pejorative context. And, when, persisting in the "what's to be done in literary criticism" vein, I opted rather peremptorily for "formalism without enfant terrible–ism," my astute hostess dotted the i's by saying, "You mean formalism without Shklovsky?"

Finally, I cannot bid farewell to the unforgettable week in Leningrad without recalling a heartwarming visit with the family that was to become immensely important to me, the Etkinds. I first met Efim Grigorievich Etkind, a splendid teacher-scholar of Russian and comparative literature, in 1967 while attending a congress in Belgrade. Efim Etkind was dropping by on his way from Vienna to say hello to his mentor and friend Viktor Maksimovich Zhirmunsky (see page 132). I asked him to join us for breakfast at our hotel. (In 1965, he had sent me a warmly inscribed copy of his pathbreaking study *Poetry and Translation*.) From the first moment, our conversation was animated, intense, and focused. I remember vividly the sense of an immediate rapport. But "rapport" is too weak a word. After fifty minutes, Iza and I were under the impression that we had known Efim Etkind for a long time. When we left the table, we both knew that we had acquired a new friend.

This sense of intellectual and moral affinity was amply affirmed in Leningrad. When we arrived at our hotel, I called Efim Grigorievich. Soon we found ourselves in a welcoming home where Efim's expansive warmth went hand in hand with Ekaterina Fyodorovna's gentle hospitality. (The two daughters, Masha and Katya, were lively and appealing. The elder was to become a very dear friend over the years.) And when our host informed us that "only last week" the living room couch on which we were sitting hosted Aleksandr Isayevich Solzhenitsyn, we felt that we had entered, to quote Boris Pasternak's novella "A Letter from Tula," "the territory of conscience."

A few years later, Etkind was to pay a heavy price for his friendship with the "enemy of the people." He was deprived of his position at the Herzen Pedagogical Institute, where he was the most influential teacher of literature, denied any opportunity to teach and publish, and forced into emigration. Ironically, his closeness to Solzhenitsyn was eventually undone by unbridgeable political disagreements. Etkind could not abide the writer's militantly conservative, neo-Slavophile stance.

On a pale, windy April day, the Etkinds suggested that we go for a ride. As all true Leningraders do, they took justifiable pride in their eerily beautiful city. Our tour of the former capital's landmarks—the Winter Palace, the Senate Square, Peter and Paul Fortress, and the islands (*ostrova*)—was for me a literary rather than sentimental journey. True, I was born there—the name of the city was then Petrograd—but I left too early to have memories of my own. For me, Petersburg–Petrograd–Leningrad is, in part, a body of family folklore but, above all, a powerful literary theme. Few cities of the world have impressed themselves so forcefully on the native literary imagination; few have been so sonorously eulogized, so eloquently denounced. Thus, as we rode through the streets of the superficially shabby and yet still poignantly graceful city, my host and I recited now alternately, now in unison, the famous Petersburg poems of Pushkin, Blok, and Mandelstam.

We had just crossed the Neva onto Vasilevsky Island, which, on the eve of the First World War, was the scene of nightly revels of Petersburg's literary bohemia, when Efim Grigorievich launched into an appropriately frenzied lyric by Aleksandr Blok. I chimed in. The haunting music of Blok's feverish lines melted into the chilly April air. We listened to the silence closely.

"Governments come and go," said Efim Grigorievich. "Poetry endures."

Russia Revisited

I visited the Soviet Union again in 1973. Iza and I were spending much of the 1972 to 1973 academic year in London. In midspring we went east. Our first objective was Warsaw. In addition to visiting her aging aunt, a former prima donna of the Warsaw opera, Iza was engaged in a research project that entailed interviewing a number of Warsaw University students. I stayed in Poland for a week and then proceeded to Moscow and Leningrad, looking forward to renewing contacts already made and to further significant encounters.

Once again I was carrying a message, this time a letter. Shortly before departing for Eastern Europe, Iza and I had occasion to meet the well-known Soviet biologist Zhores Medvedev, who had gotten into trouble for exposing the fraudulent theories peddled by the officially accredited con man Lysenko. When Medvedev heard of my intention to revisit the Soviet Union, he entrusted me with a letter to his historian brother Roy. I thought of the latter as a man of unquestionable integrity whose mildly dissident brand of Marxism was not exactly my cup of tea. Though I was not planning to look him up, I was reasonably sanguine about finding a trustworthy go-between. My optimism proved justified.

One of the first people I saw in Moscow was the impressively broad-gauged V. V. Ivanov, an erudite linguist and a man of exemplary probity whom I had enjoyed meeting back in 1969. We converged on a dinner at the Metropol, an Intourist hotel, which, according to Ivanov, could boast the largest number of NKVD agents per square foot. The main subject of our conversation, the Slavic formalist-structuralist tradition, while not exactly "safe," was by 1973 less than explosive. Once again I found Ivanov rewarding and congenial. Our fruitful dialogue proved a prelude to an equally satisfying evening—as well as a solution to the Medvedev problem. My linguist friend had just remarried—his bride, the lively and attractive Svetlana, was a daughter of the well-known Americanist Raissa Davydovna Orlova, who was married to the prominent Germanist and memoir writer Lev Zinovievich Kopelev, a real-life prototype of Lev Rubin, the personally decent if politically naive protagonist of Aleksandr Solzhenitsyn's *The First Circle.* (I understand that at some point Kopelev had acquired the habit of running around Moscow and telling whatever acquaintances he would encounter, "I'm no longer Rubin!") Ivanov assured me that his wife's stepfather was on good terms with Roy Medvedev and would be glad to convey to him the letter I was carrying. It turned out that Vyacheslav Vsevolodovich had been planning anyway to introduce me to the Kopelevs, whose apartment sounded like a beehive of intelligentsia activity.

It was to their home that we repaired after the Metropol dinner. It was a good visit. Lev Zinovievich, whose impressive beard gave him the air of a genial biblical prophet, was cordial and expansive. Raissa Davydovna was keen, quick, and articulate. The brisk and animated conversation was frequently interrupted by telephone calls. At some point, Raissa Orlova, who seemed to be at the end of her tether, exclaimed, turning to her spouse, "I can't stand it! Let's take it off the hook for a while!" As Kopelev was pondering this request, the phone rang again. "You take it!" cried Mrs. Orlova. Kopelev complied, only to emit a bloodcurdling yell, "Heinrich!" It was a long-distance call from a much-valued friend, the German novelist Heinrich Böll. When after a few minutes Kopelev rejoined us, smiling broadly, he reported rather redundantly, "It was Heinrich," and proceeded to taunt his wife good-naturedly. "You see? Had I listened to you, I would have missed this call."

Some minutes later, Kopelev's mood changed—he was visibly tense. He expected, as it turned out, the visit of the intrepid Lidya Chukovskaya, Korney Ivanovich's daughter and a fine author in her own right, a person of sterling civic courage and formidable rigor. "She is the only person," muttered Kopelev, "I am afraid of." A walking superego of the Russian intelligentsia, Lidya Chukovskaya must have been an exacting friend. Apparently, Lidya Korneyevna and Kopelev had "had words." She was coming, to use a characteristic intelligentsia expression, to "clarify the relationship." A stern-looking, taut, gray-haired woman appeared at the door. She greeted us briefly and followed Kopelev to another room. When both emerged after some half an hour, the host was beaming. The "relationship" must have been "clarified."

Yet the evening had not yet run its course. As I was contemplating an exit, there was another ring at the door. The newcomer, a tall, dark, and handsome man, was clearly a welcome guest. "Isn't our boy a looker?" exclaimed Raissa Orlova affectionately. The name of this "boy," Aleksandr Galich, had in Moscow of 1973 a considerable resonance. He was one of the three charismatic dissident poet-singers—less tuneful than Bulat Okudzhava and less harsh than Vladimir Vysotsky. Galich had put to work his rich, well-trained voice and his predominantly recitative style to contrive an apt parody of official Soviet cant. Though at the early stage of his literary career he had been a fairly conventional playwright, he became an increasingly troublesome chansonnier. By the time we met, Galich was actively contemplating emigration and was clearly interested in making contact. Before leaving the hospitable Kopelev home, he invited me to have supper at his place the following evening.

Actually, "evening" turned out to be a misnomer. I arrived at 10:00 P.M. and did not leave until 2:00 A.M. There was food, an inordinate amount of liquor, and absorbing talk. Above all, there was Galich's performance, capped by an almost unbearably moving lyric fugue celebrating the legendary Polish Jewish children's writer and pedagogue Janusz Korczak, the head of a Jewish orphanage in the Warsaw ghetto who in 1943 spurned a chance of rescue to board, along with "his" children, an Auschwitz-bound train.

Shortly before midnight, there was an odd interlude. Galich went to the phone to call a neighbor, the blatantly antiregime writer Vladimir Maksimov, who was yet to become the editor of the influential Russian émigré journal *Kontinent*. My host was brief: "Volodya, drop by. A good guy is visiting." When he returned, he told me, "Maksimov is not in good shape. He has been drinking. He may bestir himself to show up." When "Volodya" did show up, it became apparent that Galich was guilty of a vast understatement. The condition of the new arrival was deplorable. He was barely articulate, but he clearly was determined to talk politics, notably American politics. With a nearly heroic effort, Maksimov managed to stammer, "And, how . . . about . . . Vietnam?" It was clear to me what he was painfully trying to elicit was not the latest news from the battlefield but how I felt about U.S. involvement. In other words, he was trying to find out if I was really a "good guy." My answer was not easily reducible to a single sentence. I averred that to begin with I had not been entirely opposed to the U.S. stance, but that by 1973 I had concluded that the moral-political cost of "staying the course" in Vietnam was unacceptable. Maksimov seemed rather unhappy to hear this. After several aborted attempts, he dragged out of himself a staggered sequence: "No price . . . is too high . . . in the struggle against fascism." Maksimov clearly did not see any significant difference between communism and fascism. Moreover, not unlike some other single-track-minded anticommunists, he did not seem to realize that fascism sensu stricto was fascism, too. I suspect that even had Maksimov not been suffering from a severe hangover, a political discussion with him would not have been fruitful. Under the circumstances, it was unquestionably pointless. Mrs. Maksimov must have intuited that much. She appeared at the door and said sternly, "Volodya, go to bed."

About a year later, Galich left for Paris. Shortly after his arrival in the West, he came to New York to give a concert. I was eager to see and hear him on American soil. The concert was fine but the setting dispiriting. Galich's satire was intensely local and shrewdly mimetic. The audience, which consisted to a large extent of old émigrés, was appreciative, but they were not "getting it." Their inadequacy was epitomized by the chairman's embarrassingly bad Russian. His opening sentence, *"Nam podvezlo,"* intended to mean "We've lucked out" (*Nam povezlo*), was illiterate. During the milling-around period after the concert, I went up to Galich. He seemed glad to see me and introduced me to the hapless chairman in a manner which at first I found rather startling. "And this is Professor Erlich," he announced in his rich baritone, "with whom at some point we imbibed a fair amount of vodka." My first inward reaction was, "This is not how I remember that evening." I promptly realized that I was getting a character reference: "Here is a man who can hold his liquor." As I looked back to the unforgettable evening, I had to admit that the recommendation was not undeserved. We were drinking virtually all the time.

I saw Galich again a few years later at a Pasternak symposium, held at Cerisy-la-Salle, a scenic conference site in Normandy. The occasion was attended by Western scholars of modern Russian literature and recently transplanted Soviet dissident literary critics, for example, Andrey Sinyavsky, Efim Etkind, and Lazar Fleishman. I recall a somewhat tense debate between Galich and Etkind about the validity of Soviet dissent. Galich was willing to offer his moral support only to works informed by a total rejection of the totalitarian lie. Etkind argued for the legitimacy of genuine attempts to tell, under repressive conditions, *some* of the truth.

Two evenings spent in the picturesque Norman castle were devoted to Galich's recitals, ably introduced respectively by Andrey Sinyavsky and Efim Etkind. For once the poet-singer was performing in front of an audience keenly attuned to his brand of satire. I felt privileged to have been there, though I could not help feeling that the New York concert was a more typical Galich experience in the West. It was painfully apparent that this accomplished performer was paying a prohibitive price for emigration.

Several years after the provocative Normandy get-together, Galich died of an electric shock while trying to fix a TV antenna on the roof of his Paris house. On the face of it, this was an accident, but to some of his friends, the risk-taking venture smacked of suicide.

Let me return to my 1973 trip to Russia. After the intense encounters in Moscow, I proceeded to Leningrad. As soon as I settled in my hotel room overlooking the Neva, I called Efim Etkind. He urged me to come to dinner as soon as possible. As we were getting cordially reacquainted, Efim Grigorievich suggested that I join him at the meeting of the Translators' Section of the Soviet Writers' Union, at which a young literary scholar, whom I was to meet later in this country, was scheduled to speak about Pasternak. I agreed with pleasure. We were granted a warm reception; Etkind was one of the most respected members of the group. Moreover, some of those present were acquainted with my *Russian Formalism.* I was told, "You are our historian."

The subject of the presentation, the motif of the window in early Pasternak, dramatized an essential aspect of the poet's sensibility—his openness to experience. I thought the speaker's methodology overly indebted to statistics; the meticulous counting of windows in Pasternak's lyric cycle *My Sister Life* struck me as less than illuminating. Predictably, Efim Grigorievich spoke at some length during the discussion which followed. So did I, to my own surprise. When I was landing at the Leningrad airport, I did not anticipate that some eight hours later I would be taking active part in a literary debate. As it happened, Etkind's strictures and mine virtually coincided. I found this near convergence satisfying and not unexpected. Already at the early stage of our friendship, it became apparent that we shared not only a deep conviction about the indispensability of poetry but also a mode of analyzing it, which Etkind termed, half seriously, "structuralism with a human face."

We had several occasions to test this methodology within the framework of congenial scholarly encounters, be they Pasternak symposia in Normandy and Jerusalem or Akhmatova conferences on both sides of the Atlantic. The most memorable of the latter was a 1989 festival that began in Moscow and terminated in Leningrad. It was held at the height of perestroika, when all Soviet taboos were lifted. In Moscow I lectured on formalism at the Institute for World Literature (IMLI). My friend G. A. Belaya was in the chair. Both my talk and its subject were well received. In fact, a venerable-looking lady accused me of being overly critical of the formalists. Belaya had worried a bit about the possibility of some nastiness on the part of the clever, insistently chauvinistic, and insidiously anti-Semitic essayist V. Kozhinov, but his demeanor was uncharacteristically mellow. He expressed his satisfaction over my assertion, made in praising the overall achievement of the formalists, that in literary criticism individual talent was no less important than fruitful methodology. When Kozhinov hesitated to grant talent to Roman Jakobson, he was being antilinguistic rather than anti-Semitic. Virtually all the leading formalists were at least half-Jewish.

A week later, I was offering to strong applause an interpretation of a 1921 poem by Akhmatova, "How Is This Century Worse Than the Preceding Centuries?" as a somber prophecy, as uncanny anticipation of the Stalin reign of terror. Yet the high point of the 1989 Akhmatova symposium was Efim Etkind's first homecoming. I recall a long and stiflingly hot evening sequence, the only session of the conference open to the general public. Etkind was scheduled to be the last speaker. The audience's endurance was most impressive. Hardly anyone budged until midnight. When Etkind rose to pay an eloquent tribute to a great poet, Leningrad's literary community exploded in welcoming the return of one of its most distinguished members to his beloved city.

As I look back to my professional activity in the 1960s and 1970s, I am struck by the salience of the theme of the cultural and moral ferment in post-Stalin Russia. As it happened, mine was one of the first Western responses to the reemergence of Boris Pasternak and to the massive achievement of Aleksandr Solzhenitsyn. Writing in 1959 about *Dr. Zhivago,* I did not proclaim this moving if somewhat flawed novel a masterpiece but hailed "the act of composing it, in what must have been some of the darkest hours of the Stalinist inquisition [as] a magnificent triumph of the spirit over the brute force of circumstances."[1] By the same token, while assessing Solzhenitsyn as a major if not a great writer, I welcomed both his momentous debut "One Day in the Life of Ivan Denisovich" and his monumental indictment of the Soviet forced labor system, *The Gulag Archipelago,* as events of surpassing significance.

Need I insist that for such Western scholars of modern Russian literature as the French Slavicists George Nivat and Michel Aucouturier, my Dutch friend Karel van het Reve, and this writer, the rise of the human rights movement in the Soviet Union became more than an important subject of inquiry but a focus of commitment, in a word, a "cause"? When two heterodox writers, Andrey Sinyavsky and Yury Daniel, landed in the gulag for smuggling out of Russia darkly subversive stories, a collective protest was called for. Bob Jackson and I drafted a statement decrying the new wave of political repression, to be placed in the *New York Times.* The time-consuming process of collecting signatures from prominent members of the American academic community took me back to my activist days in prewar Warsaw. It helped forge ties of solidarity and friendship, most notably with the stunning and intense American Sovietologist Patricia Blake and her close associate, that remarkable Yorkshireman Max Hayward.

Let me pause briefly before the memory of this, one of the most interesting men I was privileged to meet. His death at fifty-five provided an occasion for a warm farewell. On April 17, 1979, Max's friends and admirers gathered at St. Paul's Chapel at Columbia University. As one of the eulogists, I spoke of the man who for twenty-five years had labored tirelessly and selflessly to bring to the West the good tidings about the resurgence of the free

Russian imagination. As translator of Pasternak, Solzhenitsyn, and Nadezhda Mandelstam, as an anthologist of five decades of Soviet literary nonconformity, he did more than anyone I could name to make the "dissonant voices in Soviet literature" resound in clear and graceful English.[2] In addition, in his reviews of Andrey Sinyavsky's controversial forays into Pushkin and Gogol, he proved to be a literary critic of the first order.

Yet for those lucky enough to have known Max Hayward personally, what he had done and was about to do could not be more precious and compelling than what he was. I shall always treasure my first meeting with Max, a long, leisurely conversation in his ascetic cell at Oxford's St. Anthony's College. Max was recounting his early experiences in the Soviet Union. I was spellbound by the vividness of his narrative, which brought to life a unique gallery of Soviet types, including some colorful down-and-outers. Above all, I marveled at his unerring sense of Russian culture and society, a sense epitomized by his stunning command of Russian, at the range of his intellectual curiosity and cultural empathy, at the richness of his humanity.

Heartwarming Closures

"All Is Powered by Love"

During the 1980s and 1990s, personal losses alternated with deeply gratifying closures. In 1985, I lost my brother, Alex. The lethal stroke was painless, but it was trying to see him go at the height of his intellectual powers. About a year later, Mother died at the age of 101. She was still herself at ninety-nine; at a small family gathering marking her birthday, she had a long conversation with our son Mark, with whom she had a special relationship (they were both committed left-wing socialists). Her last year was less satisfying. Her eyesight and hearing were virtually gone, her speech became blurred. At one hundred, she uttered something that had to be decoded by her attractive Polish lady companion. What she was trying to say was, "It's been too long." She would not have said this any earlier. An avid reader of the *New York Times*, she confessed at ninety-five that she no longer was prepared to worry about Africa. Almost till the end she remained lucid, concerned, fully alive.

In 1985, my teaching career came to an end; I turned seventy, which at the time spelled retirement. (Since about 1990, Yale has not had a firm cutoff date.) Though I greatly enjoyed teaching, I do not recall having felt overly deprived. I was falling behind in my publishing schedule—my last academic book, *Modernism and Revolution,* dealing with Russian prose fiction of the 1920s, which I owed to Harvard University Press, was still far from completion. I welcomed the opportunity offered by my retirement to bear down on it.

I recall fondly the heartwarming send-off I received from my colleagues. A gathering held at the heart of the campus heard generous speeches by Bob Jackson, Alex Schenker, and Ed Stankiewicz, by one of the key figures in Yale's Russian studies, the professor of Soviet and international law Leon Lipson, whose exquisite command of the English language made him a much-coveted translator from the Russian whenever a visitor's English was less than perfect, and by one of my favorite Ph.D. candidates in Slavic, Susan Amert. Susan, an active participant in our occasional "sings," injected a distinctive note when she spoke of me as probably the only American scholar of Russian literature who was known to produce now and then a zestful rendition of "I'm Proud to Be an Okie from Muskogee" by the redneck balladeer Merle Haggard.

In responding, I acknowledged the intellectual and emotional debts I had accumulated in more than four decades. The fact that one of those present was Krystyna Pomorska, Roman Jakobson's widow, who was gracious enough to journey from Cambridge to attend the occasion, was not the only reason why I felt impelled to speak of what I owed to my most distinguished and charismatic teacher.

Five years later, Iza and I were celebrating another landmark—our golden wedding anniversary—by playing host one sunny afternoon to family and friends. Henry and Mark were there with their congenial and gifted wives and their spirited children. On the front lawn where we gathered, much occasional verse was recited. (Mark, who organized the event, urged the fellow merrymakers to bring creativity rather than presents.) My colleagues Alex Schenker and Ed Stankiewicz did themselves proud, with the latter ably assisted by his wife, Florence. Henry demonstrated once more his literary flair—back at Harvard College, he showed a strong humanitarian bent only to become, somewhat to his own surprise, an internationally known geneticist. But the high point of the proceedings was a skit about Iza's and my odyssey, authored by Mark, who has become a prominent Boston-based labor official and the author of two books about the building trades in Massachusetts. His slender but deft literary effort was enacted by our grandchildren, with Mark and Bobby's nine-year-old Sonia and Henry and Brenda's eight-year-old Justin playing the leading parts. The audience was especially appreciative of the opening scene, which captured the spirit of the protagonists' encounter back in 1937 in Warsaw at the meeting of the Bundist student group. When Justin, standing in for me, produced with some effort an abstruse sentence, and Sonia, impersonating Iza, countered it playfully with, "And how about a date?" they brought the house down.

It was a serene, cloudless day. Soon, clouds began to gather. From 1994 on, Iza was plagued by sarcoidosis, a rare and increasingly debilitating disease draining the lungs and marked by frequent flare-ups. To complicate matters, Iza must have had at some point a small stroke that affected her memory. She had no trouble remembering events that had occurred, say, thirty years earlier, but often wondered at midafternoon if we had had lunch on that day (which, of course, we had). The short-term memory loss was part of a creeping mental deterioration. In some respects, Iza remained herself throughout—she never lost her sense of humor or her sound assessment of people. But her involvement in psychoanalysis, a profession she entered zestfully at a rather advanced age, was attenuated. It was painful to see a person so keen, so responsive and quick-witted, visibly reduced. Some of her closest friends and associates, such as the admirably insightful Rosemary Balsam, found this difficult to accept. Since the 1980s, Iza and I had belonged to a congenial discussion group on psychoanalysis and the humanities. As Iza's illness progressed, her interest in the group's meetings tended to wane. For the first time in the history of our friendship, Rosemary and I began to differ. She felt that I was not doing enough to counteract Iza's growing intellectual passivity. She may have been right. I'm not good at pushing, and I was not convinced it was the right thing to do.

The frequent trips to Yale New Haven Hospital were taking their toll. I felt grateful, though, that it was possible to keep Iza at home most of the time. I owed this in no small measure to our Polish housekeeper, Władzia (Gladys) Tonishefsky, who had become over the years a staunch friend—a person of remarkable warmth, effectiveness, and native intelligence. Without Władzia's invaluable assistance, I would not have been able to insure for Iza so many months of nearly normal existence. She was deeply appreciative of what was being done for her. She was grateful to Władzia; our bond was as firm as ever. Time and again, she felt the need to tell me that had she just met me, she would not hesitate to marry me. Whenever Władzia was around, she would mutter (in Polish, to be sure), "You are spoiling him."

In early February 1997, Iza had to be rushed again to Yale New Haven Hospital. This time it was heart failure. She breathed her last on February 7, with Mark and me at her side.

I was physically and emotionally drained. Since an onset of severe arrhythmia could not be controlled by medication, my doctors recommended a triple bypass. The complicated surgery was brilliantly performed. After a protracted but steady recovery, I returned to our Hamden home to face the magnitude of my loss. Alone in a big house, I was bereft, after fifty-seven years, of an irreplaceable companion, soul mate, and lover.

Let me emphasize "irreplaceable." On a number of occasions, both during and prior to her illness, Iza sought to extract from me a promise that should she be the first to go, I would remarry. She knew how much I valued female company. I was consistently evasive. In retrospect, I had a good reason to withhold commitment. There was no substitute for Iza. Moreover, at eighty-two, marriage was out of the question, the more so since when Iza died, I found myself exclusively attracted to women who were much younger than I and happily married. (This seems to be a requirement.) But in one respect, Iza was absolutely right. It has proved difficult, indeed impossible, to manage without a fervent affection for a lovely woman, be it the marvelously vital older daughter of a dear Russian colleague, the favorite niece of Władzia who several years ago journeyed from Poland to take care of me when I was ill and whose luminous smile brought me back to life, or the recently encountered charismatic Polish friend whose masterly rendition of "Night and Day" keeps reducing me to meltdowns.

The most apt and penetrating of the letters I received after Iza's death came from Efim Etkind. Nearly three years later, he, too, succumbed to a killer disease. I flew to Paris to take part in a session of l'Institut des Études Slaves honoring his memory and proceeded to Bretagne to attend his burial in a village graveyard, under a pouring rain, a singularly apposite backdrop for the inconsolable grief of Etkind's bereaved daughters.

In the eulogy I delivered in Paris, I spoke about my friend's lifelong love affair with twentieth-century Russian poetry, taking a leaf from a stunning poem by Osip Mandelstam. The persona, clearly in the throes of an emotional turmoil, is impelled by insomnia to revisit *The Iliad* and the list of the Troy-bound ships launched by the Greek chieftains in search of Helen. Toward the end of the poem, the sea of feeling, antedating the reimmersion in Homer and energized by it, overflows the text: "Both Homer and the sea, all is powered by love/Whom should I listen to?: And lo Homer falls silent/And the black sea roars rhetorically and approaches my pillow in thunder."[1] In a brief tribute to a departed friend, I argued that the key line, "All is powered by love," was an apt description of the trajectory of Efim Etkind the man and the scholar. May I suggest, as I wind up the selective record of a long journey, that the high point of the Mandelstam poem might be equally relevant to the "trajectory" of this eulogist? For what keeps me going at an unexpectedly late stage of my life is nothing less than a firm emotional bond with my wonderful family and with cherished friends who brighten my days.

The child of a lethal century, I sustained early on brutal, irretrievable losses. But I had been vouchsafed benefits for which I

shall remain grateful as long as I live. I was raised by two remarkable people who bequeathed to me a sturdy commitment
to social justice and a dedication to what Boris Pasternak called
a "life by verses." I have kept faith throughout with love of
poetry—and with poetry of love.

Notes

In a World of My Own

1. Sophia Dubnova-Erlich, *Stikhi raznykh let* [*Verses of Different Periods*] (New York: 1973), 43.
2. NKVD was the acronym for the name of the Soviet secret police, the precursor to the KGB, in the mid-1920s.
3. Boris Pasternak, *Sochineniya* [*Works*] (Ann Arbor: University of Michigan Press, 1961), 3:63.
4. Adam Mickiewicz, "Sonety Krymskie" ("Crimean Sonnets"), in *Dzieła poetyckie* [*Poetic Works*] (Warsaw: Czytelnik, 1997), 224.

Between Socialist Politics and Neo-Romantic Literature

1. W. H. Auden, "September 1, 1939," in *Selected Poems,* edited by Edward Mendelson (New York: Vintage Press, 1990), 86–88.
2. As quoted in Victor Erlich, *Modernism and Revolution* (Cambridge, MA: Harvard University Press, 1994), 202.
3. As quoted in Erlich, *Russian Formalism: History — Doctrine,* (New Haven, CT: Yale University Press, 1981), 111.
4. *The History of Polish Literature* (London: Macmillan Company, 1969).
5. Ibid., 376.

On the Road

1. Sophie Dubnov-Erlich, *Bread and Matzoth* (Tenafly, NJ: Hermitage Publishers, 2005), 247.

2. Since our stay in Kobe was very brief, we did not come into contact with the group of German Jews who were residing there at the time. We heard that when a few of our fellow Polish-Jewish refugees tried to establish such a connection, they were roundly rebuffed. "We have nothing to talk about," they were allegedly told, "since our countries are at war."

On the Other Shore

1. *Henryk Erlich and Victor Alter,* translated from the Yiddish by Samuel A. Portnoy (New York: KTAV Publishing House in association with the Jewish Labor Bund, 1990), 100.

2. Ibid., 106.

3. Ibid., 184–88.

4. Ibid., 107.

5. Ibid., 108.

6. Ibid., 167.

7. Ibid., 332.

8. Ibid., 330.

9. Ibid., 337, 336.

10. Ibid., 342.

11. Victor Erlich, "A Belated Tribute," in *Henryk Erlich and Victor Alter,* 362–63.

12. Mark Erlich, "Honoring the Past to Change the Future: Solidarity and the Warsaw Ghetto," *Tikkun,* September 1988, 25.

13. Erlich, "A Belated Tribute," 363.

14. "NKVD Documents Shed New Light on the Fate of Erlich and Alter," *East European Jewish Affairs* 22, no. 2 (1992): 76.

15. Ibid., 83–84.

16. Ibid., 67.

17. *The Poems of Stanley Kunitz 1928–1978* (New York: Little Brown and Company, 1978), 92.

"You're in the Army Now"

1. The "hook" meant a hypodermic needle. The rookies were in for a number of injections.

Back to School

1. Victor Erlich, *Russian Formalism: History — Doctrine*, (New Haven, CT: Yale University Press, 1981), 183.

2. Ibid., 172.

3. Ibid., 193

4. Ibid.

5. Ibid., 196.

6. Ibid., 77.

7. Ibid.

8. Ibid., 198.

9. Lili Brik, *Almanakh o Mayakovskom* [*Almanac About Mayakovski*] (Moscow, 1934), cited in Erlich, *Russian Formalism*, 69.

10. Viktor Shklovsky, "Isaac Babel: A Critical Romance," translated by John Pierson, in *Isaac Babel: Modern Critical Views* (New York: Chelsea House Publishers, 1995), 12.

11. Actually, when revising my Ph.D. thesis for publication, I chose to abridge the chapter rather drastically. In his own ruminations on the genesis of formalism, Jakobson, who among many other fields of specialization was an accomplished medievalist, tended to trace the movement as far back as Kievan Russia, in whose culture—strongly influenced by Byzantium— the sense of form loomed larger than it did in Muscovite Russia. In getting my first book into shape, I regretfully dispensed with "sailing to Byzantium."

A Year on the East Coast

1. Victor Erlich, "Stil-und Formprobleme" (paper presented at comparative literature congress, Heidelberg, 1958), 371.

2. Ibid., 371–72.

3. Victor Erlich, "The Place of Russian Futurism Within the Russian Poetic Avant-Garde: A Reconsideration," in *Russian Literature* (Amsterdam), Jan. 1, 1983, 2.

4. Ibid., 10.

5. Isaiah Berlin to Victor Erlich, letter in the author's possession.

6. Isaiah Berlin, *Four Essays on Liberty* (Oxford: Oxford University Press, 1977).

7. Ibid.

8. Noel Annan, introduction to *Personal Impressions,* by Isaiah Berlin (New York: Viking Press, 1980), xiv.

9. Ibid., 174.

10. Ibid., 207.

Outreach in Seattle and a Continental Interlude

1. Anna Akhmatova, *Sochinenya* [*Works*] (Washington, D.C.: Inter-Language Literary Associates, 1969), 1:321–22. The translation is mine.

From Seattle to Yale, with Visits to Israel and Russia

1. Nadezhda Mandelstam, *Hope Against Hope: A Memoir,* translated from the Russian by Max Hayward, with an introduction by Clarence Brown (New York: Atheneum, 1970), 333.

2. Osip Mandelstam, *Sobranie sochineniy* [*Collected Works*] (Washington, D.C.: Inter-Language Literary Associates, 1964), 1:85–86. The translation is mine.

Russia Revisited

1. "A Testimony and a Challenge: Pasternak's Doctor Zhivago," in *Problems of Communism,* Nov.–Dec. 1959, 30.

2. *Dissonant Voices in Soviet Literature* is the title of an anthology edited by Patricia Blake and Max Hayward.

Heartwarming Closures

1. Osip Mandelstam, *Sobranie sochineniy* [*Collected Works*] (Washington, D.C.: Inter-Language Literary Associates, 1964), 1:48–49.

About the Author

Victor Erlich is a distinguished literary critic and a professor emeritus of Russian literature at Yale University. He is the author of several books, including *Russian Formalism: History — Doctrine* and *Modernism and Revolution: Russian Literature in Transition.*

Jewish Lives

GERTRUD KOLMAR
My Gaze Is Turned Inward: Letters, 1934–1943

ARNOŠT LUSTIG
The Bitter Smell of Almonds: Selected Fiction
Children of the Holocaust
The House of Returned Echoes
The Unloved: From the Diary of Perla S.

LIANA MILLU
Smoke over Birkenau

THOMAS NOLDEN AND FRANCES MALINO, EDS.
Voices of the Diaspora: Jewish Women Writing
in Contemporary Europe

BERNHARD PRESS
The Murder of the Jews in Latvia, 1941–1945

WIKTORIA ŚLIWOWSKA, ED.
The Last Eyewitnesses: Children of the Holocaust Speak (volume 1)

ISAIAH SPIEGEL
Ghetto Kingdom: Tales of the Łódź Ghetto

JIŘÍ WEIL
Life with a Star
Mendelssohn Is on the Roof

JOANNA WISZNIEWICZ
And Yet I Still Have Dreams: A Story of a Certain Loneliness